Appalachian Speech

Walt Wolfram

Donna Christian

Center for Applied Linguistics

Library of Congress Catalog Card No.: 76-15079
ISBN: 87281-050-X

June 1976
Copyright © 1976
By the Center for Applied Linguistics
1611 North Kent Street
Arlington, Virginia 22209

Printed in the U.S.A.

"Everybody lives in the mountains has an accent all to theirself."

DATE DUE

Preface

Although the focus on social dialects during the past decade has greatly
advanced the theoretical and descriptive base of sociolinguistics, it is
apparent that the descriptive concerns have often been quite selective.
Descriptive accounts of some varieties proliferate rapidly while other
varieties remain virtually ignored. In this book, we hope to expand the
descriptive base of dialect diversity in American English by focusing on
an often-neglected geographical area of the United States--the mountain
range of Appalachia. While we have adopted a particular sociolinguistic
model for our description, we have endeavored to present our findings in
a way that would make them accessible to specialists in fields other
than professional linguistics and still be of use to linguists. We are
primarily interested in providing a meaningful reference work for edu-
cators--particularly reading specialists, English teachers, language
arts specialists, and speech pathologists. We are further concerned
with the educational implications of such diversity, and therefore discuss the educational significance of dialect diversity at some length.
We would like to think of our description of Appalachian English as comprehensive, but we are well aware of the fact that there are a number of
descriptive aspects which we have treated in little or no detail.

This book originally developed from one part of a final research
report, *Sociolinguistic Variables in Appalachian Dialects*, carried out
under contract NIE-G-74-0026 with the National Institute of Education
(NIE), from June 1974 - August 1975. Detailed formal descriptions of
a number of the features treated in the final research report are not
included here, but they can be found in the second part of the final report submitted to the NIE.

There are many people to whom we are indebted for assistance and
consultation. Prominent among them are those individuals in Monroe and
Mercer Counties who aided us in our initial contacts in the area. Mary
Compton and William McNeel in Monroe County and C. D. Lilly and Harold
Okes of Mercer County were most gracious in helping us establish contacts in the area. They generously opened up the schools in these
counties for those aspects of the research which were conducted in that
connection. We could not have participated in a more cordial working
relationship. They also offered their kind assistance in extending our
contacts to other individuals in the area who assisted us in this ven-
ture, including Haskell Shumate, county clerk of Monroe County, West
Virginia, who provided us with invaluable insight into the history of
the region.

The study could not have been conducted without the assistance of
our fieldworkers from the two counties: Nora Mann and Gary Pence, of
Monroe County; Harless Cook, Brenda Lohr, Agnes Pietrantozzi, and
Rebecca Michael, of Mercer County. They each demonstrated that indi-

genous fieldworkers can be used to great advantage in a study of this type.
Their adaptation of the questionnaire and general knowledge of the area
proved to be a rich, useful resource in this investigation.
We owe our greatest debt to them and the informants who provided the
interviews that serve as our data base for this analysis. Although the
informants, who remain anonymous in this report, may have been puzzled
by the seeming inanity of our probing, they willingly tolerated the
intrusion into their everyday world.

We are further indebted to our professional colleagues. Roger W.
Shuy, Peg Griffin, and Rudolph Troike, of The Center for Applied
Linguistics, interacted with us at many stages in the formation, analysis, and completion of the study. Hugh Rudorf, of the University of
Nebraska, and Terrance Graham, of Virginia Polytechnical Institute,
worked with us in setting up the original project and consulted with
us during various stages of the research. William Labov, Ralph W.
Fasold, Raven I. McDavid, Jr., and Crawford Feagin made many helpful
comments on various aspects of our analysis. No doubt, we will regret
that we have not always followed their advice.

Finally, we express our gratitude to those who took an active
interest in the form of the finished work. Peggy Good was committed
to seeing our original research project through to completion at some
inconvenience to her own schedule of activities, and Begay Atkinson
and Diane Bartosh were given the task of editing our sometimes unwieldy
prose. Our list of those who helped in one way or another could no
doubt be expanded considerably but it would still be incomplete. It
is often the brief question about a particular point of analysis, or
the quick reference to another work to consult, or a passing word of
encouragement that turns out to be a significant contribution to the
final product.

Walt Wolfram
Federal City College and
Center for Applied Linguistics

Donna Christian
Center for Applied Linguistics and
Georgetown University

March 1976

Table of Contents

Chapter One: Introduction

*My sister Aggie looked at it too when I
was through and she yelled out surprised,
"Here's a story about where we live!"*

—Jim Comstock, *Pa and Ma and Mister Kennedy*

OVERVIEW

   Language variation in American English is something that all speakers
of our language notice in one way or another. People notice it and comment
about it as they interact with individuals from different regions of the
United States and different social and ethnic groups. Educators also
confront it as they encounter the effect that dialect diversity may have
on language skills relating to the education process. And professional
linguists are concerned with it as they attempt to give a formal account
of the rules of English.
   While language diversity among English varieties has been of interest
for some time, we have witnessed an extended descriptive concern for
social and ethnic varieties of American English in recent years. Despite
the growing concern for understanding the linguistic structure of social
varieties, certain needs are still apparent. Some non-mainstream varieties, such as Vernacular Black English, have been the object of a great
deal of attention while others, particularly those with strong regional
ties, have been virtually ignored. One of these still neglected geographical areas is Appalachia. It is well known that this area is one
of the most linguistically divergent, yet it has been accorded minimal
descriptive attention in contemporary studies.
   The difference between the English spoken in this loosely defined
area and other varieties is well recognized by people from other areas
as they travel through the Appalachian region or have occasion to meet
people who have come from there. Unfortunately, poor imitations and
stereotypes of the language have been popularized in media presentations
depicting life in this mountain range. Such differences are also noticed
by the people of Appalachia as they compare their own speech to that

of speakers from other areas, or those among them who have lived in other areas and then returned. Educators have been concerned with the possible relationship of this variety and the acquisition of certain educational skills relating to language. As in other non-mainstream speaking communities that have been studied in the United States, there appears to be a high correlation between the level of literacy and the use of socially stigmatized language varieties. The literacy level in Appalachia is, for example, critically low when compared with that of other U.S. areas.

From the standpoint of the professional linguist, there is considerable impetus for having a description of this variety which can complement the current descriptions of other social and ethnic varieties of the language. In addition to the expansion of our descriptive base of American varieties, such studies provide an important source for investigating the theoretical nature of language variation. Recent research in sociolinguistics has developed important new models for describing language variation, particularly as evidenced in the formulation of variable rules and implicational relations. Data from this variety may serve as an extended empirical base to investigate the nature of linguistic variation.

The purpose of the present study is to add to our descriptive and practical knowledge of the range of language varieties in American English. On a descriptive level, we are concerned with providing an accurate sociolinguistic description of Appalachian English (henceforth, abbreviated as AE) as typified by one representative variety of the area. For the features of this variety which have been given minimal linguistic attention, we are concerned with giving a fairly detailed description of their structure. For linguistic features which have already been studied in some technical detail, we are also concerned with comparing our findings here with analyses of data from other areas. On a practical level, this descriptive study should provide a base for looking at a number of educational concerns, including the role of dialect differences in reading, composition, and language testing. Any concern for the role of language diversity in education must start with a solid descriptive base of the language diversity in question, and this study should provide such a base for a representative area of the Appalachian Mountain range.

A Sociolinguistic Framework

In order to place the description of AE in the subsequent chapters within an appropriate context, it is necessary to set forth a framework for viewing linguistic diversity. Some aspects of this model involve the consideration of social factors, whereas others deal primarily with linguistic considerations.

Perhaps the most significant contribution of sociolinguistic studies in the past decade has been the discovery that various social dialects in the United States are differentiated from each other not only by discrete sets of features but also by variations in the frequencies with which certain features or rules occur. This observation was in many respects at variance with popular perceptions of how varieties of English were differentiated. It was commonly thought, for example, that certain low class groups always used a particular linguistic form and high class groups never did. Studies of U.S. social dialects in the mid- and late sixties, however, clearly revealed that varieties of English could not be distinguished by simple "categorical" statements. In many cases, it was inaccurate to say that one group *always* used a particular form and another group *never* did. Instead, social dialects were more typically differentiated by the *extent* to which a certain rule applied, and many sociolinguistic studies ultimately involved a quantitative as well as a qualitative dimension.

Most of the linguistic features or rules we discuss for AE are variable rather than categorical. The term *variable,* as used here, refers to the fact that a speaker who has a particular form or rule will not use it in every instance where he might include it, but will instead fluctuate between it and an alternant form. For example, one of the characteristics of some AE speakers is the use of the "a-prefix" with certain verb + *ing* constructions, as in a sentence such as *He was a-runnin' across the field.* However, there are also many cases where the *a*-prefix does not occur but could have been used. Therefore, the same speaker who utters the above sentence may also use its non-*a*-prefixed counterpart, *He was runnin' across the field.* This type of fluctuation is quite common and does not imply any inherent structural weakness in the system. Analogous types of alternation can be observed within any of the varieties designated as standard English. For example, the relative pronoun *that* may occur in some cases as in *There's the boat that I built,* though it could be deleted in other cases as in *There's the boat I built,* resulting in a similar fluctuation between the presence and absence of a particular form. The difference between this example and the alternation illustrated for AE is that the alternant form in the one case is socially obtrusive (that is, it is more likely to be noticed and commented on) whereas in the other case it is not. Variation of this type is a common and widespread phenomenon that is simply an integral part of the organization of language systems.

That we observe variation between alternant forms does not necessarily mean that fluctuation is completely random and haphazard. Although we cannot predict exactly which form may be used in a given instance, sociolinguistic studies reveal that there are factors which systematically affect the likelihood that a particular variant will occur. When this takes place, we have what may be referred to as *structured variability.* Part of this effect on variability may be accounted for by certain social factors which may influence the relative frequency of a given form. Other aspects of structured variability can be accounted for by looking at linguistic context, such as the preceding or following linguistic environment. In these cases, certain linguistic contexts can be found to exert a fairly consistent influence on the frequency level of a given form. The systematic effect of these social and linguistic factors on linguistic variability is the touchstone of much of the current investigation of different varieties of American English.

Phonological Features

This study presents an overview of the linguistic features of AE in an attempt to highlight the major aspects of this system which may differentiate it from other varieties of English. Chapters Three and Four discuss the phonological and grammatical aspects of AE. Of necessity, our description has had to be somewhat selective, so there are aspects that have not been covered.

As will be seen in our descriptive account there are often intricate and complex rules that govern the various forms found in AE. In many cases, the rules governing these forms can be shown to have a relationship with rules found in other varieties of English, differing in relatively minor ways. It should be apparent that differences between AE and other varieties of English are highly systematic and regular; in no sense can AE be considered as an unworthy or haphazard approximation of more socially prestigious varieties of English. Some features of AE,

however, have taken on social significance, so that many of the variants
we discuss may be socially stigmatized. Social stigma is attached to
a particular language form not because of any inherent structural weakness of the form, but because of the relative social position of the
speakers who use it.

The description includes a number of the features of AE which are
retentions of forms that at one time were more generally characteristic
of a number of varieties of English. In these cases, changes affecting
other varieties of English may not yet have taken place in AE. We must
be careful, however, to avoid statements which simplistically relegate
AE to an earlier stage in the development of the English language, since
there are also cases where some of the features of AE may be candidates
for new developments in the grammar and phonology of American English.
Because of their current rejection by those who are in a social position
to set language norms, it may seem unlikely to some that stigmatized
forms of a language should be candidates for future developments. But
it should also be noted that the most formal styles of best-educated
speakers are the most conservative with respect to linguistic innovation,
so that new developments do not always (or even usually) begin with the
upper classes. Of course, those speakers in a position to set norms
for socially acceptable language must ultimately accept such innovations,
thereby limiting the number of changes introduced by the non-mainstream
groups, and their eventual establishment as part of the standard language.
No doubt, there are features that we discuss here which some day will be
considered as a part of the standard phonology and grammar of American
English. We find, then, that it is possible for a variety such as AE
to preserve some older forms of English while at the same time revealing
progress beyond the current development of standard English in other
aspects of the system.

We have attempted to give a linguistically accurate, but non-formal
account of the various features of AE that we describe. This particular
orientation is taken in order to provide a useful reference document for
language arts specialists, reading specialists, speech pathologists, and
educators, as well as a description that may be of use linguists. More
formal accounts for some of the features discussed here can be found in
the various references cited in our description. Obviously, the depth
of the technical analysis underlying the various features differs from
item to item. Since it was not feasible to examine the speech of all
informants for each of the variables treated, various subsets of the total
sample were utilized in many cases. These subsets differ in number and
composition in terms of individuals included. The selection criteria,
however, was informal and based largely on considerations of distribution
by age and sex, quality of tapes, amount of speech, and other practical
matters during the course of analysis. In each case, it is felt that a
representative sample resulted. There are some aspects of our description
based on a considerable amount of formal analysis, while there are others
still awaiting more detailed investigation. We view this description
from the perspective of an ongoing project, which can be complemented
and revised on the basis of additional investigation.

Grammatical Features

Like the description of phonological features, we find that there
are often intricate and complex rules which govern the grammatical forms
of non-mainstream varieties. In some respects, the discussion of socially
diagnostic grammatical variables is more important than phonological
variables, since it has been demonstrated (Wolfram, 1970a) that grammatical

features tend to stratify the population socially more sharply than
phonological features. As with the phonological features, many of the
grammatical variables which may distinguish different social groups of
speakers within Appalachia intersect with regional characteristics.
Therefore, some grammatical characteristics which are quite obtrusive
to an outsider may cut across different social classes within this area.
     It is most often found that AE speakers use what might be considered
a standard English variant and nonstandard one variably. That is, there
is not exclusive use of the socially stigmatized variant, but fluctuation
between this and the non-stigmatized alternant form. Unlike socially
diagnostic phonological variables, however, where many of the stigmatized
variants may be observed to some extent even among middle class speakers,
there is a general tendency of middle class speakers to categorically
avoid socially stigmatized grammatical forms. In the light of our previous discussion, the definition of what constitutes the formal standard
English rule for a region such as Appalachia may differ considerably from
that found in other regions of the United States, although there does
not appear to be as much regional flexibility in the establishment of a
standard variety with respect to grammatical patterns as is found in
phonological features.

Educational Implications

After presenting a sociolinguistic framework for the discussion of language diversity and a descriptive account of the linguistic features of
AE, we discuss some of the educational implications of the language situation found in Appalachia. A number of the educational implications
discussed relate to the general nature of dialect diversity rather than
to AE as such, but the specific application to AE should be apparent
throughout our discussion in Chapter Five. Topics included in our discussion are language attitudes, testing, reading, and language arts.

AN HISTORICAL SKETCH

     The Appalachian Mountain region covers territory from Maine to
Alabama, but the area most typically referred to as *Appalachia* has generally been considered to encompass parts of Kentucky, Virginia, North Carolina, Tennessee, and all of West Virginia. Parts of bordering states are
also included in more official definitions.[1] In all delineations, however, West Virginia is the only state which lies totally within this
region. Thus, those features which are most often associated with the
Appalachian area will apply in most cases to the entire state (e.g. the
predominance of a rural population with few metropolitan centers).
     A brief overview of the history of the central and southern Appa-
lachians, and of West Virginia in particular, can give some general indication of the roots of conditions found there today.[2] In the eighteenth
century, settlers began moving west from the Atlantic seaboard over certain routes found through the mountains where some remained and settled
in homes in valleys and on mountainsides. Few permanent settlements
survived until after the Indian population was forced out of the area,
even though a number of forts were established to protect the settlers
(Motley, 1973:39). In addition, difficulties were compounded by the
rugged mountain environment, and when settlements were maintained, the
people were largely cut off from other areas. The romantic picture of
the mountaineer, living up in the hills as his ancestors did, is for
many people in this area, not completely inaccurate.
     Many of the early settlers in this region were Pennsylvania Dutch
who migrated south, often continuing on to North Carolina. In addition

to the Germans, there were also English, Dutch, and smaller groups from other parts of Europe. However, a large and influential group--the Scottish--began arriving in America about 1640 and steadily moved to the South and West (Weatherford and Brewer, 1962:2). Those who passed through or remained in West Virginia are thought to have been mainly the Scotch-Irish, so named because their migration pattern included a stop in North Ireland before continuing on to northern American ports. It is not clear how homogeneous the early population of the area was. Some writers claim that "the mountain people [are] today largely native-born Americans of Scotch-Irish and Highland Scot lineage" (Weatherford and Brewer, 1962:4) while others feel that little evidence is available to support such a claim, maintaining instead, that "the probability is that the settlers of the mountains were representative of the population of the nation in the early nineteenth century (Belcher, 1962:39)."

Once permanent settlements were established, two basic life styles developed. The earlier settlers were largely self-sufficient farmers, whose families lived as comparatively independent units. When the country as a whole was growing rapidly during the nineteenth century, the resources of the region--particularly its lumber and coal--brought some industry to the area. The earlier settlers' agricultural life style was then complemented by the development of industrial mining and lumber camps which grew into towns that served the needs of farmers. Coles (1972:494) describes four kinds of communities that developed:

> First there are the hollows, with scattered pockets
> of people up in the hills--people usually related
> to one another and people with little to do but
> farm and hunt. Serving a number of these hollows
> is usually a larger community...able to offer the
> surrounding area a crossroad store, a post office,
> a school....Then there are the towns--mill towns.
> Here lumber and coal are gathered and loaded on
> their way out of the region....Finally, there
> are the real urban centers. They are usually
> prosperous and again, able to draw upon the wealth
> of the region's forests and mines....

The two counties we are specifically considering are Monroe and Mercer Counties, West Virginia which include the range of communities indicated above except for the urban center, and thus seem representative, on this level at least, of West Virginia and the larger Appalachian region. They are located in the far southern part of the state, each bordering on the state of Virginia (see Figure 1), and are similar in terrain, lying within "the most rugged parts" of what is termed the "Ridge and Valley Province" of the southern Appalachian area (Vance, 1962:1). However, factors involving other physical features and related aspects of historical development have led to some significant differences between the counties today.

Prior to the Civil War, the two counties were quite similar, although Mercer County seems to have been settled somewhat later than Monroe. Monroe County consisted of small communities of subsistence farmers when it was incorporated in 1799 (still a part of Virginia). When mineral water was discovered in the mid-1800's, a small, resort-type industry flourished briefly due to its claimed healing powers. This was relatively short-lived since more accessible treatments were found for the various ailments and--more importantly--since the predominantly southern upper class clientele diminished after the Civil War. Because of the extensive forests in the area, lumber became an important resource, and some in-

Figure 1

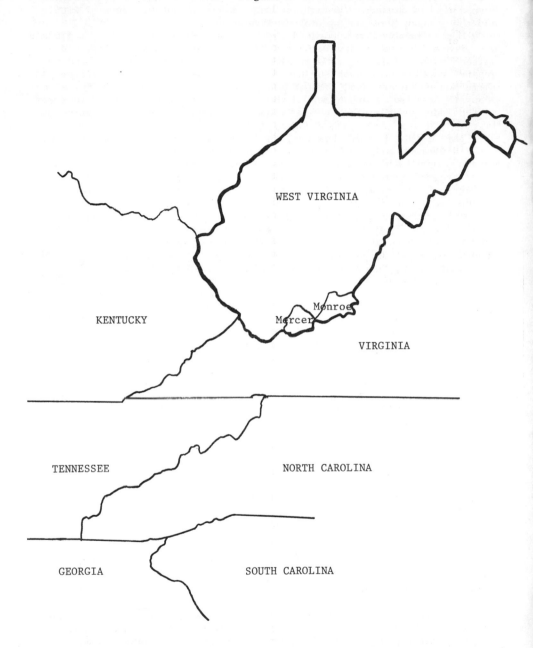

The Region as Defined in 1960 (from Ford,
The Southern Appalachian Region, A Survey)

dustrial development took place. However, since the lumbering that has
been done has been fairly small-scale, Monroe County has changed little
and the economy remains agriculturally-based.

Mercer County, incorporated in 1837 (also still a part of Virginia),
experienced its major development after coal was discovered. This resulted in the growth of industrial mining towns which naturally led to
greater population growth for the county. By 1900, it had 23,023 people
while Monroe County had 13,130 (Sizer, 1967). The mining industry also
brought a degree of urbanization to Mercer County since this is inherent
in the industrialization process. Monroe County, meanwhile, remained
largely isolated from such changes.

This is not to say, however, that the counties as a whole are radically different today. The rural sections of Mercer County are much like
Monroe County, and probably fairly typical of rural Appalachia in general,
consisting of a number of small communities and relatively isolated groups
living in the mountains. The main differences are found in the areas of
Mercer County which can be classified as *urban* according to the 1970 census. This urban area consists of approximately one-third of the total
population of 63,206, and represents only two cities, Princeton, the
county seat (population 7,253), and Bluefield (population 15,921). Monroe
County, with a 1970 population of 11,272 had no urban areas at all, and
its county seat, Union, with 566 residents, is the largest town.[3]

As greater attention is being given to the situation in Appalachia
today, Kentucky and West Virginia are often focused on because so much
of the discussion revolves around the mining industry. However, in comparing the two counties being considered here, it can be seen that the
rural counties in this area have faced many of the same difficulties,
except that the changes in the farming economy may have been less dramatic than those in mining. The nature of the physical environment, for
example, affects all areas, leading to problems like the one pointed out
by Ter Horst (1972:37) who notes that the development of transportation
systems is difficult because of the expense involved in building high-
ways. Coles (1972:495) discusses the convergence of factors giving rise
to economic problems:

> ...difficult terrain that has not made the entry of
> private capital easy, progressive deforestation,
> land erosion, periods of affluence when "coal was
> king," followed by increasing automation of the mine
> industry (and a decreasing national demand for coal),
> pollution that has ruined some of its finest streams
> so that strip mining can go full speed ahead...

Changes in population reflect the economic state of an area, with
prosperity generally coninciding with increases in population. One of
the most striking facts about Appalachia is the rate at which it has lost
population in the last 25 years, through a combination of out-migration
and decrease in the birthrate. Of those states affected by out-migration and birth decrease, West Virginia has been the hardest hit (Brown,
1972:131). Figure 2 gives the population figures for Monroe and Mercer
counties for the years 1900-1970, showing clearly the recent decline.
It can be seen that Monroe County, with its farming base, remained relatively stable (except for a decline during the Depression) in population
until recently. Mercer County, on the other hand, shows a rapid growth
period from 1900 to 1950, coinciding with the development of coal mining
and then a more dramatic decline. The influence of coal is also evident
from the number of people employed in mining, which in Mercer County dropped
from 3,808 in 1940, to 2,690 in 1950, to 427 in 1960 (Sizer, 1967:100).

Figure 2

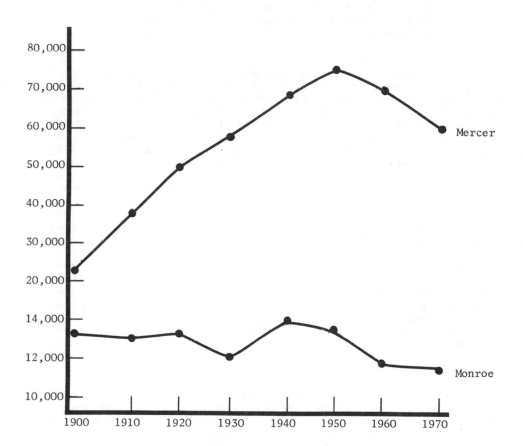

Population Figures for Monroe and Mercer Counties, West Virginia 1900-1970
(from Sizer, 1967; the 1970 census).

High rates of migration, thus, have been a major result of the economic situation in the area, with coal mining usually considered the prime cause. Brown (1972:142) notes:

> In eastern Kentucky, southern West Virginia and
> southwestern Virginia, the drastic decline of em-
> ployment in coal mining during the 1950's con-
> tinued on into the 1960's as a result of mechani-
> zation and the growth of strip mining. Together
> with availability of employment in metropolitan
> industrial centers outside Appalachia itself,
> notably in the Midwest, this resulted in a virtual
> stampede of migrants out of the region in the
> 1950's. Although the number of migrants leaving
> declined in the 1960's, the rate of migration
> loss from most of this area was still very high.

There are two significant consequences of this process which will not be discussed extensively, but should be mentioned. First, migration of great numbers to large midwestern and northern cities naturally leads to some problems in these locations. The migration to large cities adds to their labor pool and often to their unemployment statistics, so that many of the out-migrants ultimately return to their home states. A number of studies have been done on the Appalachian migrant in the city (e.g. Walls and Stephenson, 1973; Glenn, 1970; Photiadis, 1969) which document the kinds of problems that are created in such contexts. The second consequence is that many of those who leave the area are the young adults, often the more educated, who either cannot find employment or who see more attractive opportunities elsewhere. This leaves some areas with an unbalanced distribution of population among various age groups, a matter which has led to a certain amount of concern.

The brief picture of these Appalachian counties given above mirrors to a large extent that of the entire region, both historically and presently, with the physical environment a very important determining factor of the area's development at all times. The isolation of the past has been to a great extent overcome but by no means completely, and this has brought an increased contact between the culture which had evolved here and that of other parts of the nation.

THE LINGUISTIC SAMPLE

In order to provide an adequate data base for our linguistic analysis, a fairly extensive collection of tape-recorded samples of spontaneous conversation has been obtained from Monroe and Mercer Counties in West Virginia. In all, 129 tape-recorded samples have been obtained. Five different age levels are represented by the informants:[4] 7-11 years, 12-14 years, 15-18 years, 20-40 years, and over 40 years. The majority of the informants would be considered to be of the lower socio-economic level according to current indices, although there is some representation of the entire social range of the population in this area. Our sample is, however, somewhat out of proportion with the entire population since recent figures indicate that approximately 25 percent of the population falls below the federally defined poverty level. Our concentration on the lower socio-economic classes is motivated by the fact that we are primarily concerned with the language variety which might be considered *most* divergent from some of the more mainstream varieties of English.

The informants in this study were all interviewed by fieldworkers from the area, nonlinguists who were trained specifically to do socio-linguistic interviews. A broad outline of questions was prepared in consultation with some of the fieldworkers in order to focus on topics of local interest. Interviewers were instructed to be flexible with the outline and pursue topics of interest, following the guidelines for obtaining relatively natural spontaneous conversation outlined in Wolfram and Fasold (1974:46-54). Local themes found frequently in our tapes include childhood games, hunting, fishing and ghost stories, the mining industry and local farming customs (see Appendix A for a copy of the questionnaire and Appendix B for a typescript sample).

In all, six different fieldworkers from Monroe and Mercer Counties participated in the collection of interviews. Interviews were carried out in a number of locations, including the informant's home, the fieldworker's home, or a location convenient to both. The location of the interview was left up to the discretion of the fieldworker, although each was instructed to conduct the interview in a setting where the informant would be most apt to be comfortable. For reasons beyond our control, some younger children had to be interviewed within the context of the school.

The different fieldworkers represented considerable range in their ability to elicit the type of spontaneous conversation which was necessary for this descriptive study. Several of the fieldworkers were extremely ingenious in how they carried out the interview, and had considerable advantage over the type of interview that would have had to be conducted by the authors. They fully utilized their indigenous status through their previous knowledge of interests of the informant and their ability to pick up cues about activities in the area. There are, of course, also instances where the fieldworker felt too constrained by the interview outline and did not elicit adequate amounts of spontaneous conversation for our purposes. But the excellence of the good interviews by some indigenous fieldworkers seemed to adequately compensate for the formality of others. In anticipation of a range of interviewing capabilities, we purposely arranged to have considerably more interviews conducted than we could analyze thoroughly.

The informants used for this analysis were not chosen randomly. Rather, we set up a profile of the type of individual we were interested in for the sake of this study, and asked the indigenous fieldworker to choose individuals who were typically of the lower socio-economic classes and who were lifetime residents of the area. For the most part, fieldworkers complied with our requests, as indicated in the background information data sheets filled out for each informant.

In an attempt to pare down the original collection of tapes to a more usable size in terms of a corpus for more extended technical analysis, each of the original tapes was evaluated by the researchers in terms of the quality of the interview. Primarily, we were concerned with the amount of speech found in the interview and the rapport which the fieldworker had with the informant. An additional concern was the fidelity of the recording for detailed listening. Each tape-recorded interview was listened to by these researchers and a judgment made of its potential for quantitative sociolinguistic analysis in terms of a basic three-grade rating system. A grade of 1 was assigned to interviews which were judged to have a good representation of spontaneous conversation and good interviewer-informant rapport. Typically, these recordings consisted of 45-60 minute interviews, with the majority of the conversation carried by the informant. A grade of 2 was assigned to interviews with a fair amount of spontaneous conversation and adequate rapport between the field-

worker and the informant.   A grade of *3* was assigned to short interviews
(30 minutes or less) and/or those in which the interviewer-informant rapport seemed inadequate to produce the type of spontaneous, relatively informal speech in which we were interested.   While these ratings were ultimately subjective, a survey of the two evaluators of tapes indicated
that there was a good deal of agreement between researchers as to the
value of the tape for the purposes of this investigation.

From the original sample, 52 taped interviews were chosen for more
intensive linguistic analysis.   These tapes were chosen to represent the
specified age categories for each sex.   Within each cell (with five age
categories and two sexes) all interviews with a rating of *1* were chosen
to be a part of the *primary* corpus.   Interviews which did not receive a *1*
rating were chosen in terms of a decreasing rating scale until at least
five informants in each cell were chosen.   All interviews with a rating
of *3* were automatically assigned to the *secondary* corpus.   In addition,
interviews rated *2* were assigned to the secondary corpus after the limit
of five informants in each cell had been chosen.   In this study, the
secondary corpus was utilized for extraction of forms which provided a
basis for some of the aspects of AE studied only qualitatively.   The primary corpus was used for both the qualitative and quantitative aspects
of this study.

In Table 1, the distribution of interviews chosen to serve as the
primary corpus is given.   It should be noted that two of the cells do
not have five informants in them.   One cell, 20-40 year-old males, has
only four informants due to the fact that our original sample did not
provide us with an adequate representation of males in this category.
The cell with more than five informants, females above 40, has eight
informants due to the fact that more than five received ratings of *1*
for the adequacy of the interview.   (See p. 13.)

The way in which we have selected our primary corpus is, of course,
biased in favor of those interviews which produced a considerable amount
of spontaneous conversation and those that had evidenced good rapport
between the interviewer and the informant.   And, as mentioned earlier,
there was a bias in terms of who the fieldworkers might have conceived
as fairly representative speakers from the area in the various age categories designated for study.   While such a bias might hinder us from
getting a representative cross-section of the population, it seemed appropriate in terms of the goals of the study.

Notes
1.   The Appalachian Regional Commission, for example, also lists counties
     in New York, Pennsylvania, Maryland, Ohio, South Carolina, Georgia,
     Mississippi, and Alabama.
2.   In addition to the bibliographic resources cited, information in this
     section was provided by Haskell Shumate, county clerk of Monroe County,
     West Virginia, in a conversation about the history of the area.
3.   The statistics in this section from the 1970 census were obtained from
     a U. S. Department of Commerce publication, *Characteristics of the
     Population: West Virginia* (January 1973) where this information as
     well as comparative figures from earlier censuses can be found.
4.   The term *informant* is used traditionally in linguistics to refer to
     someone who furnishes the researcher with samples of language.   It
     should not be equated with the connotations of the term *informer*
     as it is used outside linguistic circles.

Table 1

Age Group	*Male* Tape No.	Age	Interview Rating	*Female* Tape No.	Age	Interview Rating
7-11	47	7	1-	73	8	1-
	48	9	1-	74	11	1-
	49	9	1-	75	10	2+
	51	10	1	77	11	1
	124	11	1-	80	9	2+
12-14	2	13	1	61	14	2+
	4	13	1	70	13	2
	6	14	1-	148	13	2
	10	14	1-	150	13	2
	44	14	1	154	13	1-
15-18	1	15	1-	64	15	1-
	7	17	2	65	15	2+
	17	16	2+	66	17	2+
	46	15	2+	149	18	2+
	155	17	2	151	18	1-
20-40	87	24	2-	29	33	2+
	158	25	2-	35	22	1
	159	20	1-	36	27	1
	164	33	1-	40	39	1
				156	20	1
40+	22	60	1	28	42	1
	30	50	1	37	45	1
	31	67	1	160	56	1
	32	54	1-	83	93	1
	146	52	1	85	78	1
				152	64	1
				153	83	1
				157	52	1

List of Informants Used for Extensive Study of Appalachian English, by Tape Number, Age, and Interview Rating

Chapter Two: A Sociolinguistic Framework for the Study of Appalachian Speech

There is a growing realization that the basis of intersubjective knowledge in linguistics must be found in speech — language as it is used in everyday life by members of the social order, that vehicle of communication in which they argue with their wives, joke with their friends, and deceive their enemies.

—William Labov, *Sociolinguistic Patterns*

SOCIAL ASPECTS OF VARIATION

When we speak of the *social variable* we are referring to the various behavioral factors that may be correlated with linguistic diversity. Obviously, there are a large number of these, and any study is somewhat limited by the social factors that it chooses to consider. Although it may be theoretically possible to isolate various social variables for the sake of study, it must be understood that this is often an artifact of the way in which a study is conducted, for it is the interaction of various social factors that ultimately accounts for linguistic diversity.

Region

A central factor in terms of accounting for diversity within American English is *geographical region*. Regionally-correlated differences emerge for several reasons. First, there are different patterns of settlement history. Dialect areas in the U.S. often indicate the migration of the early settlers, and this is no different for those varieties found in the Appalachian Mountain range. The effect of the relatively large and influential Scotch-Irish settlement in the area as described in Chapter One still lingers today. Another factor affecting regional differences is the general pattern of population movement. For example, the major drift of the White population of America has been east to west, a fact reflected by many of the dialect boundaries that can be isolated as they delineate different U.S. regional groups today. As a result of movement like this, it is very likely that a number of the linguistic characteristics of AE might also be found in areas of the Ozarks, given the fact that there was considerable migration from Appalachia to the Ozarks during one period

15

in American migratory history.

Finally, there is the matter of physical geography. At one point in
U.S. history, natural physical barriers were an important factor in sep-
arating groups, thus allowing discontinuities in communication patterns to
emerge. Whenever such discontinuities emerge--whether due to geographic
or social factors--a natural situation exists for linguistic divergence
to arise. Although modern technological advances may have greatly reduced the obstacles that the physical parameters posed, the previously ,
established lines of communication still show the effects of separation.
In many cases, geographically isolated areas of this type are seen to
preserve some older forms of the language, and thus become so-called
relic areas. While it cannot be denied that modern communication and
transportation systems have had an effect on Appalachia, their influence
seems to be somewhat exaggerated, for geographical patterns often go
hand in hand with other social factors. There are, for example, particular life styles in Appalachia which have been maintained despite the
greater accessibility of the area. Therefore, the geographical distribution and the maintenance of a particular life style can still be seen
to set this region apart from others in the United States. One aspect
of this difference is, naturally, reflected in language.

Status

Region is obviously an essential variable in accounting for certain
aspects of linguistic diversity, but it does not stand alone. Within a
given geographical region all individuals do not talk alike. In order
to account for these differences in a systematic way, other social parameters must be examined. Even a work as heavily oriented toward settlement history and geographic distribution as the *Linguistic Atlas of the
United States and Canada* recognizes the intersection of *social status*
in accounting for linguistic diversity within a geographically-defined
locale.

Although there is little doubt that social status differences correlate with linguistic differences, a precise definition of social status
in our society is rather elusive. Various attempts to define it through
objective parameters such as occupation, education, residency, and in-
come have proved useful, but not foolproof. On the other hand, attempts
to define it in terms of the subjective evaluation of individuals actually
participating in the community's social relations also are not without some
pitfalls. It is a concept which ultimately combines subjective and objective parameters of many types of behavioral roles.

Several approaches have been utilized in terms of correlating linguistic differences with social status differences. In some cases, various social classes are delimited before linguistic analysis, so that linguistic features are correlated with predetermined social groups. In other
cases, the population is delimited on the basis of linguistic differences
then examined in terms of the social characteristics of the various linguistic groups. It is also possible to use a combination of methods,
starting with a finely stratified group of subjects, but combining and
manipulating the social groups in such a way as to most clearly reveal
patterns of correlation between linguistic phenomenon and social stratification. To the extent that social status is a variable to be considered
in our description, our general approach has been to determine linguistic
groups first and then look at the various social characteristics of these
groups. Our main goal, however, is to give a description of the variety
of English spoken in Appalachia which would be more distant from mainstream varieties of standard English. As a result, we have focused more

on the speech of individuals typically assigned lower social status in the
area.

Any linguistic variable whose distribution differs on the basis of
social status may be referred to as *socially diagnostic*. Naturally, socially diagnostic features will differ in terms of how they correlate with
various social status groups. One of the differences between socially
diagnostic linguistic variables is related to their intersection with regional differences as discussed above. There are some socially diagnostic
linguistic variables which are only found to be socially significant in
a particular region. In other regions, the variable may have little or
no socially diagnostic value. For example, the absence of a contrast
between the vowel *i* and *e* before nasal segments (e.g. *pin* versus *pen*)
may be diagnostic in some more northern areas, but it is not particularly
diagnostic in many regions of the South, including apparently this area
of Appalachia. On the other hand, there are some variables which apparently have a more general socially diagnostic value which is not characteristic of any particular U.S. region. It is likely that, for example, multiply-negated sentences (see Chapter Four) would be socially
diagnostic in any area.

There are, in addition, differences in the way diagnostic variables
relate to differentiation according to social class. Some sharply differentiate social classes so that there is a fairly discrete separation
of social classes on the basis of the linguistic variable. In such a
case, members of one group would tend to use a particular feature a great
deal while members of another group might use it rarely or not at all.
On the other hand, there are cases in which social classes are not as
discretely differentiated, showing instead a progressive increase in the
frequency with which forms are used as various social classes are compared. Here, members of one group would be likely to fall within a
certain range in the usage of a particular feature, and this range would
differ, but not radically, from that of another group. The case of sharp
demarcation between social groups has been referred to as *sharp stratification* and those which involve less discrete differences as *gradient
stratification* (Wolfram and Fasold, 1974:80-81).

In terms of the social significance of various features, we may
distinguish between *socially prestigious* and *socially stigmatized* features. Socially prestigious features are those which are adopted by high
status groups as a linguistic indication of social status, whereas stigmatized features are associated with low status groups. It is important
to note that the absence of a prestige feature does not imply that the
alternant form is stigmatized nor vice versa. Thus, for example, the
avoidance of multiple negation in constructions such as *He didn't do
nothing* does not necessarily mean that the singly negated counterpart is
prestigious. In our description of the features of AE, the difference
between stigmatized and non-stigmatized forms is discussed much more frequently than that between prestigious and non-prestigious alternants.
While this may be attributable in part to the focus of our study, this
is also characteristic of how social differentiation in language operates
in American society. Status groups are more often differentiated by the
usage of socially stigmatized features than they are by the usage of
socially prestigious ones. In fact, it is tempting to define standard
varieties of English in terms of their relative absence of socially stigmatized features used by non-mainstream groups as opposed to the socially
prestigious features which may be found among high status groups. This
pattern would contrast with that of a society which emphasized differentiation in terms of socially prestigious features rather than stigmatized
ones.

Perhaps more important than the objective stratification of features

in terms of socially diagnostic features are the subjective reactions that
various groups have to them. Labov (1964:102) has classified subjective
reactions into three main types: social indicators, social markers, and
social stereotypes. *Social indicators* can be correlated with social class,
but have little effect on a listener's judgment of the social status of
the speaker. Wolfram and Fasold (1974:83) note:

> One of the most important clues for social indicators
> is the lack of variation in different styles. If speak-
> ers show a conscious or unconscious awareness of a
> socially diagnostic feature they will generally vary
> its frequency in more formal styles. Thus, a presti-
> gious variant would become more frequent in more for-
> mal styles of speech and a stigmatized one less
> frequent. In the case of social indicators, this
> does not generally take place because of relative
> unawareness of the socially diagnostic variable.

Social markers show both social and stylistic variation and have a
regular effect on a listener's judgment of a speaker's social status. It
is not necessary for social markers to be recognized on a conscious level;
in many cases, they may evoke an unconscious effect on a listener.
In the case of *social stereotypes*, however, particular linguistic
features become the overt topics of social comment in the speech community. Features such as the use of *ain't*, multiple negation, or the use of
an item like *'tater* for *potato* may be social stereotypes. There are
actually a number of social stereotypes found in AE, many of which would
be the object of comment from outsiders, but also some which are commented
on by people from the region. Since there are, however, a number of
stereotypes that do not correspond to actual linguistic behavior, we
must caution here that we are referring only to those features that relate to actual speech. In many cases, stereotypes involve a legitimate
observation but an interpretation which has no basis in fact. For example,
it may be an accurate observation to note that AE speakers tend to reduce
certain glided vowels in English (e.g. as in *time*) but to attribute it
to climate or ambition has absolutely no basis in fact. By the same
token, it may be valid to note that some AE speakers tend to use intensifying adverbs to a greater extent than other varieties of English (e.g.
as in *plumb stupid* or *right smart*) but claiming the source of this to be
an innate concern for vividness and preciseness in AE is also unwarranted.
The types of stereotypes that evolve concerning the linguistic features
of a variety such as AE are an interesting and important topic for study,
but beyond the scope of this description.

Style

Another important social variable is style. It does not take any
particular sociolinguistic expertise to realize that speakers show considerable flexibility in their use of style. We do not need to be informed
by a sociolinguist that we talk to a casual peer acquaintance in a manner
different from the way we talk to a respected authority. Lay indications
of such sensitivity are readily available.
There are a number of ways in which we might approach the matter of
stylistic variation, but the most essential dimension appears to relate
to how much attention speakers focus on their speech. The general principle governing stylistic shifting is summarized by Labov (1972a:112)
when he observes that "styles can be ordered along a single dimension,

measured by the amount of attention paid to speech." Within an interview,
formal styles are defined as those situations where speech is a primary
focus, whereas informal styles are defined in terms of the contexts where
there is the least amount of audio-monitoring of speech. At one end of
the continuum is the careful speech that one might use in a tape-recorded
interview with a respected stranger; at the other end of the continuum is
the informal style one would use with a trusted peer group member without
an outsider present. Naturally, every tape-recorded interview situation
creates a somewhat artificial situation which has a tendency to lead to
more formal styles, and this study is no exception. If more informal
speech styles are desired, certain strategies must be utilized to overcome the built-in obstacles of the tape-recorded interview situation.
One method of overcoming this is through the use of indigenous fieldworkers, people from the area who are personal acquaintances of the informants. In this particular study, indigenous fieldworkers were used
to considerable advantage since they pursued topics of interest to the
informants and events which were part of their common experience. Such
topics allow subjects to minimize the attention they give to the form
of their speech. This involvement in the subject matter proved to be
advantageous for the elicitation of more informal speech styles since
it provides a focus on content, rather than form of speech. Naturally,
subjects still indicated somewhat of a range of formality, but typically,
they responded with speech which was relatively casual, especially as
the interview proceeded.

Socially diagnostic features typically show parallel behavior along
a social class and style continuum. In particular, a feature which is
more common in the lower social classes than it is in the upper classes
will be more common in more informal styles than in formal styles for all
speakers. That is, a stigmatized form would be expected to show decreased
frequencies and a prestigious variant increased frequencies as one moves
from informal to formal styles.

Related to style shifting along the continuum of formality is the
notion of *hypercorrection*. In general, hypercorrection is characterized
by the overextension of a feature to contexts where the feature is not
used by native speakers of a language. This overextension is due to a
situation where the constraints on formality make the speaker aware of
the need to use socially acceptable forms. Wolfram and Fasold (1974:87-
88) note two types of hypercorrection, one which is quantitative and one
which is qualitative. In *statistical hypercorrection*, the structural
placement of forms follows that of the more prestigious groups, but the
relative frequency of the forms exceeds the norms of the more prestigious
social groups. This typically takes place in more formal styles, where
the linguistic security of the lower middle classes makes them use frequency levels higher than the more secure upper middle classes when speech
is the primary focus. *Structural hypercorrection*, on the other hand, involves the extension of a form to structural contexts where it would not
normally be used. A speaker may realize that a feature is socially favored, but not be aware of its restriction in terms of linguistic environments and thus use the form in linguistic contexts where it is inappropriate in terms of the rules of the language variety which the speaker is
trying to emulate. Most of the examples of hypercorrection cited in our
study involve structural rather than statistical hypercorrection.

Age

There are actually two types of age-related phenomena that must be
distinguished in any discussion of age differences. One type relates to
generational differences. In this case, older generations may not have

undergone linguistic changes that have affected the younger generation.
Although we may not always have access to detailed accounts of specific
language behavior of various generations at different time periods, it
is possible to observe language changes that are taking place through the
apparent time. From this perspective, we view different generations
within a population as a reflection of different time levels. Thus, the
speech of a group of AE speakers over 40 may represent one period in the
history of the language while a younger group, say, 17-20, represents another time period. To a large extent, the linguistic change in progress
in Appalachia is observed by appealing to the dimension of apparent time.
By the same token, stability of certain features in AE is noted by observing the occurrence of similar forms for all the different age groups
delimited in this study.

When we say that particular forms in AE characterize the older generation, we are, for the most part, maintaining that the features are
undergoing change, and may be lost or changed by the current generation.
In some ways, the change currently taking place within AE may appear more
rapid than that observed in some other varieties of English. This should
not be interpreted without qualification, however, since there are still
many features characterizing AE which indicate a good degree of stability.

In addition to generational differences, it is important to recognize the phenomenon of *age-grading*. This refers to characteristic linguistic behaviors appropriate for different stages in the life history
of an individual. Within the life cycle of an individual, there are behavioral patterns that are considered appropriate for various stages.
Language, as one aspect of behavior, is a way in which these can be mani-
fested. Age-grading, as we have defined it here, should be clearly differentiated from *language development*. Language development refers to
the initial acquisition of a language system, whereas age-grading refers
to age-related differences once acquisition has taken place. Thus, post-
acquisitional adolescent speech may differ from teen aged or adult speech
because of different linguistic expectations in different life cycle
stages. While age-grading is to be differentiated from generational differences, there is, of course, an intersection, and the isolation of these
aspects can sometimes be made only on the basis of a comprehensive analysis of the language system. Some age-grading differences have been observed in AE but generational differences tend to be more prominent.

Sex

Finally, we should mention the parameter of sex differences in relation to language. Although some cultures prescribe important differences between men's and women's speech, including entire grammatical categories, differences in English tend to be somewhat more subtle (see Labov,
1972b). With reference to socially diagnostic linguistic features, it
has been noted that women tend to avoid socially stigmatized features
moreso than men. To a large extent, this difference is quantitative
rather than qualitative, so that women simply tend to reveal lower frequency levels for socially stigmatized forms. There are, of course, a
number of sociological reasons why this might be the case, given different behavioral role expectations in our society. While the use of
socially stigmatized variants on the part of males may be viewed as an
indicator of masculinity, positive values are not as readily attached
to the use of such variants by women. Furthermore, women often tend to
be the innovators of language change, given their culturally designated
sensitivity to language norms. This may often result in their taking
the lead with respect to the spread of socially prestigious features.
Sex-related differences are not as apparent in our study of AE as

they have been in some other studies, although it appears that the general avoidance of socially stigmatized features by women is found to some extent. The differences between the men and women in our sample, however, appear to be mostly quantitative, and of lesser importance than other social variables, such as age and status.

LINGUISTIC ASPECTS OF VARIATION

Structured Variability

Not all the effects on the variability of linguistic forms can be accounted for on the basis of the types of social factors cited above. As mentioned previously, there are some systematic effects on variability which are related to the linguistic context in which items may occur. It is observed that some linguistic environments tend to favor a particular form or rule as opposed to other environments. This can best be understood by way of illustration, taking the case of word-final consonant cluster reduction as found in some varieties of American English. This particular rule has been studied in a range of settings, with the various studies showing an impressive regularity in the operation of the rule. The rule in question affects the final stop member of a word-final consonant cluster such as *st, nd, ld, sht, md*, and so forth (for a complete list of the clusters affected by this rule, see Chapter Three). Thus, items such as *west, find*, or *cold* may be realized as *wes', fin'*, or *col'*.

In addition to the effect of social variables such as those discussed above, there is a systematic effect on the relative frequency of consonant cluster reduction which is related to the preceding and following linguistic environments. These linguistic factors include whether the following word begins with a consonant as opposed to a vowel and the way in which the cluster has been formed. With reference to the following environment, we find that a following word which begins with a consonant will greatly increase the likelihood that the reduction process will take place. Thus, for example, we find reduction more frequent in a context such as *west road* or *cold cuts* than in a context such as *west end* or *cold apple*. While some reduction may be found in both contexts, it is clearly favored when the following word begins with a consonant.

As mentioned above, we also find that reduction is influenced by the way in which the cluster is formed. To understand this relationship, we must note that some clusters are an inherent part of the word base, as in items like *guest* or *wild*. There are, however, other cases where a cluster is formed only through the addition of an *-ed* suffix, which is primarily formed phonetically through the addition of *t* or *d*. When the *-ed* suffix is added to an item such as *guess*, the form *guessed* is pronounced the same as *guest*, so that it now ends in an *st* cluster. Or, an item like *called* may actually end in an *ld* cluster as it is pronounced something like *calld*. In these cases, the cluster is formed because of the *-ed* addition, since neither *call* nor *guess* have basic word forms which end in a cluster. When the degree of variation for base word clusters is compared with those formed through the addition of *-ed*, it is found that the former case clearly favors consonant cluster reduction. That is, we are more likely to find word-final consonant cluster reduction in an item such as *guest* or *wild* than in one like *guessed* or *called*. Again, we note that fluctuation can be observed in both types of clusters, so that the favoring effect of base word clusters on reduction is simply a matter of relative frequency. The systematic effect of the linguistic influences observed here is quite regular from speaker to speaker in terms of the relative effect, although of course, the actual percentage figures may differ somewhat. It is further observed that the relative effect of these influences on reduction cuts across various social classes of the varieties of English where the consonant cluster reduction rule operates.

When linguists have actually looked at the influence of various linguistic factors on the relative frequency of rule operation, they have found that not only are there many influences which favor the operation of certain rules, but some of these will effect the rule to a greater degree than others. Although we have already noted the influences of the following environment and the way in which the cluster is formed, we have yet to establish which of these effects on reduction is greater. For example, is the effect of the following consonant on reduction greater than that of a base word cluster or vice versa? One way to determine the relationship between various influences is to order them along a progressive dimension, in which the extent of rule operation is differentiated according to all the possible environmental combinations. For example, the possible combination of environmental influences which are found for consonant cluster reduction are (1) a following consonant when the cluster is part of the basic word, (2) a following consonant when the cluster is formed through the addition of the *-ed* suffix, (3) a following vowel when the cluster is part of the basic word, and (4) a following vowel when the cluster is formed through the addition of *-ed*. As an illustration, we can cite the actual incidence of cluster reduction as found in a previous study of this phenomenon reported by Wolfram (1969:57-74). See Table 2, p. 23.

The highest percentage of reduction is observed, as expected, where both of the influences favoring the operation of the rule are found: with a following consonant and the cluster as part of a base word. The lowest frequency--equally predictably--is found where neither of the factors favoring reduction are found: with a following vowel in a cluster formed through the addition of the *-ed* suffix. The important cases for determining the relationship of the influences are, however, those where the influences conflict; that is, where a following consonant, which favors reduction, is combined with a *-ed* formed cluster, which inhibits it, and a base word cluster, which favors reduction, is combined with a following vowel, which inhibits it. When these are compared, we find that the effect of the following consonant appears to be greater than that of the base word cluster, as indicated in the progressive pattern of reduction for the combination of influences. The relationship of the influences is readily seen by placing them in a hierarchical display such as Figure 3 on p. 24. If the hierarchical display were arranged so that the influence of the base word clusters was considered the more important influence, the hierarchical display would not match the progression in frequency, as in the figure.

Whenever we isolate a systematic linguistic influence on the variability of a rule, we refer to this influence as a *linguistic constraint*. If there are two or more constraints which can be ordered with respect to each other in terms of the relative importance or their effect, we refer to them as *first order constraint*, *second order constraint*, and so forth.

In many instances, the linguistic constraints and their ordering can be found to operate across different social variables, such as class, sex, and age. Thus, we see the same relations of consonant cluster reduction for different classes of Black speakers in Detroit, as indicated in Table 3 (p. 23).

The differences between the social classes seen in Table 3 are related to the actual frequency level of rule operation rather than the type of constraint or the ordering of the constraints. The important aspect of structured variability is the relationship of various constraints to variation rather than the actual frequency figures of rule operation.

Table 2

Environment	Example	Percent Reduced
Following Consonant, Basic Word	*wes(t) road*	97
Following Consonant, *-ed*	*guess(ed) five*	76
Following Vowel, Basic Word	*wes(t) end*	72
Following Vowel, *-ed*	*guess(ed) at*	34

Percentage of Consonant Cluster Reduction in Different Combinations of Environmental Influences for Working Class Black Detroit Speakers

Table 3

Environment	Upper Middle % Reduced	Lower Middle % Reduced	Upper Working % Reduced	Lower Working % Reduced
Following Consonant, Basic Word	79	87	94	97
Following Consonant, *-ed*	49	62	73	76
Following Vowel, Basic Word	28	43	65	72
Following Vowel, *-ed*	7	13	24	34

Consonant Cluster Reduction for Four Different Classes of Detroit Black Speakers (Wolfram, 1969)

Table 4

A	B
0	0
0	1
1	1

Tabular Display of an Implicational Relation

Figure 3

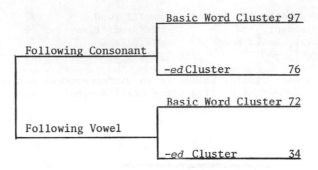

Correct Hierarchical Arrangement of Linguistic Influences on Consonant Cluster Reduction

Figure 4

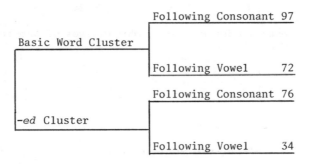

Incorrect Hierarchical Display of Linguistic Influences on Consonant Cluster Reduction

There are important dimensions of structured variability as we have
discussed which relate to how one gives a formal account of the rule for
a given variety. However, there are important considerations of variability which must be kept in mind regardless of the level of technical description that we give for AE. For example, in a general description of AE such
as that given in Chapters Three and Four, it would be inaccurate to assume
that the rules of AE were categorical. But it would also be incomplete
without some recognition of the systematic effect of various linguistic
constraints. Although we do not give a formal account of structured variability, these dimensions must always be kept in mind when we discuss variable aspects of the features of AE.

Implicational Relations

In the preceding section, we have discussed the systematic variation
in the frequency with which various forms occur. This is, however, not
the only way in which socially significant variation can be viewed. Another way to examine socially significant linguistic data is by looking
at variation in terms of combinations of features. This approach deals
with the implication of the presence of certain features for the absence
or presence of others, and is therefore sometimes referred to as *implicational analysis.*
A relationship of implication with respect to variation in language involves the existence of one linguistic feature *implying* the existence of another. This relation holds when a form *B* is always present
when another form, *A*, is found, but not vice versa. Given this relationship, we may say that "*A* implies *B*." A tabular display of this relationship may be indicated by a representation where *1* stands for the categorical presence of a feature, and *0* the categorical absence as in Table 4
on p. 23.
In the display in Table 4, it is possible for neither *A* nor *B* to
occur, or both *A* and *B* to occur, but if only one occurs, then it must be
B. That is, *A* implies *B* since *A* can never occur if *B* does not also occur.
If the situation were such that *A* occurred when *B* did not, then the implicational relation between *A* and *B* specified above would be the opposite
(i.e. *B* implies *A*).
To illustrate how this type of implicational relation specified above
relates to language entities, we can consider the case of copula deletion,
somewhat simplified for illustrative purposes here. It is observed that
copula deletion of present tense forms such as *He nice* or *You ugly* is
found to operate on both forms of the copula which come from *IS* and *ARE*.
As its usage is observed among different groups of speakers, we find that
there is, however, an implicational relationship between copula deletion
for *IS* and *ARE*. First of all, there are some speakers who have copula
deletion for both *IS* and *ARE* and there are speakers who have copula deletion for neither. On the other hand, if a speaker is to have copula
absence for only one form, then it will be *ARE* and not *IS*. We therefore
have an implicational relationship between *IS* deletion and *ARE* deletion,
in which *IS* deletion implies *ARE* deletion. The tabular arrangement for
this would then be as in Table 5 (p. 27).
In an arrangement such as this, the rows typically represent different groups of speakers, as indicated in different varieties of English.
The vertical dimension, then, defines the relationship among different
varieties of English. An implicational relation such as this can, of
course, be much more extensive than what we have portrayed in Table 5.
In the discussion so far, we have described implicational arrays as
if they pertained only to categorical usage. That is, either a given

form will always occur or it will never occur. In the light of our previous discussion of variability we know that there is an important variable dimension which is a part of language. This variability can be built
into implicational analysis by recognizing a category of variability.
If we symbolize variability between features as *X*, we may then have three
values, categorical absence *O*, categorical presence *1*, and variability
between presence and absence *X*. We may, then, for example have a display
such as the one displayed in Table 6.

For some of the features in this scale, we find categorical presence
or absence, whereas for others we only find a variable parameter. There
is, in addition, an implicational relationship which pertains to variability, when variability characterizes two or more successive entities in a
particular row. For example, we find that all four entities in the third
row of Table 6 show variability. In a situation like this, there is an
implication that the frequency is greater (that is, closer to categorical
1) for those features to the right of a given variable entity and less
for those to the left. For example, in the third row, we find that the
frequency in *D* will be greater than that in *C*, which in turn will be greater than that found for *B*, which will in turn be greater than that found
for *A*. Thus, we see an implicational pattern which relates to the variable parameter as well as to the categorical aspect. It is also noted
that not all the logical possibilities in this three-valued display in
Table 6 need be realized in terms of how language systems function at
a given point in time. For example, Table 6 actually characterizes the
structure of the variability of final consonant cluster reduction as discussed earlier. This pattern is found in Table 7, which shows the relationship that various varieties of English may have in terms of consonant
cluster reduction when the environments discussed previously are delimited.
In this table, we distinguish four different environments for consonant
cluster reduction, and the relationship to each other as found in different varieties of English. The environments are: (1) an *-ed* formed
cluster followed by a vowel, (2) a base word cluster followed by a vowel,
(3) an *-ed* cluster when followed by a consonant, and (4) base word cluster when followed by a consonant. (See p. 27.)

As indicated in Table 7, there are varieties (most typically standard
English) which have no deletion when followed by a vowel and variable deletion when followed by a consonant. However, when followed by a consonant, there is more reduction when the cluster is part of a base word as
opposed to a cluster formed through the addition of an *-ed* suffix. On
the other end of the continuum, there are varieties of English (some
varieties of Vernacular Black English) where there is categorical reduction when a base word cluster is followed by a consonant and variable
reduction in all other environments. A progressive dimension in the relationships of these variable environments is also found. After the categorical environments, the most frequent incidence of reduction will occur
when an *-ed* formed cluster is followed by a consonant, the next most when
a base word cluster is followed by a vowel, and the least when an *-ed*
formed cluster is followed by a vowel. The inclusion of this dimension
into an implicational array allows us to fit the picture of systematic
variability into a framework in which the variable relationships can be
seen as a part of the total picture.

In the preceding discussion of implicational relations, we have only
included those items which are structurally related. For example, *IS*
and *ARE* as given in Table 5 are related to the structural process of copula deletion and the linguistic environments given in Table 7 are all related to consonant cluster reduction. Entities which enter into implicational relations may include particular linguistic rules, classes of

Table 5

IS Deletion	ARE Deletion
0	0
0	1
1	1

Implication Relationships of ARE *and* IS *Copula Deletion*

Table 6

A	B	C	D
0	0	X	X
0	X	X	X
X	X	X	X
X	X	X	1

Tabular Arrangement of Implicational Scale Including Variability

---

Table 7

-ed __ V	Base Word __ V	-ed __ C	Base Word __ C
0	0	X	X
0	X	X	X
X	X	X	X
X	X	X	1

Implicational Array for Consonant Cluster Reduction Including Variability and Categoricality

---

Table 8

	Unstressed Syllables	Stressed Syllables
Stage 1	1	1
Stage 2	X	1
Stage 3	X	X
Stage 4	0	X
Stage 5	0	0

Stages of Language Change for Intrinsic h *in* it *and* ain't

forms which may occur, and various linguistic environments. It is, however, possible to draw up implicational relationships between linguistic
entities which are not structurally related. For example, we observe
that there is an implicational relationship between the incidence of *a*-
prefixing and the occurrence of unstressed *ing* forms as *in'* (see Chapters
Four and Three) even though these are related to different linguistic
structures. It is observed that if *a*-prefixing takes place, it implies
that we will categorically get the *in'* form as opposed to the *ing* form
(e.g. one gets forms like *a-workin'*, but not *a-working*). In non-*a*-pre-
fixed cases, *in'* may fluctuate with *ing*. Thus, we see an implicational
relationship between *a*-prefixing and the categorical use of *in'*, features
which are not linguistically related.

There are two important reasons for considering implicational relations of the type we have described above in the treatment of a variety
such as AE. In the first place, it provides a framework for viewing relationships of entities which comprise the system. And, as a variety
of English which shows relationships with other varieties of English, it
often allows us to see where AE fits in terms of the continuum of English
dialects. Implicational relationships, then, may provide a picture of
the relative linguistic distance between AE and other non-mainstream varieties of English and standard English. We thus find a systematic basis
for comparing various dialects of English.

A second reason for investigating the implicational relationships
relates to language change. Language change is an ongoing, dynamic process which takes place in a systematic way. One way of observing various
stages in the process of change and which steps may have preceded or will
follow a given stage is to look at the implicational relationships. For
example, consider the case of intrinsic *h* in words such as *hit* for *it*
and *hain't* for *ain't*. At one point in the English language, *h* was found
for these items in both stressed and unstressed syllables. The presence
of *h* then apparently became variable in unstressed syllables while remaining categorical in stressed ones. At the present time in AE, it is
found to appear mostly in stressed syllables, but we may find speakers
who have some incidence of *h* in items which do not receive primary stress.
If, however, speakers have this "intrinsic *h*" in less stressed syllables,
then it implies that they will also have it, and to a greater extent, in
primary stressed syllables. Eventually, however, before being lost, it
will only occur in stressed syllables. We may represent the various
stages in Table 8 where *1* indicates the categorical presence of *h*, *X*
the fluctuation between presence and absence, and *0* categorical absence.

The implicational relationships as seen above then represent the
stages in the change of this item through time. We know historically that
Stages 1 and 2 existed, and we still may find speakers who are in the latter
stages of 3, a number of speakers in Stage 4 and some in Stage 5. Implicational relations, then, give important insight into how languages change
systematically with respect to various items, showing the direction of
previous change and predicting how future changes may proceed. (See p. 27.)

THE DESCRIPTION OF AE

In the preceding section, we have attempted to provide the framework on which the following description of AE is based. There are, of
course important implications of the model we discussed which relate to
linguistic theory (see Labov, 1969; Fasold, 1970; Bickerton, 1971; Bailey,
1973; Wolfram and Fasold, 1974), although we have not specified them here
in detail. It should not, however, be thought that these pertain to matters only of linguistic theory, for there are ways in which this model is

essential for viewing the general description of AE given in Chapters Three and Four. The various features we account for in the subsequent chapters must be seen in terms of the systematic effects that the social and linguistic constraints have on the relative frequency of the items, if we are to arrive at an accurate picture of AE. And, as we shall see, there are some educational implications of the data we describe which are related to the model that we have assumed for their description.

The implicational relations found among linguistic entities are also essential in accounting for AE within the continuum of linguistic diversity in American English. Dialects do not stand alone as isolated entities, but show systematic relations to other dialects in the continuum of linguistic diversity. One way of seeing this picture accurately, therefore, involves a consideration of implicational relations. For example, there are a number of cases in which we summarize the relation of AE with respect to other non-mainstream varieties and standard English through an implicationally arranged table. As mentioned previously, this type of arrangement also relates to the observation of change in progress within AE, putting it into a dynamic perspective. Certain changes, for example, may be expected and are, in fact, imminent based upon the current status of forms we have found in AE. Such information is important in terms of understanding where AE has come from and where it may be going. This knowledge, furthermore, has important consequences in terms of developing educational strategies which make use of the linguistic description we outline here.

TOWARD A DEFINITION OF APPALACHIAN ENGLISH AND STANDARD ENGLISH

Throughout this description, we have used the term *Appalachian English* (AE) in a rather loose way. Like terms used with reference to other non-mainstream varieties, this designation is somewhat of a misnomer which needs to be qualified. Ultimately, we would have to restrict our use of the term to the particular variety of English which we have found in the region of Appalachia studied. Even within this context, however, the designation needs to be qualified since there are obviously differences within the region we are discussing. Our focus has been on the working class rural population, so that our restricted interest would preclude many middle class speakers from the region who do not use the forms that we account for here. Specifically, then, we use the term AE to refer to the variety of English most typically associated with the working class rural population found in one particular region of the Appalachian range. Although this qualification is necessary, there is evidence, both from our own informal comparisons of working class speakers from other rural areas and available descriptions of other sections of Appalachia, that many of the features we describe have relatively wide distribution within the central Appalachian range. In our designation, we have chosen to err in the direction of generality, realizing that we may have created a somewhat fictitious designation. As shall be seen in Chapters Three and Four, there are differing varieties even with the restricted definition of AE we give an account of.

There may be some question as to whether it is justifiable to differentiate an entity such as AE from other (equally difficult to define precisely) varieties of American English, particularly some of those spoken in the South. Quite obviously, there are many features we have described which are not peculiar to speakers within the Appalachian range. On the other hand, there also appear to be a small subset of features which may not be found in other areas. Even if this is not the case, we may justify our distinction of AE on the basis of the combination of features. It is

doubtful that other southern varieties of English which compare favorably
to what we have designated as AE share the particular set of features in
the way that they are found within regions of Appalachia. Fully cognizant
of the pitfalls found in any attempt to attach terminological labels to
varieties of English, we shall proceed to use the designation AE as a convenient, if loosely-defined notion.

Of necessity, the description of what we designate here as AE is
made with reference to some comparative norm. It would be a prohibitive
and, indeed, a redundant task to describe for AE all those aspects of this
variety that are identical to those found in mainstream varieties of
English.[1] It thus becomes necessary to decide what aspects of the complete system to describe. For the most part, the normative guide for our
description is what we may refer to as *informal standard American
English*. (Reference to standard English throughout the remainder of this
work should be interpreted in terms of this norm.) The notion of informal standard American English is to be distinguished from what is sometimes referred to as *formal standard English*. Formal standardization
is described by Wolfram and Fasold (1974:19) as follows:

> Formal standardization refers to what is prescribed
> for a language by grammar and usage books, diction-
> aries, ortheopical guides, and language academies.
> Invariably, these formal codes are drawn up so that
> almost no one speaks the standard language. Formal
> standardization is based on the written language
> of established writers, which automatically limits
> it to the most formal style of older, highly educa-
> ted people.

Given the removed, prescriptive nature of formal standard English,
it does not appear to be useful to appeal to it as a comparative norm in
highlighting the features of AE. Informal standardization, on the other
hand, is a more difficult notion to define, since it is based on the
actual language behavior of speakers, including aspects of the variable
parameter we have discussed above. On one level, it may be a rather in-
dividualistic notion, so that one person may consider a form to be standard, depending on a person's subjective reactions to particular language forms. But on another level, there are certain unifying aspects
which may help us arrive at a more workable definition of informal standard English. As has been noted by Wolfram and Fasold (1974:21), in
every society there are people who are in a position to use their judgments about what is good and bad in language in making decisions which
affect other people (e.g. school teachers and employers in American society). Since their judgments about language affect people's lives, our
notion of informal standard English refers to the informal standard language of people, like teachers and employers, who are in a position to
make such decisions about language appropriateness. This definition
must, however, be qualified by noting that it assumes that such individuals will not enforce language forms that are not actually used by them.
To the extent that the speech of an educated West Virginian speaker differs from that of an educated Bostonian, we may speak of differing varieties of informal standard English. Some of these regional types of
differences will also be discussed in what follows, particularly as they
contrast with northern varieties of English. Given such flexibility,
which we point out at various intervals in our description of the features of AE, we must hasten to point out that there are many grammatical
and phonological features that uniformly would be rejected as nonstandard
by educated speakers in all parts of the country.

Notes

1. *Mainstream* will be distinguished from *standard* (and *non-mainstream* from *non-standard*) in the following way. When we speak of particular forms of a language, they can be considered to be standard if they conform to the type of informal norms discussed in this section. To characterize a variety of the language, the terms used will be mainstream and non-mainstream, which indicate more accurately the social factors that enter into this kind of label. It follows that mainstream varieties include predominantly standard linguistic forms, while non-mainstream varieties have varying degrees of non-standard usage. Standard English is, then, an artifact containing only standard forms which is represented by a number of mainstream varieties.

Chapter Three: Phonological Features

"—What are some of the things people grow here in their gardens?"
"—Oh, potatoes and tomatoes—or did you want me to say 'maters and 'taters?"
(31:4)

CONSONANT CLUSTERS

Consonant Cluster Simplification

The simplification of word-final consonant clusters or blends is one of the features which has occupied considerable attention in recent studies of social dialects. When we speak of consonant cluster simplification or reduction here, we are referring to the deletion of a stop consonant such as *t*, *d*, *p*, or *k* when it follows another consonant at the end of a word. It is important to distinguish two basic types of clusters that are affected by this type of reduction. First, there are clusters in which both consonants in the cluster are an inherent part of the same word. Thus, when this reduction process operates, words like *test*, *hand*, *desk*, and *wasp* may be produced as *tes'*, *han'*, *des'*, and *was'*. A second type of consonant cluster has a final *t* or *d* resulting from the addition of an *-ed* suffix to a word. It should be noted that when the base form of a word ends in a consonant other than *t* or *d*, the addition of an *-ed* ending usually results in a consonant cluster. The cluster will end in *d* if the preceding consonant is a voiced sound (such as *m*, *b*, *z* in words like *rammed* [ræmd], *rubbed* [rəbd], or *raised* [rezd] and *t* if the preceding consonant is a voiceless sound (such as *p*, *s*, *k* in words like *ripped* [rIpt], *missed* [mIst], or *looked* [lUkt]). (This kind of alternation in forms due to the nature of sounds in the environments is called phonological conditioning.) In a number of studies of social dialects, it has been observed that consonant cluster simplification applies as well to clusters resulting from the addition of the *-ed* suffix, so we may get forms like *ram'*, *rub'*, *raise'*, *rip'*, *miss'*, and *look'* for *rammed*, *rubbed*, *raised*, *ripped*, *missed*, and *looked* respectively. The list of clusters affected by consonant

cluster reduction and the examples of the two types of simplification are
given in Table 9, taken from Wolfram and Fasold (1974:130). In this table,
Type I refers to those clusters that do not involve *-ed* and Type II represents clusters that result from the addition of the *-ed* suffix. Where
logically possible combinations are omitted from the list, the cluster
does not occur word-finally in English (e.g. *šp, šk*, etc.).

Table 9

Phonetic Cluster	Type I	EXAMPLES Type II
[st]	test, post, list	missed, messed, dressed
[sp]	wasp, clasp, grasp	
[sk]	desk, risk, mask	
[št]		finished, latched, cashed
[zd]		raised, composed, amazed
[žd]		judged, charged, forged
[ft]	left, craft, cleft	laughed, stuffed, roughed
[vd]		loved, lived, moved
[nd]	mind, find, mound	rained, fanned, canned
[md]		named, foamed, rammed
[ld]	cold, wild, old	called, smelled, killed
[pt]	apt, adept, inept	mapped, stopped, clapped
[kt]	act, contact, expect	looked, cooked, cracked

Consonant Clusters in Which the Final Member of the Cluster May be Absent
(*Where there are no examples under Type I and Type II, the cluster does
not occur under that category.)

It should be noted that the table does not include all the possible
clusters involving a final stop. Clusters such as *mp* (*jump, ramp*), *lt*
(*colt, belt*), *ŋk* (*crank, rank*), and *lp* (*gulp, help*) are not affected by
this process. Some linguists have suggested that the process does not
operate on these clusters due to the fact that one of the members of the
cluster is voiced (e.g. *m* in an *mp* cluster) and the other voiceless (e.g.
p in the *mp* cluster). Other linguists have suggested that the reason it
does not affect these clusters is due to the fact that the lateral *l* or
nasals *m, n,* and *ŋ* are not realized as true consonants when preceding certain voiceless sounds. While linguists disagree as to the reason for the
failure of some clusters to be affected by this process of simplification,
they are in basic agreement as to those clusters that can and cannot undergo simplification.

A certain amount of consonant cluster reduction is typical of standard
varieties of English as well as those considered to be nonstandard, but
the conditions for the deletion of the final member of a consonant cluster
tend to be somewhat different. In most standard varieties of English, the
final stop consonant is deletable when the following word begins with a
consonant. This means that we would get forms like *res' stop, col' cuts,*
or *tes' case*. When followed by a vowel, however, the final member of the
cluster is usually present, so that we might get *rest afternoon, cold egg,*
and *test over*.

In many cases, differences between varieties of English with respect
to final consonant cluster simplification turn out to be quantitative

rather than qualitative. That is, differences are based on the frequency
with which simplification is observed to occur rather than the categorical
(i.e. 100 percent) incidence or non-incidence of simplification as such.
In this regard, it is important to note that there are two major linguistic
constraints which affect the frequency of simplification. One constraint
relates to the presence of a following consonant or vowel. All studies
of this phenomenon have shown that simplification is much more frequent
when the following word begins with a consonant than when it begins with
a vowel. As mentioned above, for some varieties the rule for reduction
may operate only when a consonant follows. Another constraint is related
to the presence or absence of the *-ed* suffix. If the cluster is an inherent part of a word, simplification tends to be more frequent than when
a cluster is formed by the addition of the *-ed* suffix. Thus, simplification in *We will have a gues' for dinner* would be expected to be more frequent than *We guess' the wrong answer*, although a degree of simplification may be found in both contexts.

With the variable nature of word-final consonant cluster simplification and the two main constraints on this process in mind, we can now
look at the simplification of clusters as revealed by a small subset of
our sample of AE speakers. In Table 10, the observed number of simpli-
fications is given for each of the main contexts cited above out of the
total number of clusters that might have been simplified. Figures are
given for six representative speakers in this table.

As indicated in Table 10, consonant cluster reduction in AE is largely restricted to contexts where the following word begins with a consonant.
The incidence of simplification when the following word begins with a
vowel is relatively small but it does occur to some extent. Although a
further breakdown of the different types of clusters is not included in
the figures given, it should be noted that the majority of clusters
which have been simplified before a vowel include clusters like *ld*, or
a nasal *m*, *n*, and *ŋ* plus *d* rather than a cluster involving an *s*-like
(i.e. sibilant) sound such as *st*, *sht*, *sk*, or *zd*. The latter type of
cluster tends to remain relatively intact before a vowel and cumulative
tabulation of these types of clusters for the informants given above indicates that less than seven percent of all sibilant plus stop clusters
are simplified before vowels. In fact, one is impressed with the high
frequency of *st* retention before vowels. Even items like *just*, reduced
to *jus'* in many casual standard English varieties, may sometimes retain
the *t* in AE. (See p. 36.)

In the preceding discussion, a crucial breakdown of linguistic environment was made between a following consonant and vowel. This does
not actually cover all the relevant types of following environment since
it is possible for a potential consonant cluster to occur at the end of
an utterance (e.g. *Did you get some rest?*); that is, followed by a pause.
One of the interesting aspects of other studies of final cluster reduction
relates to whether a following pause behaves more like a following vowel
or consonant in its effect on clusters, since there are apparently dialect
differences in this regard. For example, Fasold (1972:67) has shown that
in Vernacular Black English, the simplification of clusters before pauses
tends to approximate the frequency levels observed when the following
environment is a consonant, while Guy (1974:39) concludes that pause
functions more like a vowel in its effect on consonant clusters for White
Philadelphia speakers. A cumulative tabulation of our six speakers indicates that 24.5 percent of all potential clusters before a pause have
been simplified, suggesting that in AE the effect of a following pause

Table 10

Inf No.	Age/Sex	Not -*ed* Follow-ed by Consonant		-*ed*, Followed by Consonant		Not -*ed*, Follow-ed by Vowel		-*ed*, Followed by Vowel	
		No. Simp/T	%	No. Simp/T	%	No. Simp/T	%	No. Simp/T	%
36	27/F	17/21	81.0	11/16	68.8	2/20	10.0	3/47	6.4
31	67/M	35/45	77.7	12/17	70.6	6/28	21.4	2/39	5.1
2	13/M	29/36	80.6	8/12	66.7	6/21	28.6	1/16	6.3
64	15/F	26/38	68.4	5/9	55.6	5/22	22.7	1/17	5.9
48	9/M	11/14	78.6	11/16	68.8	3/34	8.8	3/52	5.7
77	11/F	30/46	65.2	9/14	64.3	4/25	16.0	1/31	3.2

Consonant Cluster Reduction for Six Representative Speakers

Table 11

Language Variety	Not -*ed*, Follow-ed by Consonant	-*ed*, Followed by Consonant	Not -*ed*, Follow-ed by Vowel	-*ed*, Followed by Vowel
	% Simp	% Simp	% Simp	% Simp
Middle Class White Detroit Speech	66	36	12	3
Working Class Black Detroit Speech	97	76	72	34
Working Class White New York City Adolescent Speech	67	23	19	3
Working Class White Adolescent, Rural Georgia-Florida Speech	56	16	25	10
Working Class Black Adolescent Rural Georgia Florida Speech	88	50	72	36
Southeastern West Virginia Speech	74	67	17	5

Comparison of Consonant Cluster Reduction in Different Regional and Social Varieties of American English

is more like that of a following vowel than a following consonant.

Although it is quite clear that AE favors retention of intact clusters when the following word begins with a vowel, there are several exceptions to this pattern which seem to relate to individual lexical items.
For example, the form *kept* and, in some instances, *except* categorically
ends in *p* rather than a *pt* cluster. These patterns relate to particular
words as such and do not appear to be part of a general pattern in which
clusters are reduced before vowels, since we do not observe the type of
structured variability revealed by other clusters.

At this point, we may compare consonant cluster simplification in
AE with that which has been observed in some other varieties of American
English. These include several northern urban varieties from Detroit
(adapted from Wolfram, 1969:62; 68) and New York City (from Labov et al,
1968:147), and two southern rural varieties (adapted from Summerlin, 1972:
97-98). Figures are broken down according to the two important constraints
on the frequency of simplification given above. Although slightly different procedures for tabulation were utilized in the different studies,
these figures are still useful for a rough comparison.

Table 11 indicates that AE, as represented by our speakers from
southeastern West Virginia, is most comparable to the various standard
and nonstandard White varieties indicated in the table. This is particularly true with respect to the effect of a following vowel which
strongly inhibits the simplification of clusters. Before a following
consonant, however, simplification is quite frequent, like most other
standard and nonstandard varieties of English. The only surprising
aspect of simplification before a following consonant is the relatively high frequency of simplification involving *-ed* clusters preceding a
word beginning with a consonant. On the whole, consonant cluster reduction in AE does not appear to be particularly socially diagnostic
and speakers from different age and social group levels do not differ
significantly from each other in terms of the extent of simplification.

Final Consonant Clusters and Plurals

In most varieties of English, the *regular* plural represented in
spelling by *-s* or *-es* actually takes several different forms in pronunciation, depending on the final segment of the base word. (Again,
this is a type of phonological conditioning, like that discussed for
the *-ed* suffix.) If the item ends in a voiced sound other than an *s*-
like sound (i.e. a sibilant sound such as *s*, *z*, *sh*, or *zh*) the plural is
produced like a *z*. That is, the plural formation of items like *bud*,
ham, *bee*, and *tub* would be produced something like *budz* [bədz], *hamz*
[hæmz], *bees* [biz], and *tubz* [təbz]. If the item ends in a voiceless
sound other than an *s*-like sound, the plural is produced
as *s*, giving us items like *kits* [kIts], *racks* [ræks], or *maps* [mæps].
When the item ends with a sibilant, however, the plural is formed by
adding a vowel plus *z*, giving us *buzzes* [bəzIz], *busses* [bəsIz], or
bushes [bUsIz] for the singular forms *buzz*, *bus*, and *bush*. For some
speakers of AE, there is a slight modification on the conditions under
which the *-es* or [Iz] plural may be added. In addition to the occurrence
of the [Iz] plural produced on items which end in a sibilant, this plural
form may occur when the sibilant is followed by a stop such as *t*, *p*, or *k*
at the end of a word. That is, the [Iz] plural may be added to items ending in *sp*, *st*, or *sk*, resulting in forms like *deskes* [dɛskIz], *ghostes*
[gostIz], or *waspes* [waspIz] for *desks*, *ghosts*, and *wasps*. We thus get
the following examples from various speakers:

(1) a.   She stretched it all across the *deskes* [dɛskIz] and everything.
          1:28[1]
     b.   ...cause people tell you it's *ghostes* [gostIz].   9:(994)
     c.   ...you could see *ghostes* [gostIz].   28:32
     d.   ...I really like *roastes* [rostIz] or the steak.   38:14

The occurrence of the *-es* or [Iz] plural form following *st, sk,*
or *sp* in AE seems to be a special condition on the regular plural formation. Other dialects seem to use this formation in different ways. For
example, in Vernacular Black English as described by Wolfram and Fasold
(1974:132), it is noted that the predominant form of plural formation for
forms ending in *st, sk,* or *sp* in standard English eliminates the final
stop and adds the [Iz] plural. We thus get forms like *desses* [dɛsIz],
ghosses [gosIz], and *wasses* [wasIz] as the predominant plural rather than
the forms we cited above for AE. Only occasionally do forms such as
deskes or *ghostes* turn up in a dialect like Vernacular Black English,
and these occurrences are attributed to special conditions which arise
when speakers attempt to learn standard English.

> Attempting to learn Standard English pluralization pat-
> terns, speakers will sometimes pluralize words like *desk*
> and *test* as *deskes* and *testes*, respectively. These
> forms result from a tendency to pluralize the same words
> in the same way, even when the cluster is maintained
> intact. This is an example of structural hypercor-
> rection... *(Wolfram and Fasold, 1974:132)*

While such forms may be accounted for in this manner in varieties
such as Vernacular Black English, the predominance of forms like *deskes*
and *testes* in AE does not make this a plausible explanation. It is
forms like *desses* and *tesses* which are quite rare among AE speakers who
have fully acquired their language. We thus conclude that the *-es* or
[Iz] following consonant clusters results from a regular and integral
difference on the conditions for the addition of plurals in AE when
compared with standard English and some other social and regional varieties of American English.

Because the addition of the [Iz] plural following *sp, st,* or *sk*
appears to be socially stigmatized, it is more characteristic of working
class than middle class speakers. Even among working class speakers,
however, its use is somewhat selective and it is apparently now used
less frequently than it was at an earlier period. A more frequent production of clusters like *st, sk,* or *sp* that include a plural marking involves a lengthening of the duration of the *s* preceding the stops *t, k,*
and *p* and a retention of the stop, resulting in forms like *ghosst*
[gos:t], *tesst* [tɛs:t], and *wassp* [was:p] for *ghosts, tests,* and *wasps.*
Examples of this pronunciation are given below:

(2) a.   ...even though some people don't believe in *ghosst* [gos:t] some
          do.   7:19
     b.   They's *ghosst* [gos:t] that come up out the grave.   16:(817)
     c.   ...cause you don't have to worry about homework and *tesst* [tɛs:t]
          150:19

It should be noted that the production of clusters involving *sts,*
sks, or *sps* at the beginning or end of a syllable involves fairly complex
articulatory movements for the speaker of any dialect, due to the transition from an *s* to a stop *t, k,* or *p* and then back to *s* within the same

syllable. Speakers may deal with this complexity in several ways since
there is a natural tendency to avoid such complex transitions in casual
speech style. One way, of course, is to insert a vowel to break up the
transition, as in the case of *testes* or *ghostes* cited previously. Another
alternative is to simply eliminate the stop *t*, *k*, or *p* and lengthen the
s so that you get something like *ghoss* [gos:], *tess* [tes:], or *wass* [was:].
There are a number of dialects of American English that seem to favor
this pronunciation (e.g. Vernacular Black English, which favors consonant
cluster reduction to a much greater extent than AE, prefers this production when avoiding the more stigmatized forms like *tesses* and *ghosses*).
Another alternative is to lengthen the *s* and retain the original *t*, *k*, or
p. This is the option most often chosen by AE speakers when not using
socially stigmatized forms such as *testes* and *ghostes*. The lengthened *s*
followed by a stop carries no apparent social stigma.

Intrusive *t* in Clusters

We previously described a process whereby certain consonant clusters
may be simplified or reduced in AE. Such simplification, it was seen,
is a regular process which takes place to some extent in all varieties
of American English. Although the general process of simplification
operates as described, it should be noted that there are certain clusters
in AE not typically found in a number of other varieties of English.
That is, there are words that end in clusters in AE which do not end in
clusters in other regional and/or social varieties of English. For the
most part, this feature is restricted to a small set of items, including
once, *twice*, *across*, and *cliff*. In this variety, they may be produced
with a final *t*, so that we get *oncet* [wənst], *twicet* [twa^{1}st], *acrosst*
[əkrost], and *clifft* [klIft]. Following are examples of these items with
the inclusion of the final *t*.

(3) a. Four could only get on the barrel at *oncet*. 73:2
     b. ...*oncet* a day.   69:(267)
     c. ...feed him *twicet* a day.   37:7
     d. ...seen him *twicet* every week.   56:(44)
     e. I got out there and I started *acrosst*...   22:10
     f. I got them two *acrosst*...   22:11
     g. ...ever which way I'd go it was a *clifft*.   17:17
     h. ...and there's a big *clifft*.   34:(450)

Quite clearly, the presence of *t* on these items is related to earlier
forms which developed in British English dialects and simply survived
in current American English dialects as more archaic forms. Items like
oncet and *twicet* seemed to develop along with a set of items like *amidst*,
amongst, and *against* during an earlier period of English. Some historical
sources (e.g. *The Oxford English Dictionary*) suggest that the item *acrosst*
developed from a blending of *across* and *crossed* several centuries ago.
The pronunciation of *clifft* for *cliff*, was related to the form which
eventually became the word *cleft* in modern English (at an earlier stage,
cleft was *clift*). Although some sources attribute the form *clifft* to
a confusion between *cleft* and *cliff* during the 16th century, it may also
be hypothesized that these items originally broke off from the same item
and evolved in different directions. Whatever the etymology for this
item, the production *clifft* must be considered as a particular case of
retention from an earlier period.
     The presence of *t* on the items cited above is still fairly common
among different age and social groups from Appalachia, and does not appear
to be particularly stigmatized as such. Following the regular pattern

for cluster simplification, it can be observed that the presence of *t* in
these items is considerably more frequent when the following item begins
with a vowel than when it begins with a consonant.

In addition to the fairly regular pattern of so-called "intrusive *t*"
in items such as those cited in sample (3), there are occasional instances
where *t* may be found on other items, as illustrated by the following examples:

(4) a. We're very *closet*. 29:10
     b. ...even though you're *closet*. 29:11
     c. ...that's the best *stufft* you ever eaten. 31:31
     d. ...up at the top of the *hillt*. 51:5
     e. ...I'd die of a heart *attackt*. 37:29
     f. ...but any wild animal will *attackt* you if you corner it. 40:42

Cases such as those illustrated in (4) appear to be formed by analogy
with other types of intrusive *t* patterning and may be a type of hypercorrection. Whereas the examples given in (3) are observed quite regularly among different speakers, those given in (4) tend to be quite idiosyn-
cratic.

COPULA AND AUXILIARY

Copula Absence

Another phemenon of some non-mainstream varieties of English that
has been very thoroughly studied is the deletion of the present tense
forms of the copula. Although copula and auxiliary deletion are often
thought of as grammatical features, we include them here since detailed
technical analyses have shown them to be a result of phonological processes. Copula deletion has been described for Vernacular Black English
by Labov (1969), while a comparison of this phenomenon in Vernacular
Black English and White southern speech has been offered by Wolfram
(1974b). In Labov's seminal article on copula deletion, he argued that
copula absence in sentences like *He ugly, The men gonna do it*, etc.,
resulted from a deletion rule which operated on the output of contraction
(i.e. *He is ugly →He's ugly →He ugly*). To summarize, it was concluded
that wherever the contraction of *is* and *are* could take place in standard
English, a variety such as Vernacular Black English could delete the
copula, and wherever standard English could not contract, Vernacular
Black English could not delete it. That is, deletion could take place
in sentences such as those given above since it corresponded to a con-
tractable form in standard English, but it could not take place in sentences where the full form of the copula was required, such as with the
past tense (e.g. *He was home yesterday* but not *He home yesterday*), in
clause-final position (e.g. *I know that's what they are* but not *I know
that's what they*), or in non-finite constructions (e.g. *They want to be
good* but not *They want to good*).[2]
Wolfram's (1974b) study of copula deletion among White southerners
in Mississippi indicates that there are both important differences and
similarities between a variety such as Vernacular Black English and White
southern speech. With respect to the deletion of *are*, the White southern
speakers differed mainly in the frequency levels at which *are* was deleted,
typically showing lower frequency levels of deletion than those found in
Vernacular Black English. Many of the White southern speakers, however,
did not have *is* deletion at all, thus differing qualitatively from speakers
of Vernacular Black English.

One of the interesting questions regarding AE is how it compares to other southern varieties of English and Vernacular Black English in the operation of copula deletion. In order to answer this question, we have analyzed in some detail the incidence of copula deletion for 15 different speakers in our corpus, supplementing this detailed analysis with observations from all the speakers in our corpus. The 15 subjects chosen for detailed study of copula deletion represented a cross section of age and sex differences among the working class subjects in our sample.

To begin with, we may note that copula deletion for *is* does not typically take place in AE. In this respect, it is more like other southern White varieties of English than Vernacular Black English, although, as noted above, there is a subset of White speakers in the deep South who do have *is* deletion to a limited degree. AE does not, however, have a corresponding subset of speakers for whom *is* deletion operates even to a limited extent. The deletion of *are* does take place to some degree in AE but it does not completely parallel the way it operates in whole varieties investigated in the deep South. In the analysis of copula deletion in the deep South by Wolfram (1974b), it was shown that *are* deletion may typically take place following a noun phrase (e.g. *the men ugly*) as well as a pronoun (e.g. *you ugly*), but in AE it is found to operate only when following a pronoun. That is, we do not typically find examples such as *The men ugly*. Examples of copula deletion following pronouns such as *we*, *you*, and *they* are given in (5).

(5) a. We _interested in baseball. 22:1
     b. We _just dreamin'. 1:15
     c. You _playin' right here. 74:2
     d. Man, you _crazy. 4:5
     e. They _afraid. 159:23
     f. They _good and straight. 30:12

In previous studies of copula deletion, it has been demonstrated that there are important linguistic constraints that influence the relative frequency of deletion. Among these is the structure that follows the copula. Both Labov, for Vernacular Black English, and Wolfram, for White southern speech in the deep South, have shown that there is a continuum in which the following types of constructions show a progressively greater relative effect on copula deletion: Predicate Nominative (e.g. *You a man*); Predicate Adjective (e.g. *You nice*); Predicate Locative (e.g. *You in the woods*); Verb + *ing* (e.g. *You standing there*); and Special lexical form *gonna* (e.g. *You gonna like it*). Previous studies have shown that the greatest incidence of copula deletion will be found with the lexical item *gonna* and the least with predicate nominative constructions.

Within the range of copula deletion in AE, it is important to note that the same general constraints on its variability observed in other studies are found for AE. That is, the greatest incidence of deletion is found with *gonna*, the next greatest with verb + *ing* forms, the next with predicate locatives, the next with predicate adjectives, and the least with predicate nominatives. This is a pattern which has been duplicated in virtually every study of copula deletion, regardless of the particular variety of English.

With this information in mind, we may now look at the incidence of copula deletion of *are* for the 15 speakers examined here in detail. Table 12 indicates the actual incidence of copula deletion in relation to the potential cases where it might have taken place. The breakdown is given in terms of the occurrence in those types of constructions delimited above. Table 12 is arranged in terms of rank frequency, with the totals

Table 12

INF No.	Age/Sex	Nom. No. Del/Tot	Adj. No. Del/Tot	Loc No. Del/Tot	Verb-ing No. Del/Tot	gonna No. Del/Tot	Total No. Del/Tot	% Del
164	33/M	0/1	9/14	2/3	3/3	--	14/21	66.7
85	78/F	--	--	--	2/2	0/1	2/3	66.7
74	11/F	0/2	1/2	0/1	2/4	1/1	4/10	40.0
4	13/M	0/2	1/2	0/3	--	1/1	2/8	25.0
156	20/F	--	1/3	--	2/11	--	3/14	21.4
146	52/F	0/1	2/13	0/1	1/6	1/1	4/22	18.2
31	67/M	0/4	1/11	--	2/5	0/2	3/22	13.6
40	39/F	0/3	1/6	0/5	1/8	1/3	3/25	12.0
154	13/F	1/1	0/5	0/2	--	0/2	1/10	10.0
64	15/F	--	0/10	1/1	0/6	--	1/17	5.9
151	18/F	0/4	0/13	1/2	0/12	--	1/31	3.2
TOTAL		1/18	16/79	4/18	13/57	4/11	38/183	
% Del		5.6	20.3	22.2	22.8	36.4	20.8	

Speakers With No Incidence of ARE Deletion

INF No.	Age/Sex	Nom. No. Del/Tot	Adj. No. Del/Tot	Loc No. Del/Tot	Verb-ing No. Del/Tot	gonna No. Del/Tot	Total No. Del/Tot	% Del
51	10/M	0/1	0/4	0/1	0/1	0/8	0/15	0.0
77	11/F	0/1	0/4	0/1	0/3	0/1	0/10	0.0
7	17/M	--	0/2	0/1	0/1	0/2	0/6	0.0
2	13/M	0/1	--	--	--	0/1	0/2	0.0

Incidence of Copula Deletion for are in the Spontaneous Speech of 15 AE Informants

for those subjects who have some incidence of *are* deletion separated from those subjects who do not indicate copula deletion at all. (See p. 42.)

There are several important observations to be made on the basis of Table 12. First, we note that there is considerable range in the incidence of *are* deletion, ranging from 2/3 out of all cases deleted to no deletion at all. Unlike other varieties, such as some varieties of White southern speech in the deep South and Vernacular Black English, there are no informants who have categorical *are* deletion. On the other hand, there is a subset of speakers for whom copula deletion does not take place at all. The overall incidence of *are* deletion following pronouns is considerably less than that found in the deep South variety of non-mainstream English studied by Wolfram (1974b). In fact, the frequency of copula deletion for *are* following a pronoun was over three times greater in Wolfram's study than that observed here. When this limited frequency range is considered along with the fact that there is no deletion of *is* and no deletion of *are* following noun phrases, we get a picture of the limited extent to which deletion is found in AE. While the overall picture emerges in which copula deletion is restricted in AE, it is interesting to observe that there are occasional speakers who have *are* deletion to a considerable extent. Quite clearly, there are several different varieties of AE with respect to the deletion of *are*. However, no clear-cut social variables emerge which can account for these different varieties. For example, all of the informants in Table 12 would be considered "working class" according to current indices for assessing social status, yet there is still a considerable range of *are* deletion; younger speakers tend to be less prone to have extended copula deletion than the older generation, yet age differentiation is not clear-cut. Furthermore, an attempt to correlate the differences in terms of specific geographical location within the West Virginia counties studied did not turn up a specific pattern.

We may summarize how copula deletion operates for various non-mainstream varieties of English in Table 13. In the table, *1* indicates the categorical operation of copula deletion (i.e. it is deleted wherever it is possible to delete it), *X* substantial but non-categorical incidence of the deleted form, *x* limited fluctuation of the deleted form with the non-deleted one, and *0* the presence of only the non-deleted form.

Table 13

	IS	*ARE* NP	Pro
*VBE	X	X	1
SWE$_1$	x	X	1
SWE$_2$	0	X	1
SWE$_3$	0	x	X
AE$_1$	0	0	X
AE$_2$	0	0	x
AE$_3$ & NWNE	0	0	0

Varieties of Non-Mainstream English with Respect to Copula Deletion

(*VBE: Vernacular Black English; SWE: Southern White English; AE: Appalachian English; and NWNE: Northern White Nonstandard English)

What we see in Table 13 is a continuum of varieties with respect to
copula deletion in American English. The most divergent variety from
standard English is Vernacular Black English and the closest to standard
English is White northern non-mainstream varieties. The varieties of AE
fall between these extremes, more removed from standard English than most
northern White varieties but not as divergent as Vernacular Black English
and White southern varieties found in the deep South.

Auxiliary Deletion

Varieties of English share a process which allows auxiliary forms
(such as *have* and *will*) to be contracted in many circumstances. The
operation of this process results in forms like *he's* for *he has* or *he
is* and *you've* for *you have*. Contraction, particularly when the auxiliaries are paired with pronouns, is very common in most styles of speech.
Some varieties, in addition, allow certain of the auxiliary forms to be
deleted. In AE, it is possible to delete the auxiliary *have*, in constructions like:

(6) a. First time I ever *been* out in the woods with a gun. 10:11
     b. I think she *been* down here maybe twice. 85:6
     c. Well, I've just been lucky I never *been* bit. 159:31

This process of deletion occurs variably, even within the same utterance
as in (6c), and is more frequent in some situations than others.
     Auxiliary *have* deletion is most common when the *have* combines with
been, as in the utterances in (6). It is found with a few other verbs
in the corpus, but much less often. These cases include:

(7) a. That was the prettiest tree that ever he *seen*. 157:18
     b. I *seen* several pictures in the paper where people *been* snake-
         bitten. 37:29
     c. I've got a horse, saddle horse and we take it and I *got*
         another horse, quarter horse... 7:4

It is somewhat difficult to determine which of the utterances of this
type are in fact cases of *have* deletion. Due to the variation that
exists in past tense forms of verbs, the actual shape of the verb cannot
be assumed to be the deciding factor, since it could, in some cases,
represent the simple past tense (see Chapter Four). In the case of *got*,
(7c), the form could represent either the standard past form or the deletion of *have* from *have got*. Surrounding context must help in deciding
whether a form is derived from *have* deletion or not.
     Like contraction of auxiliaries, deletion is favored when preceded
by a pronoun, as seen in (8), but this is not an absolute restriction on
the process.

(8) a. These girls *been* there for a long time. 17:(190)
     b. One of 'em *been* averaging about 20 points a game. 87:(1048)

The pronoun constraint has also been found to influence the deletion
of copula forms. Finally, it can be observed that *have* deletion occurs
for the most part in main clauses, with a few exceptions like (9):

(9) They'd a-knowed right there, you know, what to *done*. 36:10

Since the past tense can be represented by *have* in infinitival forms as
in (9) above, it seems likely that the deletion process operated to

produce this construction.

When the term *auxiliary deletion* is used, this refers to a combination of processes, not simply deletion of the full form of *have*. The rules that result in contracted forms first apply, giving, for example, *I've been*; then the contraction *'ve* is deleted, resulting in *I been*. The absence of *have* in a surface form is then due to the operation of phonological rules. This sequence accounts for the fact that deletion in non-mainstream varieties typically takes place only in those cases where contraction in standard English is possible (as in the case in copula absence). Thus, we do *not* find contraction or deletion in sentences like (10):

(10)   a. If anybody's been there, they *have*.
       b. *If anybody's been there, *they've*.[3]
       c. *If anybody's been there, *they*.

An exception to this restriction seems to be in questions, where the auxiliary form can be deleted even though contraction is impossible. For example, sentence (11) is a report of a direct question:

(11)   She said, "Well, how long you *been* up?" 6:21

This process is also common in formal standard English, and may occur with other auxiliaries in addition to *have*, as pointed out by Wolfram and Fasold (1974:160). It results in direct questions like "What you *[whatcha]* been doing?" (*have* deletion) in informal speaking styles.

It has been noted (Wolfram and Fasold, 1974:158) that different varieties of English may extend auxiliary deletion to forms other than *have*, including *will* and *would*. There is evidence that AE permits auxiliary deletion of modals such as *will* and *would*, although apparently not to the extent that it may be found in a variety such as Vernacular Black English. Cases such as *will* and *would*, however, appear to be derived through the operation of a different set of phonological processes which may affect contracted forms.

R AND *L* DELETION

R-lessness

The deletion of *r* is a characteristic of a number of different varieties of American English. To a large extent, *r* deletion, often referred to as "r-lessness," closely correlates with geographical distribution, although the parameter of social class invariably intersects with regional distribution to some degree. The incidence of *r*-lessness is quite sensitive to word or syllable position, and varieties of American English can be differentiated on the basis of the types of contexts in which *r*-lessness occurs. At the beginning of the word, *r* is always present in all varieties of American English, as in *run* or *rob*. In other positions, however, *r* is sometimes "vocalized" and pronounced something like *uh* (phonetically close to the schwa [ə]). While there are many cases in which a phonetic vestige of the *r* remains, there are also some contexts where there is no phonetic residue of the *r* at all (see Wolfram and Fasold, 1974:149).

AE participates to a limited extent in the deletion of *r* (which we shall use here to refer to both cases where a phonetic vestige of the *r* remains, and to those where no vestige remains), but in ways which are somewhat different from that found in other varieties. One of the main contexts in which *r*-lessness has been observed is post-vocalic position.

We may therefore look at one aspect of *r*-lessness in AE by examining deletion patterns in post-vocalic position for a representative group of
speakers.

In Table 14, figures for *r*-deletion are given for 10 different
speakers from our corpus. These figures are broken down according to
several different contexts in which post-vocalic *r* might occur. First
of all, post-vocalic *r* deletion is tabulated within a word when followed
by a consonant (e.g. *beard, start, court*). This context is differentiated from word-final position, where several different subclasses are
delimited. In word-final position, a distinction is made between those
items occurring in stressed (e.g. *before, prepare, four*) and unstressed
(e.g. *father, camper, regular*) syllables. Within the stress category,
a further distinction is made between those items which are followed by
a vowel in the next word (e.g. *before eight, father asked, regular animal*)
and those followed by a consonant (e.g. *before five, father brought,
regular guy*). The delimitation of different contexts such as these appears essential to understanding various contextual influences on the
relative frequency of *r*-deletion. For each of the contexts delimited
above, 15 items were tabulated for each of the informants. The table is
arranged according to the rank frequency of *r* deletion. (See p. 47.)

The picture of post-vocalic *r*-lessness which emerges from Table 14
is fairly clear-cut. It is observed that there is little *r*-lessness
within a word when followed by a consonant. The figures are so low that
we can rule out this aspect as an important part of AE as spoken in
this region. There may, however, be a few lexical items in which an
r-less form corresponds to an *r*-full form in other varieties of English
(e.g. *futhuh* for *further*), but these are apparently lexical differences.
Although we have not tabulated *r*-lessness within a word when followed by
a vowel, we have observed in our corpus occasional instances in which an
r may be absent inter-vocalically (e.g. *du'ing* for *during*, *ba'él* for
barrel, *ma'y* for *marry*). While the incidence of such items is quite
infrequent and limited to very few speakers, the occurrence of such
forms at all is somewhat surprising given the overall preference for retaining *r* within a word. In other studies of non-mainstream varieties,
such cases have been found only when a great deal of *r*-lessness in other
contexts was characteristic of the variety.

Table 14 also indicates that *r*-lessness does not occur to any great
extent when *r* occurs in a word-final stressed syllable. However, in
word-final unstressed syllables, a somewhat different pattern emerges.
We find that *r*-lessness does occur to some extent, although it is much
less frequent than the levels of *r*-lessness found in many other varieties
of English which are characterized by post-vocalic *r*-deletion. As has
been found in other studies of post-vocalic *r*-deletion, the deletion of
r is strongly favored when the following segment is a consonant. We
conclude, then, that post-vocalic *r*-lessness is found to a very limited
extent in this variety of AE and is largely restricted to word-final
position in unstressed syllables. We should be careful not to extend
this observation to other areas within Appalachia, since this may be
a feature that is quite sensitive to regional differences within this
territory.

Our discussion of *r*-lessness in this variety of AE should not be
concluded without mentioning post-consonantal *r*-lessness. It is noted
that post-consonantal *r* absence has been observed in several specialized
contexts. One of these contexts is an item preceded by *th* and followed
by a round vowel such as *o* or *u*. We thus get examples such as *th'ow* for
throw and *th'ough* for *through*. (Note that we do not observe post-consonantal *r* absence in items like *three* or *prone*.) The incidence of this
r-less pattern is surprisingly high, especially in light of the fact that

Table 14

Word Final

Inf No.	Age/Sex	Within Word C		Stressed Syllable ##V		Stressed Syllable ##C		Unstressed Syllable ##V		Unstressed Syllable ##C		Total	%Del
		No D/T	%D	No D/T	%D	No D/T	%D	No D/T	%D	No D/T	%D		
85	78/F	1/15	6.7	1/15	6.7	2/15	13.3	3/15	20.0	11/15	73.3	18/75	24.0
164	33/M	1/15	6.7	1/15	6.7	1/15	6.7	3/15	20.0	8/15	53.3	14/75	18.7
40	39/F	0/15	0.0	0/15	0.0	0/15	0.0	4/15	26.7	7/15	46.7	11/75	14.7
77	11/F	0/15	0.0	0/15	0.0	1/15	6.7	3/15	20.0	6/15	40.0	10/75	13.3
4	13/M	0/15	0.0	1/15	6.7	0/15	0.0	3/15	20.0	5/15	33.3	9/75	12.0
64	15/F	0/15	0.0	0/15	0.0	0/15	0.0	2/15	13.3	6/15	40.0	8/75	10.7
154	13/F	0/15	0.0	0/15	0.0	1/15	6.7	1/15	6.7	5/15	33.3	7/75	9.3
51	10/M	0/15	0.0	1/15	6.7	0/15	0.0	2/15	13.3	4/15	26.7	7/75	9.3
152	64/F	0/15	0.0	0/15	0.0	0/15	0.0	0/15	0.0	4/15	26.7	4/75	5.3
31	67/M	0/15	0.0	0/15	0.0	0/15	0.0	0/15	0.0	2/15	13.3	2/75	2.7
TOTALS		2/150	1.3	4/150	2.7	5/150	3.3	21/150	14.0	58/150	38.7	90/750	12.0

Incidence of Post-Vocalic r Deletion Among Appalachian English Speakers

post-vocalic *r*-lessness is so restricted. Many speakers who show very infrequent post-vocalic *r*-lessness consistently reveal *r*-lessness in items
like *throw* and *through*. It may be, however, that there are simply a few
lexical items in which this pattern is related to the particular word
rather than a productive pattern of post-consonantal *r*-lessness. The other
context in which post-consonantal *r*-lessness may take place is in an unstressed syllable, where we occasionally get items like *p'ofessor* or
p'otect for *professor* and *protect*. Here again, we are dealing with a
limited number of items which may actually be affected by this process,
but there does appear to be a generalizable phonological context which
can account for the absence of *r*.

L-lessness

   The vocalization of *l* (a vocalized *l* sounds like *oo* with *l*-coloring)
or its complete deletion is also possible in different varieties of American English, although this characteristic has been studied much less extensively than *r*-lessness. Like *r*-lessness, this phenomenon is most
typically found in various post-vocalic positions. In fact, most studies
report it exclusively in this context. Analogous to *r*-lessness, AE participates in this process to a very limited extent, so that we may occasionally get vocalization in items such as *table*, *battle*, *candle*. Although *l* vocalization is quite restricted, it is interesting to note that
there are contexts in AE where *l* may be completely deleted. If the following segment is a labial sound such as *p*, *b*, or *f*, *l* may be completely
deleted. This occurs in items such as *wolf*, *help*, or *shelf*, making words
such as *woof* and *wolf*, *hep* and *help*, or *chef* and *shelf* homophonous. Somewhat like the relationship between different aspects of *r*-lessness discussed in the preceding sections, this is somewhat different from our expectations, since we would expect that the complete loss of *l* before
labial sounds would correlate with a relatively high incidence of other
types of *l* vocalization. What we find is a system in which there is
relatively little post-vocalic *l* vocalization that allows a specific environment for *l*-deletion.
   Some aspects of grammar may be attributable to the loss of *l*. The
most important of these concerns the loss of *l* on a contracted form of
the future modal *will*. We may occasionally get examples such as *Tomorrow,
he be here*, accounting for the use of *be* as an indicator of future time.
This construction, then, would not be due to a grammatical process, but
would instead be a result of the phonological process of *l*-deletion.

TH

Th Sounds

   There are actually two sounds that are represented by the spelling
th in English. One of these sounds is a voiced apico-dental fricative
sound in words such as *this*, *either*, or *bathe*; the other is a voiceless
apico-dental fricative sound in words such as *thing*, *ether*, or *tooth*.
Words such as *thy* and *thigh* are pronounced identically except for these
initial sounds, the former being the voiced, and the latter the voiceless
consonant. Both of these sounds have alternant pronunciations in non-
mainstream varieties as well as variants that may be acceptable in standard English.
   At the beginning of a word, the most notable socially diagnostic
pronunciations involve the corresponding stops for ð, (the phonetic representation for the voiced apico-dental fricative) and θ (the phonetic

representation for the voiceless apico-dental fricative). There are cases
in most non-mainstream varieties of English where ð may be produced as *d*
and θ something like *t*. Note, however, that the corresponding stops are
not exactly identical to the *d* of *dog* or the *t* of *taught*. They are typically pronounced slightly more front in the mouth, being produced with
the tongue tip against the back of the teeth. They are also not produced
with quite as much pressure as the stops of *dog* or *taught*. In the case
of *t*, the characteristic puff of air, called aspiration, following the
t of *taught*, is also not present. AE is like most other varieties of
non-mainstream English in allowing the pronunciation of the corresponding
stops for ð and θ, except that they do not appear to be quite as frequent
as in some other varieties. The lower frequency of the stop counterpart
for ð may be due, in part, to the greater frequency of initial ð's which
may be deleted completely. In the case of θ, there simply appears to be
a lower frequency of *t* for θ, especially as compared with some northern
White varieties.

It has also been observed that there are non-mainstream varieties
of English where the corresponding stop production may occur in the middle
of a word between vowels. This is especially true of ð, where it may
become *d* in items such as *mother*, *brother*, or *bother*. The stop pronunciation is less frequent at the end of a word, but it can also occur in
items like *lathe* or *bathe*. This particular pronunciation is not found
to any extent in AE, and the majority of ð's that occur intervocalically
or at the end of the word are pronounced as they would be in standard
varieties of English.

There is another nonstandard variant for θ in word medial and final
position which is occasionally found in AE, namely *f*. We therefore observe the following types of examples from some AE speakers.

(12) a. He shoots this juice stuff in your *mouf* and it numbs your
         mouf. 17:10
     b. ...if I get back *wif* 'er. 9:(395)
     c. I had a *birfday* party. 20:(203)
     d. ...in a phone *boof*. 123:(180)
     e. ...it took off a-rollin' *wifout* that woman in it. 124:(490)

This particular variant has been found in other non-mainstream varieties of English, and is particularly prominent in Vernacular Black English. Its distribution in AE is somewhat different from Vernacular Black
English in that it is found much less frequently and appears to be more
age-graded. That is, it is typically found to a limited extent among
younger AE speakers. For example, the samples given in (12) are all from
subjects between the ages of 11 and 16. Even among younger speakers, it
is found much more sporadically than it would be found in a variety such
as Vernacular Black English. It is noted only rarely among older speakers
of AE, mainly in the item *with*.

Th Contiguous to Nasals

There is a rule in AE whereby a voiceless *th* sound (phonetically [θ])
may be produced as a *t* next to a nasal segment. This rule is quite like
a rule found in other non-mainstream varieties of English. The process
changing *th* to *t* accounts for the fact that *arithmetic*, *month*, or *nothing*
may be pronounced as *aritmetic*, *mont'* or *nutt'n*. With respect to the
item *nothing*, the *th* is not immediately followed by a nasal segment in
standard varieties of English. In non-mainstream varieties of English,
however, the vowel of the *-ing* sequence is deleted, leaving a syllabic

nasal following the voiceless *th*. This change must take place before the rule changing *th* to *t* can operate, since it is dependent on the nasal segment immediately preceding or following the sound.

INITIAL SEGMENTS

Unstressed Syllable Deletion

In casual speech styles, most varieties of English allow the deletion of some unstressed initial syllables. This process may affect both standard and non-mainstream varieties of English but the extent to which the process operates differs somewhat, depending on the variety. In casual spoken standard English, speakers may delete the initial vowel of prepositions or adverbs like *around* or *about* so that they become *'round* and *'bout*. This is a fairly common phenomenon and is apparently not socially stigmatized. Likewise, an initial consonant and vowel (i.e. *CV*) or vowel plus consonant (i.e. *VC*) syllable may be deleted, giving items like *'cause* and *'til* for *because* and *until*. Sentences like (13) are not uncommon in the casual speech style of most standard English speakers:

(13) a. He liked him *'cause* he was nice.
      b. He went *'til* he was exhausted.
      c. He told her *'bout* the book.
      d. It took her *'round* three years.

While AE speakers are like most standard English speakers in their ability to delete these initial unstressed syllables, the process is somewhat extended in AE. This extension applies to both the classes of items (e.g. nouns and verbs) which are included in the operation of this process and the sequences of unstressed initial syllables that can undergo this deletion. For example, consider the range of unstressed word initial syllables in Table 15 which can be deleted in AE.

Table 15

Initial Unstressed Sequence	Examples
a/e	Kids should be *'llowed* to hear that. 22:2 He's a *'lectrician*. 30:31 *'mergency* 68:(58) *'ccordin'* to what size they are. 159:24
un-	I stood there *'til* her husband come home. 35:42 She won't get in the 'frigerator *'lessn* I do. 17:14
be-	I've throwed 'em out *'fore* he got here. 35:28 It's *'tween* each individual. 28:28 He done lived there a year or two *'fore* I knowed. 22:19
re-	I don't *'member*. 36:7 She won't get in the *'frigerator* 'lessn I do. 17:14
su-	And the professor *'posed* to been Cary Grant. 15:(535) I don't *'spect* that you'd want to hear it. 39:(243)
po-/to-	...it just has *'tatoes* in it. 47:5 ...corn, *'maters*,'tatoes. 50:(41)
con-	He *'fessed* up and made the people take notice. 11:(988)

Illustrative Examples of Initial Unstressed Syllable Deletion in AE

In Table 15, we note the similarities and differences in the process of initial unstressed syllable deletion found in AE and the process which we would expect in the casual speech style of many standard English speakers. For example, unstressed *be-* deletion is quite common with the item *because* in standard English, but it would occur rarely if ever with an item like *before*. Similarly, we expect initial unstressed vowel deletion in adverbs or prepositions like *'bout* and *'round* in standard English, but it is not nearly as typical in nouns like *'lectrician* or *'mergency*. We further note that the list is expanded to include sequences like *re-*, *su-*, *po-*, *to-*, and even *con-*. Sequences of this type are not typically subjected to the initial unstressed syllable deletion rule in most standard English varieties. The deletion of some of these sequences has, in fact, become rather stereotyped in AE. For example, *'taters* for *potatoes* and *'maters* for *tomatoes* can certainly be considered to be stereotypes, and they are sometimes the topic of comment by outsiders and even by some AE speakers. In fact, one of the informants in our sample responded to an interviewer's question as follows:

> Fieldworker: What are some of the things people grow
>   here in their gardens?
> Informant: Oh, potatoes and tomatoes - or did you
>   want me to say 'maters and 'taters? 31:4

In Table 16, we have tabulated the incidence of unstressed initial syllable deletion for 13 of the subjects in our sample. In presenting this table, it is necessary to make two distinctions, since these may affect the relative frequency with which unstressed initial syllable deletion takes place. First of all, we distinguish between the type of syllable the initial unstressed sequence is, delimiting initial *V* and *CV* sequences. The second distinction concerns the type of sound that precedes the initial unstressed syllable. A preceding vowel (i.e. where the preceding word ends in a vowel, such as *the 'lectrician*) is distinguished from a preceding consonant (i.e. where the preceding word ends in a consonant such as *bad 'lectrician*). In each case, the number of actual instances of unstressed initial syllable deletion is tabulated out of all the possible cases in which it might have taken place. Thus, a case like *the 'lectrician* is tabulated as an instance of actual deletion while a case such as *the electrician* would be counted as a potential case in which deletion was not realized.

Several important observations can be made on the basis of Table 16. To begin with, we note that the frequency range of unstressed initial syllable deletion typically falls between 20-60 percent. While this is a fairly wide range of deletion, it is important to note that this phenomenon is quite variable. There are no speakers who never delete unstressed initial syllables. Differences between speakers are found only in terms of frequency levels. We also note that there is a quite regular effect related to the preceding context; a preceding vowel regularly favors the deletion of the unstressed syllable over a preceding consonant. (We are more likely to get a form like *He's the 'lectrician* than *He's a bad 'lectrician*.) This may be attributed to the fact that there is a natural preference in language to separate successive consonants with an intervening vowel. Finally, we should note that the deletion of an initial *V* syllable is generally preferred over the deletion of *CV* sequences. (We are more likely to get deletion in a form like *'lectrician* for *electrician* than in a form like *'frigerator* for *refrigerator*.) The *CV* sequence appears to be more stable in its resistance to the operation of this deletion rule. (See p. 52.)

Table 16

Inf No.	Age/Sex	Initial V						Initial CV						OVERALL TOTAL DELETION	
		PRECEDING CONSONANT		PRECEDING VOWEL		Total		PRECEDING CONSONANT		PRECEDING VOWEL		Total			
		No Del/Tot	%	No Del/Tot	%	Total	%	No Del/Tot	%	No Del/Tot	%	Total	%		
31	67/M	6/36	16.7	4/13	30.8	10/49	20.4	2/6	33.3	2/6	33.3	4/12	33.3	14/61	22.9
83	93/F	6/21	28.6	4/5	80.0	10/26	38.5	0/6	0.0	0/3	0.0	0/9	0.0	10/35	28.6
85	78/F	6/17	35.3	8/14	57.1	14/31	45.2	5/18	27.8	0/2	0.0	5/20	25.0	19/51	37.3
153	83/F	14/37	37.8	10/13	76.9	24/50	48.0	3/10	30.0	1/1	100.0	4/11	36.4	28/61	45.9
22	60/M	17/48	36.4	8/11	72.7	25/59	42.2	6/13	46.1	3/5	60.0	9/18	50.0	34/77	44.2
152	64/F	11/44	25.0	5/8	62.5	16/52	30.8	2/15	6.7	1/3	33.3	3/18	16.7	19/70	27.1
157	52/F	9/33	27.3	8/15	53.3	17/48	35.4	0/14	0.0	3/8	37.5	3/22	13.6	20/70	28.6
30	50/M	7/27	25.9	8/10	80.0	15/37	40.5	2/21	9.5	3/10	30.0	5/31	16.1	20/68	29.4
44	15/M	12/25	48.0	5/5	100.0	17/30	56.7	9/16	56.3	2/2	100.0	11/18	61.1	28/48	58.3
124	11/M	11/24	45.8	6/6	100.0	17/30	56.7	3/6	50.0	-/-	--	3/6	50.0	20/36	55.6
146	52/M	14/35	40.0	5/7	71.4	19/42	45.2	3/12	25.0	0/2	0.0	3/14	21.4	22/56	39.3
2	13/M	15/31	48.4	3/6	50.0	18/37	48.6	8/11	72.7	3/4	75.0	11/15	73.3	29/52	55.7
29	33/F	23/51	45.1	6/12	50.0	29/63	46.0	5/20	25.0	1/3	33.3	6/23	26.0	35/86	40.7
TOTALS		151/429	35.2	80/125	64.0	231/554	41.7	48/168	28.6	19/49	38.8	67/217	30.9	298/771	38.7

Unstressed Initial Syllable Deletion

While our previous discussion has focused only on unstressed initial
syllables, it should be observed that there is a related phenomenon in
which an unstressed schwa vowel [ə] within a word can be deleted. This
process, like the one discussed above, is found to some extent in the
casual speech style of all varieties of English, but it appears to be
extended somewhat in AE. Items like *s'posta* for *supposed to*, *prob'ly*
for *probably*, *rel'tive* for *relative*, and *(A)mer'ca* for *America* are all accounted for by this general process. The exact difference between the
operation of this process in AE and its operation in casual spoken standard English, however, remains to be studied.

Deletion of Initial ð

In most varieties of English, the initial segment of some words beginning with ð (typically spelled *th*) can be deleted. The number of words
actually beginning with ð is relatively small in English, but some of
these may occur with considerable frequency in conversation. Included
in the inventory of items beginning with ð are the demonstratives such
as *this, that, these*, and *those*, third person plural forms such as *they,
them*, and *their*, the comparative form *than*, and the form *there*--which
may function as a locative (e.g. *It's up there*) or an existential pronoun (e.g. *There are five students who passed*). All of these forms may
undergo ð deletion under some circumstances. In this regard, they are
different from other forms beginning with ð, such as *thus*, which appear
never to delete the ð. In between these extremes are forms such as *then*
and *the* where the initial ð may be absent under restricted conditions.
    In examining this deletion phenomenon as it occurs in many main-
stream varieties of English, it is necessary to specify certain conditions which appear to enhance deletion. To begin with, we must note
that it is something which tends to take place in relatively fast, informal speech. It is not nearly as characteristic in slower, more
formal styles of speech. Within the context of casual speech, there
are linguistic factors which affect the relative frequency of initial
ð deletion. One of these factors is stress. The deletion of ð is
much more characteristic when the form is unstressed than when it is
stressed; in fact, it appears that it cannot take place when the form
in question receives strong or emphatic stress. We thus get ð deletion in sentences like (14a), but not typically (14b):

(14)   a. He'll stop *'em*.
       b. He'll stop *thém*, but not me.

It is observed that ð deletion is much more characteristic of some forms
like *them* as opposed to a form like *that*, a fact which may be related to
relative degrees of unstress.[4] We thus get a sentence such as (15a)
more frequently than a sentence such as (15b):

(15)   a. Will you kick *'em* for me?
       b. Will you kick *'at* for me?

There is also an effect related to the preceding segment, so that a preceding consonant appears to favor the deletion over a preceding vowel.
That is, deletion is more frequently found in a sentence like (16a) than
it is in a sentence like (16b);

(16)   a. I thought he would pick *'at* up.
       b. I thought he would do *'at* for me.

Finally, it is observed that this type of deletion is more characteristic in the middle of a sentence than it is at the beginning of a
sentence. We find sentences like (16a) more common than (17):

(17) ...'at's all I can say.

This effect may, of course, ultimately be due to the different types of
stress that may be assigned to forms at the beginning of a sentence, but
it appears that there are some mainstream varieties where sentence initial
ð is deleted rarely, if at all. (The exception to this is certain set
phrases such as *Atta boy* or *Atta way*.) While there are more detailed
effects that might be cited (cf. Christian, 1973; Cofer, 1972), these
constitute the main constraints which affect the relative frequency of
ð deletion in the casual style of some mainstream varieties of English.
    The deletion of ð in AE operates in much the same way as in main-
stream varieties, except that its application has been somewhat extended. Examples of ð deletion for the forms mentioned above are given
in sentences (18) through (21):

Demonstratives *(this, that, these, those)*
(18)   a. I done filled up on 'is ham. 84:(439)
       b. And this boy grabbed a great big cinder block -- 'bout like
           'at and throwed 'at in on me. 2:3
       c. She's get on 'ose skates. 84:(697)
Third Person Plural Forms
(19)   a. You could pick 'em good while 'ey was hot. 85:8
       b. But 'ey wasn't right 'at day. 84:(107)
Comparative *than*
(20)   a. You can't bat more 'n one eye at a time. 146:19
       b. I mean things are gettin' worser anymore 'n what they used
           to be.[5]
Locative and Existential *there*
(21)   a. 'ere's 'at high priced knife, Chester. 84:(37)
       b. They said they's gonna ride up 'ere, get on Sukis, push 'em
           up to the top of the hill up 'ere. 20:(1259)

    Most of the AE examples cited in (18) through (21) are also found
in casual mainstream varieties of English. There are, however, some differences between mainstream varieties and AE in their use of ð deletion.
One difference is found in the increased frequency with which it occurs
in AE. The deletion of ð appears to be more frequent in AE than it is
in many mainstream varieties of English. As a function of this increased
frequency, there is also greater likelihood that it may be used to some
extent even in more formal styles of speech. Another difference between
ð deletion in AE and other mainstream varieties is in the expansion of
contexts in which it occurs. We previously mentioned that ð deletion
does not usually occur in more stressed contexts in mainstream varieties
of English. This contraint is not as strong in AE as evidenced by sentences like (22):

(22)   a. You wanna use 'is or you wanna use 'at. 84:(46)
       b. ...but 'at was it. 84:(1023)

Likewise, the constraint which prohibits or greatly restricts the use of
ð deletion sentence initially is not as strong in AE, as seen in sentences
like (23):

(23)   a.   *'at* was Daddy's mother.   85:4
       b.   *'ere's* 'at high-priced knife, Chester.   84:(37)
       c.   *'at* old man jumped 'at big buck.   84:(3)

Generally, then, restrictions which are found in some mainstream varieties
are not quite as strong in AE.

The case of the conjunction *then* and the article *the* is somewhat
different from other types of ð deletion and there is some question as
to whether it can be considered a deleted form at all.   What appears is
a general restriction in which the ð is absent when following a nasal
sound such as *n* or a lateral such as *l*.   For example, we may get utterances such as (24):

(24)   a.   An' *'en* he started to run.
       b.   An' *'e* one I was gonna shoot disappeared.
       c.   All *'e* way home he cried.

What actually appears to take place in cases like (24) is a special
assimilation of the initial ð to the preceding *n* or *l* (e.g. *an' 'nen*'--
'and then,' *all 'le*--'all the') rather than a complete deletion of the ð.
While a preceding *l* and *n* appear to affect an increase in the deletion
of ð for the forms mentioned previously (i.e. sentences (18) - (21), a
specifically defined context must be cited for the absence of ð in *the*
and *then* to be found at all.   With respect to the assimilation of ð
when preceded by a *l* or *n*, AE does not appear to be different from fast,
informal style in varieties of mainstream English.

It is interesting to note that although ð deletion in AE is only
an extension of a general process found to some extent in all varieties
of English, it has become a characteristic stereotype of the area.
Literary representations often use it prominently in their portrayal
of AE, and teachers concerned about mainstream norms often cite it as
one of the crucial differences between the AE sound system and that of
mainstream varieties.   Apparently, the extension of this process in the
ways mentioned earlier is sufficient to make it a matter for overt comment.

Deletion of Initial *w*

In most varieties of English, there are conditions under which the
initial *w* of certain items can be deleted.   Most commonly, this process
affects modals such as *will* and *would*.   Once the initial *w* is lost in
these modals, the following vowel may also be deleted, so that we end up
with a contracted form such as the following:

(25)   a.   He'*ll* go downtown.
       b.   He'*d* go downtown if he could.

In these cases, the initial *w* can be lost only when the modal is unstressed, or not in a syntactically exposed position (e.g. clause final)
so that we do not find the process operating in cases like (26) and (27):

(26)   a.   He *will* go downtown.
       b.   He *would* go downtown if he could.
(27)   a.   He'll go downtown, I know he *will*.
       b.   He'd go downtown if he could, I know he *would*.

Some linguists (cf. Zwicky, 1970 for details) consider the *w* de-

letion in cases such as these to be part of a more general rule of initial
semi-vowel deletion. This general rule includes the deletion of *h* in
auxiliaries, as will be discussed (e.g. *He's* been here). The deletion
of *w* in the modals *will* and *would* is a very common phenomenon of English
and is in no way socially stigmatized.

In AE, there are two additional aspects of initial *w* deletion which
are noteworthy. These aspects are not governed by linguistic rules that
are drastically different from the rules operating for mainstream English
varieties, but are simply extensions of the rule which operates to some
extent in practically all varieties of English. The first type of extension involves the past form of the copula or auxiliary *be* form, namely
was or *were*.[6] The examples given in (28) illustrate the extension of *w*
deletion for *was* in AE.[7]

(28)   a.   We took off when we seen him a-runnin', he *'uz* runnin' up
            the road a-hollerin'. 10:26
       b.   We *'uz* sittin' up 'ere laughin', couldn't stop a-laughin'
            he *'uz* sittin' back 'ere cryin' about 40 bees stinged him.
            10:26

In cases like (28), we notice that the vowel (phonetically close to [ə])
is still retained so that only the initial *w* is deleted for *was*. Although
this is a pattern that can be found to some extent in AE, a more common
pattern involves the deletion of the following vowel as well, as in
sentences like (29):

(29)   a.   ...and this boy grabbed a great big old cinder block -
            'bout like 'at, and throwed 'at in on me; Boy, I*'z*
            a-hollerin'. 2:3
       b.   I guess they knew what they*'z* a-sayin'. 24:(382)

In cases such as these, we see that the contraction rule that
affects modals like *will* and *would* is simply extended to *was*. Parallel
to the restrictions on the contraction of items like *will* and *would*,
this process cannot take place when the form is stressed or in syntactically exposed positions. Thus, a full form of *was* is required in
sentences like (30):

(30)   a.   He *was* hunting turkey.
       b.   He*'z* hunting turkey yesterday, I know he *was*.

It should be noted that the contraction of past tense forms of *be*
(i.e. *was*), along with the regular contraction of third person singular
present tense forms (i.e. he *is*→*he's*), may result in past and present
contracted forms sounding identical. In both cases the actual sound of
the segment left after contraction is a *z*-type sound, as in (31):

(31)   a.   Yesterday he*'z* [z] huntin' turkey.
       b.   Right now he*'s* [z] huntin' turkey.

The contracted forms resulting in homophony do not typically lead to a
problem in distinguishing past and present tense since the surrounding
context in most cases is usually sufficient to indicate which tense is
intended.

The other extension of *w* deletion in AE involves the pronoun form
one (phonetically [wən]). It is observed that when this pronoun is in

unstressed position within a sentence the *w* may be deleted, giving us
sentences like those in (32):

(32) a. He had eight children, I think, with the first wife, six
         with the second *'un.* 85:7
     b. ...but she was pretty bad, you know, about bossing around
         the young *'uns.* 36:11
     c. She just come up *'ere* and whopped me a good *'un* with the
         paddle. 36:(40)

Like the other forms affected by *w* deletion, this operation cannot
operate when the form is stressed, so that the full form is required in
(33):

(33) I'll take *one*, if you take the other.

Most typically, the vowel following the *w* is retained, but it may be
lost under conditions where the following nasal may become the syllabic
peak, as in sentences like (34):

(34) a. I got *this'n* [n] at Ched's. 85:28
     b. *That'n* [n̩] got away from us and then the second one. 22:20

For some speakers, the deletion of initial *w* in this pronoun may be
limited to the lexical item *young 'uns*, with other unstressed contexts
of *one* following patterns in most mainstream varieties of English.
     The extension of initial *w* deletion that we have observed for AE
seems to be characteristic of a number of varieties spoken or derived
from the rural South, so that we find a similar process operating in
rural White varieties spoken in the deep South and in Vernacular Black
English.

INITIAL *H* RETENTION IN AUXILIARIES AND PRONOUNS

     In the history of the English language, there were a number of pro-
nouns and auxiliary verbs which originally began with *h*. Through a
general process starting with initial *h* of unstressed forms, however,
many of these items have deleted the *h*. As Jespersen (1933:57) notes:

> *H* tends to disappear in weak forms of pronouns and
> auxiliary verbs, not only in cases like *it* for *hit*,
> where the *h* form has totally disappeared, *'em* for old
> *hem* (not developed from *them*), *I've* for *I have*, *you'd*
> for *you had*, etc., which are frequently written, but
> also in the colloquium pronunciations like *if (h)e
> took (h)is hat*; *you must (h)ave seen (h)im*; *we see
> (h)er every day*.

To a certain extent, the deletion of initial *h* has affected all varieties
of English. In casual speech, for example, most speakers of English
varieties may delete an initial *h* in pronouns and auxiliaries when they
are unstressed, giving us sentences like:

(35) a. *I've* gone downtown.
     b. He's seen *'im*.

     While this process may operate in casual speech styles for most
varieties of American English, the *h* is still typically retained even in

casual speech style when the auxiliary or pronoun is stressed, either
because of emphasis or because of its position in the sentence. Cases
of this sort are illustrated in (36):

(36) a. I *have* seen 'im.
      b. I've seen *hím*.
      c. You may not think I've seen him, but I *have*.
      d. You may think it's me, but it's actually *hím*.

In the case of the auxiliaries such as *have* and *had*, there is an
additional deletion of the following vowel which results in the "contracted" form. (There are actually several other processes leading up
to the contracted form which have been discussed by Labov , 1969; Zwicky,
1970; and Wolfram, 1974b). The deletion of *h* in these forms is, of
course, a quite regular process in most varieties of American English
which holds no special social significance other than as a casual style
indicator.

As mentioned above, the extent of *h* deletion which has resulted
from this historical process may vary in different varieties of English.
Thus, for example, we find that many mainstream varieties of American
English have completely lost the original *h* in items like *it* (originally
hit) and *ain't* (originally *hain't*). This, however, is not the case in
AE, where *h* is still retained by a number of the older residents of the
area. We still find examples such as the following:

(37) a. When the winter set in, *hit* set in, *hit's* just like in a
          western.   22:10
      b. *Hit* was these three billy goats.   20:(830)
      c. I *hain't* got none now.   12:(186)
      d. I said I *hain't* a-gonna do it.   83:23

The retention of the initial *h* in these forms is most likely to
be found in the more stressed items in a sentence, and occurs rarely, if
at all, in unstressed items. We have referred here to the notions of
greater and lesser degrees of sentence stress since there are actually
a number of degrees of stress which can be noted within a sentence.
For example, in (37a) it appears that the item *hit* has a primary stress
in the phrase *hit set in* whereas the stress pattern of (37b) indicates
that the pronoun does not receive the degree of stress found in *billy
goats* but does receive greater stress than the remainder of the sentence.
When the pronoun form is in the least stressed form in a sentence--the
regular stress pattern for sentences such as (38)--it is questionable
whether the *h* can be retained.

(38) Hè boúght it.

In these unstressed contexts, the forms tend to be exactly like those
found in other varieties of American English, where the *h* has been lost
completely. Of course, if the stress patterns of (38) were changed to
emphasize the pronominal form, the *h* could readily be retained, as
in (39):

(39) Hè bought *hít*.

As implied in the previous description, the retention of *h* in
forms like *it* and *ain't* is a variable matter, with the relative frequency
of *h* retention sensitive to the phrase and sentence stress patterns.

The general principle which appears to govern the increased frequency
of *h* retention may be stated as follows: the greater the degree of stress
on the pronominal or auxiliary verb form, the greater likelihood that *h*
will be retained. As mentioned, *h* retention in forms such as *it* and
ain't is something which is much more characteristic of older speakers
than the younger generation. In fact, we would anticipate the complete
extinction of *h* in *it* and *ain't* within a generation or two.

FEATURES INVOLVING NASALS

Consonants Preceding Nasals

        In AE, as in many other varieties of English, there are a number of
different processes which can affect consonants when they precede nasal
segments such as *m*, *n*, or *ŋ*. The consonantal changes depend on the type
of consonant preceding the nasal sound and, in some cases, the operation
of previous processes affecting these consonants.
        Voiced fricatives preceding nasals. In AE, as in many other vari-
eties of English spoken in other parts of the South and some selected
regions of the North, it is observed that the *z* sound in items like
wasn't, *isn't*, *hasn't*, and *doesn't* is realized as the corresponding
voiced stop *d*. There are numerous instances of these variants as indicated by the following:

(40)   a. They *wadn't* [wədn̩] a dang one of them... 31:12
        b. *Wadn't* [wədn̩] but one house down there... 36:13
        c. It's a wonder somebody didn't get hurt on it, *idn't* [Idn̩]
            it? 2:5(FW)
        d. ...dangerous with that, *idn't* [Idn̩] he? 2:2
        e. She *hadn't* [hædn̩] been away from that... 31:18
        f. But it *doedn't* [dədn̩] take but about... 40:19

        The pronunciations cited above are actually the result of a more
general rule whereby voiced fricatives can become their corresponding
voiced stop. Voiced fricatives included in this process are *z*, *v*, and
th ([ð]). The fricatives *z* and *ð* typically become *d* as in *wadn't*
('wasn't') and *headn* ('heathen'), whereas the *v* most typically becomes
b as in *sebm* ('seven') or *elebm* ('eleven'). In order to understand how
this rule operates, it is necessary to note that in unaccented syllables,
the vowel preceding the nasal *m* or *n* may be lost, leaving the nasal immediately following the consonant. (This nasal now takes the syllabic
beat usually taken by the vowel and thus becomes a "syllabic nasal.")
Once the nasal sound is immediately following the fricative, it can
effect the change of the voiced fricative to its corresponding stop.
        A result of the process changing *z* to *d* is the reduction of con-
trast between the negativized past tense *hadn't* and the negativized
present form *hasn't*. The change of *z* to *d* now allows both forms to
be realized as *hadn't*. The lack of distinction between these forms
is clearly due to this pronunciation rule and should not be attributed
to a different grammatical use of the auxiliary *have*. The distinction
between the past and present forms of *have* (e.g. *He has gone* and *He had
gone*) is consistently maintained in the same fashion in AE as other varieties of English, so that the merger of *hasn't* and *hadn't* must be attributed to this pronunciation process.
        Devoicing d *to* t *preceding nasals.* Once the voiced fricatives of
items like *wasn't*, *hasn't*, *isn't* are realized as *d* due to the process
described above, there is a further process which can devoice the *d* to

a voiceless stop such as *t*. In most cases, this may be a momentarily
unreleased *t* or a glottal stop, which is produced by a closing of the
vocal bands in a rather abrupt manner. The subsequent change of *d* to
t in *wasn't*, *hasn't*, and *isn't* is part of a more general process operating
on *d*'s before nasals, and affects many more items than those *d*'s that
were originally derived from *z*'s. For example, it can affect items like
didn't, *couldn't*, or *wouldn't* in addition to *wasn't*, *hasn't*, and *isn't*,
as in the following examples:

(41)   a.   No we *coultn't* [kUtn̩].   2:5
        b.   She really *ditn't* [dItn̩] deserve that.   36:37
        c.   ...and I told her I *woultn't* [wUtn̩].   36:36
        d.   It *watn't* [wətn̩] very deep.   2:12
        e.   ...if she *hatn't* [hætn̩] raised the blinds.   36:7
        f.   Well, I *hatn't* [hætn̩] got driver's license yet.   36:40

The general process of *d* devoicing before nasals is a relatively common
phenomenon in AE, just as it is in some other regional English varieties.
    The loss of d *preceding nasals*. In addition to the above types of
options for the realization of consonants before the nasal sounds, there is
a further process that may operate on some of these consonants. This
process involves the complete loss of a segment before the nasal sound.
In actuality, it appears that the sound is completely assimilated to
the immediately following nasal. Like the devoicing of *d* to *t*, this
is a process which can affect a general class of items where *d* precedes
n, not only those that were originally derived from items such as
wasn't, *isn't*, or *hasn't*. It can thus affect items like *couldn't*,
wouldn't, and *didn't* as well as those forms of *z* which have been changed
to *d*. The following examples illustrate this process:

(42)   a.   ...I *din't* [dIn] try to get them.   31:32
        b.   ...we *coun't* [kUn] get down.   47:8
        c.   ...I *woun't* [wUn] care about it.   31:23
        d.   ...the hardest fall, *in't* [In] it?   31:22
        e.   ...I *wan't* [wən] gonna do nothing.   61:16

    The loss of the consonant preceding a syllabic nasal causes the
nasal to lose its syllabic beat. This results in a reduction of the
number of syllables in the item. For example, with the realization of
z, *d*, or *t* preceding the *n* of *wasn't*, the item will be two syllables,
waz and *nt* with the beat of the second syllable usually being carried
by a syllabic nasal. With a loss of the consonant in the preceding
syllable, however, the syllabic beat is lost from the nasal as it becomes the final segment of the preceding syllable.
    The complete absence of *d* before *n* occurs somewhat less frequently
than the realization of *d* or *t* before *n*, and is most characteristic of
more rapidly spoken, casual speech.

The Pronunciation of Indefinite Articles

    In most standard varieties of English, the pronunciation of the
indefinite article varies depending on the shape of the following word.
If the following word begins with a consonant, the article *a* (usually
pronounced as [ə]) is realized. We thus get forms like *a man*, *a fiddle*,
or *a child*. However, if the following item begins with a vowel, most
standard varieties use the form *an* (usually pronounced as [ən]), as in
an apple, *an ear*, or *an accident*. In AE, the form *a* may be generalized for both contexts, so that it can be used before both vowels

and consonants, giving us forms such as *a apple*, *a ear*, or *a accident*. While the usage of *a* before both consonants and vowels is characteristic of many non-mainstream varieties of American English, it appears to be less socially significant as a class differentiator in AE than it is in some northern contexts. The relatively minor extension of *a* to precede all forms receives considerable attention in some cases because there is a spelling difference to match the automatic pronunciation difference maintained in many standard varieties.

In cases where the generalized article *a* (pronounced as a schwa [ə]) precedes a word beginning with a [ə] phonetically, it may seem that the article is not present at all. Thus, we get forms such as *in apartment* for standard English *in an apartment* or *He's electrician* for *He's an electrician*. This effect is created by the fact that the initial vowel of the following word is eliminated by the initial syllable deletion rule previously discussed, and not due to the absence of the article. Close attention to phonetic detail will, in fact, indicate that there is a slight juncture between the article and the form which has undergone unstressed initial syllable deletion. Such sequences should then be interpreted as in (43):

(43) a. ...in *a* 'partment. 8:8
      b. He's *a* 'lectrician. 30:(613)

In cases such as (43) we see that the generalized article *a* is intact and the following schwa is simply deleted by a different phonological rule.

Unstressed *-ing*

One of the most well known and socially stable diagnostic variables of American English is that of the so-called *g-dropping* in some words ending in *ing*. Phonetically, *ng* is actually just one nasal segment [ŋ], so that what is actually meant by the reference to *g* dropping is the replacement of the nasal segment [ŋ] by [n]. The *in'* pronunciation has actually been studied in a number of different settings, and appears to be present to some extent in all varieties of American English. The main differences, then, between regional and social varieties is the extent to which this process actually takes place. It should be mentioned here that there is some historical evidence (cf. Wyld, 1936; Krapp, 1925) that the most common pronunciation of this form in early modern English was apparently the *in'* form, with the preference for the *ing* form in some varieties of English gathering momentum during the late 18th and 19th centuries.

The pronunciation *in'* is heavily influenced by the stress of the syllable. In monosyllabic words that automatically receive primary stress, *in'* is not used. Therefore, items like *sing* and *ring* will always receive the *ng* or [ŋ] pronunciation. In polysyllabic words in which *ing* is assigned an intermediate level of stress (that is, not primary stress, but not unstressed), it also appears that *ing* is the favored pronunciation in most varieties of English. Items like *anything* and *everything* will predominantly be produced with [ŋ] in most varieties of English, including AE. When the syllable containing *ing* is unstressed, however, *in'* is a very common pronunciation. Most frequently, unstressed *ing* involves the verb suffix in items such as *trying*, *fixing*, and so forth, but it also is observed in items like *nothing* and *something*. In the case of *something*, of course, the pronunciation may involve a syllabic *m*. With regard to stress patterns, it should be noted that there may be some individual differences among speakers in terms of the differentiation

between intermediate levels of stress and unstress. For example, some
speakers appear to interpret the *ing* form in an item like *morning* as
an intermediate level of stress and therefore do not reduce it to *in'*
whereas other speakers interpret it as unstressed so that they realize
it as *mornin'* at very high frequency levels.

In spontaneous, relatively casual conversation, the *in'* form is
clearly predominant in AE. While there is certainly some degree of differentiation which may be related to class or style factors, this differential does not seem to be quite as extensive as has been reported for
the *ing* in alternation in other varieties of English. Fairly typical
frequency levels of *in'* in casual conversation style are represented by
the following six speakers:

Table 17

Inf No.	Age/Sex	No. *in'*/Total	%*in'*
31	67/M	67/71	94.4
1	13/M	113/114	99.1
64	15/F	45/53	84.9
28	42/F	56/58	96.6
124	12/M	37/37	100.0
165	57/M	114/135	84.4

Frequency of in' *and* ing *in Unstressed Syllables
for Six Appalachian English Speakers*

The range of *in'* realization typically falls between 80-100 percent
of all the cases where *ing* can potentially be reduced (i.e. they are in
unstressed syllables). The observed frequency of *in'* forms from these
speakers of AE tends to be somewhat higher than the realization of *in'*
forms by speakers of White northern nonstandard varieties (as indicated
in studies of Detroit [Shuy, Wolfram and Riley, 1967:III, 67] and New
York City [Labov, 1966:396]). It is more comparable to the figures obtained for both Black and White speakers in other parts of the South (e.g.
Anshen, 1972:20) although it appears to be slightly more frequent than other
non-Appalachian White southern varieties. The historical reasons for this,
of course, may be found in the retention of the older -*in'* form from an
earlier period of English.

In addition to the cases of *in'* pronunciation for *ing*, there are
cases in which the suffix *ing* does not appear to be present at all. We
thus get examples such as the following:

(44) a. ...and he's *shine* that flashlight. 2:4
      b. ...what wasn't fishing, you know, was *swim*. 36:27
      c. ...where the water come *run* down. 31:19

These types of examples are found in relatively rapid speaking style and
appear to occur only when the base form is a nasal sound such as *m*, *n*, or
ŋ.   In cases of this type it appears that the *in'* form assimilates with
the final nasal sound of the word base. This assimiliation process takes
place in several steps. To begin with, we note that the elimination of
the vowel in *in'* is relatively common in some contexts, so that the nasal
sound takes the syllabic beat of the final syllable. We thus can get
forms like:

(45) a. He was *gettn̩* sick.
      b. She was *settn̩* there.

where the diacritic ̩ indicates that the nasal takes a syllabic beat.
The syllabic nasal takes the syllabic beat left by the eliminated vowel.
However, in items following another nasal, the syllabic nasal may be
reduced further so that it appears that the final syllable is lost entirely. In many cases, it is actually realized as a lengthened form of
the nasal of the word base (phonetically [šaIn:] 'shine,' [swIm:] 'swim,'
or [rɘn:] 'run'), but the reduction of the syllabic beat makes it seem
perceptually like there is no *ing* form at all. And, in some cases, the
lengthened nasal may be further reduced so that there is, in fact, no
vestige of the original *ing*. These types of reductions are relatively
restricted and not due to the grammatical loss of the *ing* suffix but a
regular pronunciation process for the majority of speakers revealing
this phenomenon.[9]

OTHER CONSONANTAL FEATURES

     In addition to the consonantal features discussed in the previous
sections, there are other aspects of the AE system that we might mention
briefly. One of the phonological features not discussed is the pronunciation of stops in word-final position, when they are not in consonant
clusters. In AE, as has been found for some other varieties of English,
word-final voiced stops such as *d*, *g*, and *b* may be pronounced with a
sound something like their voiceless counterparts *t*, *k*, and *p*. Phonetically, there is an abrupt cutoff of voicing with or even a little before
the stop occlusion in the mouth. In the case of *d*, the abrupt cutoff
of voicing known as a "glottal stop" may stand alone. Like many varieties
of non-mainstream English, the voiceless stop counterpart or glottal
stop is quite frequent when the final syllable of the word is unstressed,
as in items such as *hundred*, *salad*, or *decided*. In AE, as in Vernacular
Black English (cf. Wolfram and Fasold, 1974:138) the abrupt devoicing can
also occur in monosyllabic words, as in *kid*, *rag*, or *cub*. We may thus
get these forms resembling *kit*, *rack*, or *cup*. Complete homophony between items like *kid* and *kit*, *rag* and *rack*, and *cub* and *cup* does not result, since the duration of the preceding vowel is longer in those items
that have gone through "stop devoicing." That is, the vowel of an item
like *kit* corresponding to *kid* would be a few fractions of a second longer
than the vowel in an item like *kit* even though the devoicing process
here may mean that both of them end in a *t*-like sound. Although we do
not have actual figures to support our conclusion, it appears that the
incidence of final stop devoicing in monosyllabic words is considerably
less frequent in AE than it is in a variety such as Vernacular Black
English.
     There are also several consonantal features that may be socially
obtrusive but affect small sets of items or individual words. For example, AE is one of those varieties of English in which some incidence
of the older pronunciation of *ask* is retained. The pattern originally
had a different sequence of the final consonants in which the *k* preceded
s instead of following it. This older pattern is still occasionally
found so that *ask* may be pronounced like *axe*. Another phonological
pattern which apparently affects only a single item is the pronunciation
of *chimney*. Two alternant pronunciations may be found in AE. It is
possible to follow the *m* with an *l*, as in *chimley*, or have an *mbl* sequence as in *chimbley* although the former pronunciation is clearly favored in this area. There are other restricted consonant features that

might be cited, but our focus on phonological rules which affect significant classes of items has precluded them from this discussion. Ultimately,
a complete description of AE phonology must include such variant pronunciations, even if they are quite restricted in scope.

VOWEL CHARACTERISTICS

    Although there are a number of interesting vowel differences found in
AE, our discussion of the vowel system will be limited in scope. The description of vowels should, in fact, be considered as more demonstrative
and approximative than complete and precise. To give a complete and precise description of AE vowels would take us considerably beyond the level
of phonetic detail to which we have restricted our study. There are many
aspects of vowel quality that can be described only with the finest phonetic detail. Without appealing to the instrumental measurement for some
of these details, our analysis might suffer from reliability in the im-
pressionistic transcription of minute vowel differences.
    Our description is also limited by the restricted geographical region
which serves as the basis for our description of AE. Other aspects of
the AE phonological system and the syntactic system appear to cover a
wide range of territory, but there are apparent vowel differences from
region to region within Appalachia. Even within the restricted locale
we have studied here, there is evidence that several different vowel
systems must be recognized. A comprehensive description would have to
discuss different systems within their own right as well as the similarities and differences between vowel systems in the area. Certain types
of vowel quality must be viewed in terms of the systematic effect that a
given vowel quality has on the quality of adjacent vowels in the system
(e.g. the raising of one vowel quality may have a triggering effect on
other vowels in order to maintain "phonetic space" between vowels).
With the above types of reservations on completeness and detail, we may
proceed to our description of some selected aspects of AE vowels.

Glide Reduction

    The pronunciation of the so-called long *i* used in northern varieties
of English actually consists of two sounds, a full vowel such as *ah* followed by an off-glide which sounds something like *ee* (phonetically [a^i]).
In many southern varieties of English, the off-glide is absent, so that
an item like *pie* may be pronounced something like *pah*. This area of AE
participates in this reduction or loss of the *ee* glide. As found elsewhere, the absence of the off-glide is quite sensitive to the following
linguistic context. It is most likely to be absent when at the end of
a word as in *pie*, *sky*, or *tie*. If a consonant follows it, the glide is
more likely to be absent when the following consonant is voiced, as in
words such as *time*, *wide*, or *side*, than when it is voiceless, as in
words such as *sight*, *kite*, *fight*. The absence of the off-glide, particularly when at the end of a word or followed by a voiced consonant, is
not particularly stigmatized socially, and simply seems to be a regional
characteristic. It should be noted that the absence of the off-glide
does not create widespread homophony. Even when a word like *side* is
pronounced something like *sahd*, it is distinguished from items like
sad and *sod* by the quality of the *ah* vowel.
    A similar situation extends to the *y* sound in items like *boy* and
boil, where the off-glide may be deleted in AE, as in other southern
varieties of American English. Here again this deletion does not result
in homophony since items such as *boil* and *ball* and *oil* and *all*, while

closer phonetically than they are in some northern varieties, are not pronounced identically.

Ire Sequences

In a number of varieties of English, sequences which are convention-
ally spelled *ire* (as in *tire, wire,* or *fire*) or alternantly spelled *yer*
(*flyer, buyer*), *ier* (*plier*), or *iar* (*liar*), may be pronounced as two
syllables. Thus, items like *tire* or *fire* may be pronounced something
like *tayer* (phonetically [ta^{i}ər]) or *fayer* (phonetically [fa^{i}ər]). In
AE, the sequence may be pronounced somewhat differently. To begin with,
we observe that there is a loss of the up-gliding *y* on the vowel *a*. This
is part of the process previously discussed which affects many of the
up-gliding vowel diphthongs in southern varieties of English. In addition to this process, it is observed that the two syllable sequence
found in other varieties is coalesced to one in AE. Thus, the items
tire and *fire* may be pronounced more like *tahr* and *fahr* respectively.
This process makes these items appear to be relatively close to items
such as *tar* and *far* and it is not uncommon for non-AE speakers to interpret these pronunciations as identical. It is important to note, however, that these pairs of items are not pronounced identically, and
few native AE speakers would ever confuse these pronunciations. Items
like *tire* and *fire* are distinguished from *tar* and *far* by differences in
the vowel. For one, the vowel of *tire* and *fire* is produced more front
in the mouth than the vowel of *tar* and *far*, which is typically like the
a of *father*. In addition, the vowel in *tire* and *fire* is usually of
slightly longer duration than the corresponding vowel on *tar* and *far*.
It appears that the process we have described above is more commonly
found in items where the *ire* is part of the basic word as compared with
items where the construction is formed by the addition of an *-er* suffix.
The process is more likely to take place in a form like *tire* or *fire*
than a form like *buyer* or *flyer* where *-er* is a suffix. While these differences in frequency appear to be the case impressionistically, data
is still needed in order to confirm this hypothesis.
The process affecting *ire* sequences is fairly widespread among AE
speakers, and does not appear to be especially stigmatized. While we
may expect less incidence of this process among middle class speakers,
the phonological process has become well established as a regional characteristic of the area.

Ea before *r*

One of the effects of *r* on the preceding vowel sequence involves
the sound of the vowel typically spelled *ea* in words such as *bear,*
wear, or *tear*. Sequences of this type are quite sensitive to dialect
differences in American English, but in ways which are somewhat different
from that observed in AE. In AE, one of the pronunciations still found
among some speakers involves a lower front vowel, produced somewhat more
in the front of the mouth than the *a* of *father*. Although items such as
bar and *bear* may be considered to be pronounced identically by some outsiders, they are differentiated by the fronting of the vowel in *bear* as
opposed to the *a* of *father* or *bar*. This pattern is now found to be rather
sporadic, and remains in the speech of a minority of speakers from the
area. It does remain in stereotype caricatures of AE speech as seen in
the popular spelling of *bar* for *bear* or *thar* for *there*. It appears to
persist more in an item such as *bear* than *there*, a fact which may be
related to the relative frequency of these words (an item such as *there*
would occur many more times than one such as *bear*).

Final Unstressed *ow*

One of the characteristic aspects of the AE phonological system most
noticeable to outsiders involves the alternation of final *ow* forms with
er. For example, we note the following types of correspondences found
among our AE speakers:

(46) a. *holler* for 'hollow' 16:(15)
      b. *tobaccer* for 'tobacco' 30:15
      c. *yeller* for 'yellow' 34:(250)
      d. *potaters* for 'potatoes' 30:7
      e. *winders* for 'windows' 37:(100)
      f. *Narrers* for 'Narrows' 30:10

The *er* alternation is observed only on items that have potential alternants as *ow*. This does not necessarily mean that *ow* must be the only
alternant for the *er* form, but it must exist as one the potential alternants. Thus, for example, an item like *potato* may actually be pronounced
with a final schwa something like *potatuh* ([pətetə]) or with an *ow* something like *potatow* ([pətetow]) in addition to *er*.
A second condition of the operation of the rule concerns the fact
that the syllable in which the alternation takes place cannot take the
main word stress. Thus, an item like *belów* or *bestów* (contrasted with,
for example, *béllow*) would not be eligible for the operation of this rule
since the main stress in these words falls on the syllable containing *ow*.
This condition also eliminates words of one syllable, so that the *er*
correspondence would not operate on items like *flow* or *low*.
While it is noted that the *er* correspondence for unstressed *ow* in
AE typically occurs at the end of the word, it is possible to retain this
correspondence with the addition of suffixes such as plural *s* or progressive *-ing*. Thus, we may get *potaters* or *winders* for *potatoes* and *windows*,
and *follering* and *swallering* for *following* and *swallowing*. Word final
position, then, is defined in terms of the word base or stem, since we
have seen that it is possible to add a suffix after the *er* alternation.
There is, however, one exception to this general condition found in our
corpus: *Narrers* for *Narrows* (*Narrows* is a city along the southeastern
Virginia and West Virginia borders). In this case, the *s* is actually a
part of the name of the city and typically would not be considered a
suffix. The fact that it is *s*--the same form which is added in a suffix--
leads us to conclude that this form came about by analogy with other
forms in which the final *-s* was actually a suffix.
It appears that the *er* correspondence for *ow* is more frequently
found on items where it is preceded by an *l* type sound (e.g. *holler*,
yeller, *piller*, etc.) but can be found to some extent on all items that
meet the conditions we specified above. Some speakers may only show
evidence of alternation following the *l*, while the *ow* forms following
other sounds do not alternate with *er*. There are also several lexical
items where the *er* correspondence appears to be more resistant to change,
including *holler* and *yeller*. On the whole, the general application of
the *er* for *ow* correspondence is becoming much more sporadic in the
speech of the current generation than it apparently was at one time,
since it has become one of the stereotypes of AE speakers.

Final Unstressed ə

In many varieties of English, there are items that end in a schwa-
type vowel. Typically, this schwa-type vowel [ə] occurs only when the
syllable is unstressed. This final unstressed [ə] of other varieties of

English may correspond to a high front vowel (symbolized as [i] phonetically and usually *ee* or *y* in traditional spelling) for some speakers of
AE. We thus get the following types of pronunciations:

(47) a. *sody* for 'soda' 85:1
      b. *Virginny* for 'Virginia' 153:27
      c. *Santy* for 'Santa' 153:33
      d. *extry* for 'extra' 40:(429)

It is interesting to note that, in addition to the correspondences
given above, this process can affect an item like *kinda*, which is originally derived from *kind of*. We therefore note items like:

(48) a. *all kindy noise* for 'all kinda noise' 1:7
      b. *we kindy like to* for 'we kinda like to' 160:10

In the case of *kinda* it appears that the item is treated as one lexical unit, regardless of its historical origin, and as such is eligible
for the correspondence of final *y* for [ə] which affects word-final [ə]in
AE. By contrast, it is observed that we do not get examples of *y* for [ə]
in items that are apparently treated as separate even though they may co-
alesce to end in a final [ə]. For example, we do NOT get *mighty* for *might
have/of* or *wouldy* for *would have/of* or *bunchy* for *bunch of* even though we
might get *mighta*, *woulda*, and *buncha* in casual spoken speech. It should
also be noted that this process does not affect the final schwa-like sound
that may be left after a final unstressed *r* has been lost through the application of the *r*-lessness rule. That is, we do not get items like
fa(r)my or *toasty* for *farmer* and *toaster* even though the application of the
r-lessness rule may result in forms such as *fa(r)muh* and *toastuh*. Similarly, the process is not observed to apply to items which may alternate a
schwa with final *ow*. Thus, we do not get *windy* or *felly* for *window* and
fellow even though an alternant pronunciation might be *winduh* or *felluh*.
These final *ow* forms are affected by a different process discussed in the
preceding section.
  While there is a productive grammatical suffix *-y* that is used on adjectival forms (*squeaky* for *squeak* or *windy* for *wind*), the *-y* form on the
lexical items cited above seems to be different from these. It appears to
be a purely phonological phenomenon while the *-y* suffix has a grammatical
function.
  Since there are not a great many words that actually end in a schwa-
type sound as described above, this particular process is relatively
limited in scope. Its current usage tends to be limited to middle-aged
and older speakers of AE, and appears to be dying out.

Other Vowel Differences

There are actually a number of other vowel differences which might
have been cited here as a characteristic of AE. Some of these are fairly
well known characteristics, such as the collapse of the contrast between
e and *i* before nasals. This pattern, which is widespread in the South,
results in the homophony of items such as *pin* and *pen* or *tin* and *ten*.
There are other patterns about which less is known, such as the raising
of the vowel *i* to a vowel more like *ee*. Most predominantly, this pattern can be found before consonants such as *sh* or *l*, as in items like
fish and *wish* or *pill* and *fill* but it occurs to some extent before other
consonants. In some cases, there is an off-glide into a schwa-type
sound, so that an item like *crib* may be pronounced something like
creeuhb. There are also cases where a back vowel such as *oo* may be
produced more front in the mouth, gliding into a schwa-type vowel, or

even an *ee* glide. This is also predominant before consonants like *sh* or
l as in items such as *bush* or *pool* but may also take place preceding other
consonants.
    There are many other vowel differences that might be included, many
of which are more generally southern in nature but some of them are apparently unique to regions within AE. Further analysis of the vowel sys-
tem(s) awaits a more detailed phonetic investigation.

Notes
1. Sentences taken from our corpus are referenced by the informant number
   preceding the colon and the page on our typescript where the example
   is found following the colon. In the case of informants for whom we
   have no typescript, the counter number on the tape recorder is included within parentheses.
2. Unlike many varieties of English, contraction of past tense forms can
   take place in AE so that the conditions for the retention of full
   forms is slightly different in this variety. See Labov (1969) for
   a complete list of the structures in which copula deletion cannot take
   place.
3. The asterisk preceding a sentence indicates that this sentence is not
   permissible. That is, the sentence is *ungrammatical* in the linguist's
   technical definition of grammaticality.
4. Some sources (Jespersen, 1933:57) observe that *'em* developed from the
   older form *hem* rather than *them*.
5. In cases involving a form ending in a nasal sound (e.g. *than*, *them*)
   the vowel may also be deleted leaving a *syllabic nasal* (i.e. the
   nasal functions as the peak unit of the syllable).
6. Zwicky (1970:326) includes *was* and *were* in his inventory of *w* deletion for mainstream varieties of English. Whereas *w* deletion may
   affect *was* and *were* for standard English speakers to some extent in
   more rapid speech styles, its operation is much more pervasive in AE
   and does not appear to be restricted to the most rapid speech styles.
7. Due to the fact that the verb agreement rules for AE limit the ap-
   pearance of *were*, most of the forms observed to be affected by this
   process are *was* and *were*.
8. Pronouns and auxiliaries were not the only forms affected by this
   historical deletion process. The process has affected a number of
   compound noun forms (e.g. *shepherd*) and *h* in word medial position
   where *h* originally occurred between a stressed and unstressed vowel
   (e.g. *vehement*, *annihilate*). In Cockney, a rather drastic version
   of "*h*-dropping" has taken place which has become a well-known and
   stereotyped characteristic of the variety.
9. This process seems to be somewhat more general than Wolfram and
   Fasold (1974:143) had previously described for non-mainstream varieties of English. In their analysis, deletion of the *in'* is restricted to cases where two syllables are phonetically identical
   (e.g. *listenin'*, *openin'*).

Chapter Four: Grammatical Features

> *... It will be proved to thy face that thou hast men about thee that usually talk of a noun and a verb, and such abominable words as no Christian ear can endure to hear.*
>
> —**Shakespeare,** *Henry VI, Part II*

VERBS

As in other non-mainstream varieties which have been studied by socio-linguists, many of the grammatical features differentiating this variety from standard English concern aspects of the verb system. Some of the features of the AE verb system are shared by other non-mainstream varieties, but different verb parameters which distinguish AE may also exist.

A-Verb-*ing*

Of the variety of forms that characterize AE, one that holds considerable linguistic intrigue is the *a*-prefix that occurs with *-ing* participial forms. We thus encounter sentences like the following in this variety:

(1) a. ...and John boy, he come *a-runnin'* out there and got shot. 44:6[1]
     b. It was a dreadful sight, fire was *a-flamin'* everything. 16:(434)
     c. He just kept *a-beggin'* and *a-cryin'* and *a-wantin'* to go out. 83:18

While forms such as those given above have been found to occur in a number of varieties of American English, they are apparently most frequent in AE (Atwood, 1953:35).

A-*prefixing* (so-called because the *a* is considered to be a prefix attached to the following verb form) has solid historical roots in the history of the English language. Krapp (1925:268) is just one of the many writers on the history of the English language who notes the occurence of this form:

> A very frequent syntactic form of contemporary popular
> speech is that which puts an *a* before every present
> participle, especially after *go*, as in *to go a-fishing*,
> *bye baby bunting, daddy's gone a-hunting*, etc. In phrases
> like these, the construction is historical, the *a-* being
> a weakened form of the old English preposition *on* in un-
> stressed position, and *fishing, hunting*, etc., being
> originally verbal nouns which have been assimilated in
> form and, to a considerable extent, in feeling, to pre-
> sent participles. Starting with these phrases, however,
> the *a-* has been prefixed to genuine present participles,
> after forms of *to be* and other verbs, with the result
> that in popular speech almost every word ending in *-ing*
> has a sort of prefix, *a-*.

Most sources consider *a*-prefixing to be derived historically from
prepositions, notably *on*. For example, Jespersen (1933:53) notes:

> ...we start from the old phrase *he was on hunting*, which
> meant 'he was in the course of hunting, engaged in hunting,
> busy with hunting'; he was, as it were, in the middle of
> something, some protracted action or state, denoted by the
> substantive *hunting*. Here *on* became phonetically *a*, as in
> other cases, and *a* was eventually dropped, exactly as in
> other phrases: *burst out on laughing, a-laughing, laughing*;
> *fall on thinking, a-thinking, thinking*; *set the clock on
> going, a-going, going*, etc.

The status of *a*-prefixing as an archaism is relatively secure and its
historical source seems to be fairly well documented, but its current use
in AE and other varieties of English where it is found has not been subjected to a thorough analysis. In an effort to account for *a*-prefixing,
we shall therefore provide more detail than we have for some other features of AE where detailed descriptions of similar phenomena exist for
other varieties of English. Unfortunately, the common viewpoint on the
grammatical aspects of *a*-prefixed participles seems to have been represented by Krapp (1925:266) when he noted that "in popular speech, almost
every word ending in *-ing* has a sort of prefix *a-*." Such a broad claim
is clearly unwarranted, as will be illustrated by the examples we discuss
below. There are clear-cut cases where *a*-prefixing is permissible with
-ing forms in AE; by the same token, there are also cases where it is
clearly not permissible.

To begin with, we must note that the most common cases of *a*-prefixing
occur with progressives, including past tense, non-past tense, and *be +
ing* forms where the tense is found elsewhere in the main verb phrase.
Its occurrence with progressives is illustrated by the sentences in (2):

(2) a. I knew he was *a-tellin'* the truth but still I was *a-comin'*
         home...   83:1
     b. My cousin had a little brown pony and we was *a-ridin'* it one
         day. 124:19
     c. Well, she's *a-gettin'* the black lung now, ain't she? 83:25
     d. ...and he says, "Who's *a-stompin'* on my bridge?" 16:(610)
     e. This man'd catch 'em behind the neck and they'd just be
         a-rattlin'. 28:25

     f. He'll forget to spit and he'll cut and it'll just be *a-runnin'*,
        a-drippin' off his chin when he gets to catch them. 146:25

A further context in which *a*-prefixed forms can be found is that of
the movement verbs such as *come, go,* and *take off*. In these cases, the
participial *ing* form functions as a type of adverbial complement to the
verb. Cases of this type are illustrated in (3):

(3) a. All of a sudden a bear come *a-runnin'* and it come *a-runnin'*
        towards him and he shot it between the eyes. 44:18
    b. ...and then I took off *a-ridin'* on the minibike. 4:21
    c. ...they wasn't in there no more and I went down there *a-huntin'*
        for 'em. 44:20

There are also cases in which *a*-prefixing occurs with verbs of continuing or starting. Most predominantly, this involves the form *keep*,
but there are also some instances of forms like *start, stay, get to*
and so forth. Illustrations of this type are found in (4):

(4) a. He just kep' *a-beggin'* and *a-cryin'* and *a-wantin'* to go out.
        83:18
    b. Then send the rope back down, just keep *a-pullin'* it up 'til
        we got it built. 124:2
    c. You just look at him and he starts *a-bustin'* out laughing at
        you. 80:(683)
    d. ...and we'd get plowed, and we'd get to laughing and *a-gigglin'*.
        85:15

Again, it appears that the *a*-prefixed form functions as a type of adverbial complement to the verb.
    Finally, we should note its occurrence on other types of adverbial
constructions, where it is not a complement to a verb of movement or
verbs of starting or continuing. Examples of this type are found in sentences like (5):

(5) a. ...you was pretty weak by the tenth day, *a-layin'* in there in
        bed. 37:13
    b. ...one night my sister, she woke up *a-screamin'* -- cryin',
        hollerin', and so we jumped up. 156:25
    c. ...say Chuck would come by and want to spend a hour *a-talkin'*,
        I always figure I'm not too busy to stop. 30:4
    d. ...course a lotta times you can't, and grow up *a-huntin'*
        with them instead of hunting for them. 31:22

All of the examples given above represent *a*-prefixing on the form
to which the *-ing* is directly attached, but the prefixing can be extended to compound forms as well, thus giving us examples like (6):

(6) a. I went *a-deer-huntin'* twice last year. 31:31
    b. I told her I was goin' *a-pheasant huntin'*. 31:30
    c. We was goin' up there *a-squirrel huntin'*. 159:30

In order to understand precisely the systematic grammatical functions
of this form, it is also necessary to note several types of contexts
where *a*-prefixing is NOT found. For example, we do not find *a*-prefixing
on *-ing* when it is added in order to make a verb function as a noun or

adjective. These are the so-called gerund or gerundive constructions.
This means that we do NOT get constructions such as *He watched their a-
shootin'*, **A-sailin' is fun*, and **He likes a-sailin'* where the *-ing* participial form functions as a noun. Similarly, we do not observe forms like
*The movie was a-shockin' or **Those a-screamin' children didn't bother me*,
when the *-ing* participial form functions adjectively. One further syntactic restriction on the permissibility of the *a*-prefixed form concerns prepositions. *A*-prefixing does not typically occur following a preposition,
so that we do not obtain forms such as **John hit his dog for a-breakin'
the dish* or **He got sick from a-workin' so hard*. This restriction is
due to the fact that *a*-prefixing originally derives from the preposition
on or *at*, prepositions which would be in conflict with other prepositions
such as *for, from, by*, etc. We thus conclude that *a*-prefixing is restricted to *-ing* forms which function as adverbial complements and progressive forms.

      In addition to the above types of restrictions, which are related to
grammar, some phonological restrictions on the permissibility of *a*-pre-
fixing were also observed. In this regard, there is an interesting intersection of grammatical and phonological conditions that determine its
occurrence. One type of phonological restriction is related to the stress
pattern of the verb. There are no cases where the *a*-prefix is attached
to a verb that begins with a relatively unstressed syllable. For example, we do NOT get forms like **He was a-discoverin' a bear in the
woods* or **He was a-retirin' to his cage*. This condition appears to be
related to the fact that there is a general restriction of words which
begin with two relatively unstressed syllables in English. Another restriction on *a*-prefixing related to phonology concerns items which begin
with a vowel. When the verb form begins with a vowel, the *a*-prefix is
rarely, if ever, attached to the form, so that we do NOT typically get
forms like **He was a-eatin' the food* or **He was a-askin' a question*.

      In addition to these phonological restrictions on *a*-prefixing,
there is an interesting phonological constraint which has been found for
a-prefixing forms occurring in coordinate constructions. In coordinate
constructions formed with a simple coordinate such as *and* or *or*, there
is a strong tendency to place the *a*-prefixed form on all of the forms
involved in the coordination. Thus, we get constructions such as (7).

(7)   a.   ...they'll be all bushed up *a-struttin'* and *a-draggin'*.
           146:17
      b.   He just kept *a-beggin'* and *a-cryin'* and *a-wantin'* to get out.
           83:18
      c.   ...just keep *a-rockin'* and *a-rollin'*, rock the car and you
           finally can rock you a way to get out.   24:(218)

It appears that we have here an alliterative effect which is being created with the coordinate constructions. In this regard, it may be noted
that certain literary writers have used the *a*-prefixed forms for a special
alliterative effect in their dialect representations of AE, a caricature
that may have some basis in terms of how *a*-prefixing may be used. If
only one *a*-prefixed form is to be used in coordinate construction, it
is more likely to occur on the second (and succeeding *-ing* forms in a
series) construction than the first. That is, we are more likely to get
a form like *I heared her barking, and a-barkin' and a-barkin'* (22:26)
than a form like **I heared her a-barkin', and barkin' and barkin'*.

      While the grammatical and phonological considerations cited above
have been virtually ignored in recent descriptions of *a*-prefixing, the
few current attempts to describe this phenomenon in AE have focused on
its semantic properties. Some of these recent attempts have proposed

that *a*-prefixing actually has a semantic distinctiveness which has no comparable analogue in standard English. For example, Stewart (1967:10) has proposed:

> The prefix shows that the action of the verb is indefinite in space and time while its absence implies that the action is immediate in space and time. Thus, *he's a-workin'* in Mountain Speech means either that the subject has a steady job, or he is away (out of sight, for example) working somewhere. On the other hand, *he's workin'* in Mountain Speech means that the subject is doing a specific task, close by. A similar (though not identical) grammatical distinction is indicated in Negro Dialect by the verbal auxiliary *be*.

Such interpretations of the semantic distinctiveness of *a*-prefixing turn out to be unfounded speculations. The examples in (8) are fairly typical and cause us to question the interpretation that restricts *a*-prefixing to indefiniteness and/or remoteness.

(8) a. I's *a-washin'* one day and to go under the door I had to go under that spider. 28:21
     b. I's *a-cannin'* chicken one time... 153:38
     c. ...all of a sudden, a bear come *a-runnin'* towards him and he shot it between the eyes. 44:18
     d. Count to about 10 or 15 so we can see if this machine's *a-workin'*. [Fieldworker] 13:1

In cases such as (8a-c), adverbial modifiers such as *one day, one time*, and *all of a sudden* refer to a particular activity in terms of space and/or time. Each relates to an incident in which the speaker is located at a specific time or place, such as the location of the speaker in a particular room engaged in a specific activity (8a). Even more specific is the sentence used by one of our fieldworkers (an authentic *a*-prefixing speaker) in (8d). The directions given there refer to the tape recorder located at the point of the interview at that particular time.

Quite clearly, then, *a*-prefixing cannot be restricted semantically to indefiniteness and/or remoteness. It can certainly be used in such contexts but is in no way restricted to them. A fairly extensive investigation of the possible unique semantic categories for *a*-prefixing has turned up similarly negative results. We therefore conclude that there is no formal semantic distinction between the *a*-prefixed form and its non-*a*-prefixed counterpart. This is not to say that it has no stylistic effect in its usage. It appears that it is most frequently used in more animated or vivid narratives and descriptions. In these cases, an older, more rural form has given rise to a stylistic device for adding dramatic vividness to a narrative or description.

As we have mentioned earlier, the *a*-prefixed forms originally derived from an older prepositional form such as *on* or *at*. Through a phonological change, many of these forms weakened to become an *a*-prefix rather than a full preposition.[2] *A*-prefixing was, of course, quite widespread in the English language at one time. Eventually, however, the *a*-prefix was lost in many varieties. It is interesting to note that the loss of *a*- was apparently related to the general phonological process in which unstressed initial syllables could be deleted. This general deletion process can also be shown to be related to the deletion of the *a*-prefix as currently found in AE. For example, we find that AE speakers typically have less

a-prefixing following a vowel, the general linguistic constraint that
favors deletion for unstressed syllables (especially initial *V* syllables).
Speakers who have more *a*-prefixing retention also tend to retain unstressed
initial syllables more (i.e. have less deletion). What we find in AE is
that this deletion process simply did not completely eliminate the *a*-prefix
as was the case in some other varieties of English.

In Table 18, we present the extent of *a*-prefixing usage for 13 AE
speakers. For this purpose, we have tabulated the actual usage of *a*-pre-
fixing in those contexts where it might have potentially occurred. The
identification of these potential occurrences is based on the grammatical
and phonological characteristics of *a*-prefixing discussed. Actual usage
in relation to potential usage is given for the 13 speakers in our corpus
who are observed to have the highest incidence of *a*-prefixing. We have
broken down tabulation in terms of the four main grammatical contexts in
which *a*-prefixing is observed to occur: (1) progressives, (2) the special
lexical item *keep*, (3) movement verbs such as *come*, *go*, *take off*, etc.,
and (4) adverbs other than adverbial complements to *keep* or movement verbs.
The figures for these 13 informants are given in terms of the rank frequency of *a*-prefixing usage.

Several observations can be made on the basis of Table 18. To begin
with, we note that the total frequency levels of *a*-prefixing (right-hand
column) for each of the speakers are all below 50 percent. The range
typically falls between 10 and 40 percent. In terms of the various grammatical categories, we note that it is actually realized at higher frequency levels with movement verbs and *keep* than for progressives. While
most citations of this form refer to its usage with progressives, this is
a function of the fact that there are many more potential progressive constructions in which it might occur. In terms of actual usage in relation
to potential usage, however, the frequency of *a*-prefixing for progressives
is relatively low.

Table 18 also presents clear-cut support for the contention that *a*-
prefixing is a phenomenon that is dying out in Appalachia. The eight
speakers with the highest relative frequency levels for *a*-prefixing are
all age 50 or older. Only three of the 13 speakers represented in the
table are under age 30, and these three speakers all reveal *a*-prefixing
at levels under 20 percent. (See p. 75.)

In addition to the occurrence of *a*-prefixing on participial *-ing*
forms, it should be noted that it infrequently occurs on participial *-ed*
forms. We therefore have the following types of constructions:

(9) a. I went through a house that's supposed to be *a-haunted* spooky.
         17:27
     b. ...and it just looked like it had a big sheet, just *a-wrapped*
         'round him and no head. 85:18
     c. I held one leg and Lilly had the head, a-holdin' it *a-stretched*
         out. 85:29
     d. You'd lose your power the next day. After midnight, the days
         a-gone; it's a new day then. 15:(923)

Although these types of constructions are relatively rare, we do find AE
speakers who use them. We additionally find that *a*-prefixing may be used
on non-participial adjectival and adverbial constructions, as indicated in
(10).

(10) a. That's probably what's *a-wrong*. 77:2
     b. I said, "Turn 'em *a-loose!*" 77:2
     c. We'd have a stack *a-way* up high. 85:3
     d. I can make *a-many* of them. 6:(1012)

Table 18

Inf No.	Age/Sex	Progressives		Keep		Movement Verbs		Adverbs		Total	
		No a-/T	%a-	No a-/T	%a-	No a-/T	%a-	No a-/T	%a-	No a-/T	%a-
31	67/M	13/28	53.6	0/2	0.0	2/3	66.7	2/7	28.6	17/40	42.5
83	93/M	16/37	43.2	3/6	50.0	0/1	0.0	0/2	0.0	19/46	41.3
85	78/M	18/57	31.6	4/4	100.0	-/-	--	3/12	25.0	25/73	34.2
153	83/F	9/35	25.7	0/1	0.0	2/2	100.0	1/4	25.0	12/42	28.6
22	60/M	18/64	28.1	-/-	--	0/4	0.0	3/11	27.3	21/79	26.6
152	64/F	11/43	25.6	1/4	25.0	1/1	100.0	1/10	10.0	14/58	24.1
157	52/F	14/52	26.9	-/-	--	0/3	0.0	1/8	12.5	15/63	23.8
30	50/M	7/52	13.5	1/5	20.0	2/5	40.0	4/16	25.0	14/78	17.9
44	14/M	4/41	9.7	1/2	50.0	4/7	57.1	0/3	0.0	9/53	17.0
124	11/M	1/45	2.2	1/2	50.0	8/16	50.0	0/10	0.0	10/73	13.7
146	52/M	9/59	15.3	-/-	--	0/10	0.0	0/9	0.0	9/78	11.5
2	13/M	3/54	5.6	5/13	38.5	1/12	8.3	0/5	0.0	9/84	10.7
29	33/F	7/79	8.9	-/-	--	1/10	10.0	1/4	25.0	9/93	9.7
TOTALS		130/646	20.1	16/39	41.0	21/74	28.4	16/101	15.8	183/860	21.3

A-Prefixing According to Grammatical Categories

e.   ...and if she was *a-jealous*, *a-jealous* of me, she would want
      to see where they was coming.   30:29

A-prefixing on forms such as these is not as productive as it is on
participial *-ing* forms, but it does appear to be a regular part of some AE
speakers' systems.   In some cases, however, it appears restricted to certain types of lexical items, such as *a-way* or *a-many*. Apparently, forms
such as these also were derived from prepositions originally, although a
precise description of their current usage is somewhat elusive at this
point.

Subject-Verb Concord

     Many languages require that verbs in sentences be marked to agree
in various respects with the subject noun phrase of the verb.   This type
of marking, which is usually referred to as "agreement" or "concord," can
involve a fairly extensive set of inflections that reflects the person
and/or number characteristics of the subject.   In present-day English,
this process is relatively limited, but it has evolved from an agreement
system which, in earlier stages of the language, was much more extensive.
     In both Old and Middle English, the verbal agreement inflections for
the present tense typically differentiated between first, second, and
third person singular subjects and between singular and plural subjects,
although there was no distinction made for person among the plural inflections (Robertson and Cassidy, 1954:141). This more extensive set of
distinctions eventually developed into the present system, which dis-
tinguishes only the third person singular agreement from all other persons
and numbers (except for the case of *be* which we discuss later).   In standard English, concord with third person singular subjects is represented
by the *-s* inflectional suffix, all other present tense forms are identical
to the basic word stem of the verb.   This development is displayed in
Table 19.   In the past tense, no distinctions are made for person or
number of the subject noun phrase, again excepting *be*.
     As indicated, *be* departs somewhat from the paradigm described by
maintaining some of the older inflectional distinctions.   The first and
third person singular present forms (*am* and *is*) contrast with the form
used for second person singular and all plurals (*are*). Number agreement
also is retained to some degree in the past tense, where first and third
singular subjects occur with *was* and the other subjects take *were*.
In both tenses, the singular-plural distinction in the second person is
no longer observed, and the plural verb form has been adopted.   (This
coalescence is also found in the pronominal form, where both singular and
plural are represented by *you*.)

Table 19

	Old English		Middle English		Modern English	
	sg.	plur.	sg.	plur.	sg.	plur.
1st person	-e	-aʒ	-e	-e(n)	-	-
2nd person	-est	-aʒ	-est	-e(n)	-	-
3rd person	-eʒ	-aʒ	-eth	-e(n)	-s	-

Development of Subject-Verb Concord Inflections in English
(from Robertson and Cassidy, 1954:141)

In AE, as in many non-mainstream varieties of English, subject-verb concord does not always follow the paradigm given above. The cases where the pattern may be different for this variety almost exclusively involve number agreement in which a singular form is found with a plural subject. We should note that the terms "singular" and "plural" here refer to grammatical concepts, not necessarily semantic ones; for example, the pronoun *you* may be semantically singular or plural, but grammatically it follows the pattern for plural. The differing pattern of concord in these cases is influenced by the kind of plural subject that occurs, as well as the nature of the verb. This set of relationships for AE was noticed by Hackenberg (1972) and much of what will be presented here is confirmed by his data.

The type of verb appears to be the major factor in determining differences in the AE concord pattern. With verbs other than *be*, no subject-verb concord occurs other than in the present tense, so past forms of these verbs will not be discussed. For *be*, however, we have seen that both present and past tenses can show concord, with *be* retaining more of the older distinctions of person and number than other verbs. Due to the differing relationships of concord between *be* and non-*be* verbs and the historical development that led to the present system, it is not surprising that there are also differing degrees of "nonconcord."

The extent of concord as found in a variety such as AE may be indicative of further change in progress. Since concord with person or number has disappeared entirely in verbs other than *be*, it may be expected that the past tense of *be* would be farther advanced in such change in varieties where this is happening. The data from AE support such an expectation. Table 20 shows the total amount of nonconcord for the past and present tenses of *be* and the present tense of other verbs for our sample of 52 speakers.

Table 20

	BE			Non-*BE*	
Past		Present		Present	
No./Tot	%Noncon	No./Tot	%Noncon	No./Tot	%Noncon
935/1177	79.4	241/1150	21.0	100/3217	3.1

Incidence of Subject-Verb Nonconcord in AE

It is obvious from the figures in Table 20 that there is a much greater likelihood of nonconcord occurring with a past tense *be* form than with present tense *be* or non-*be* verbs. That is, *was* is more likely to occur for standard English *were* than *is* for *are* or *goes* for *go*. In AE, then, the concord system for *be* more closely approximates that for other verbs in that *was* is used predominantly for both singular and plural subjects, much like the pattern in which a single form is used for the past tenses of other verbs.

Another influence on agreement in AE appears to be the nature of the plural subject. An obvious distinction is that between a pronoun such as *you*, *we*, or *they* and other nominals. This particular distinction apparently interacts strongly with the type of verb, since a pronoun subject with *be* past shows a high incidence of nonconcord (79.8 percent) while nonconcord with present tense *be* and other verbs is almost nonexistent (0.7 and 0.1 percent, respectively). Within the class of plural subjects, there are also differences in effects on concord, but they seem more constant across types of verbs. Various classes of plural subjects

were considered in this investigation, but four general categories emerged
as influential on agreement patterns. These are illustrated in sentences
(11) - (14).

(11) *Conjoined Noun Phrase.*
      a. Me and my sister *gets* in a fight sometimes. 1:25
      b. A boy and his daddy *was* a-huntin'. 22:23
(12) *Collective Noun Phrase.*
      a. Some people *makes* it from fat off a pig. 164:30
      b. People'*s* not concerned. 30:12
(13) *Other Plural Noun Phrase.*
      a. ...no matter what their parents *has* taught 'em. 61:22
      b. The cars *was* all tore up. 77:16
(14) *Expletive* there.
      a. There'*s* different breeds of 'em. 159:22
      b. There *was* 5 in our family. 160:13

      These examples contain grammatically plural subjects. Conjoined
noun phrases are those with two or more constituents each of which may
be singular or plural, joined by a conjunction like *and* or *or*. These
typically function as plural subjects.[3] The second type of noun phrase
distinguished is referred to as "collective." This term was chosen to
indicate those subjects which refer to an indeterminate group, and which
do not have singular and plural forms but act grammatically plural. The
prime example is *people*. Other noun phrases were simply grouped together
since no other distinctions seemed to be significant at this point. The
final category--expletive *there*--is somewhat different from the others
since it fills the surface subject slot but does not determine the agreement relationship in the sentence. Sentences with this use of *there*
are instead related to other sentences in the following way:

(15) a. Four cows are in the barn.
      b. There are four cows in the barn.

The subjects in sentences like (15a), before the *there* is inserted,
govern agreement. In that way, a sentence with *there* can have verb concord for either singular or plural, depending on a following noun phrase.
Although *there* can be inserted in sentences with other verbs, it predominantly occurs with *be*. The fact that the subject is removed from its
usual position preceding the verb may contribute to the higher degree
of nonconcord with *there* in AE.
      The incidence of nonconcord for the sample is presented in Table 21.
The table is broken down by verb type and subject category as described
above. These figures indicate that the past form of *be* has consistently
higher rates than the present tenses, with no great differences among
subject types. The distinction among subjects shows up clearly in the
present tenses of *be* and other verbs--showing conjoined noun phrase subjects and *there* to be the most favorable contexts for this process. After
those two, there are collective noun phrases and other noun phrases, in
that order, and pronouns with only a slight amount of nonconcord. This
display appears to indicate that agreement operates differently in the
two tenses in AE. First of all, in the past tense, pronouns participate
in the process comparably with other types of subjects, while they do
not in the present tenses. In addition, there is a relatively small
difference among subject types in the *be* past, but a clearer separation
in the present tense verbs. What may be happening is that the form *was*
is being generalized for all number subjects with the past tense of *be*
in conformance with the pattern for past tense in other verbs. For the

present tenses, it is not the verb form (third person singular) that is
generalizing (since *they* is relatively unaffected); instead, various subjects in differing degrees depending on type, are given singular agreement, and the present tense of *be* acts like other present tense verbs in
this respect. (See Table 21, p. 83.)

The operation of agreement in AE does not appear to be related to the
social variables of age or sex, since the groups based on those characteristics show considerable uniformity in the rate of nonconcord for the various linguistic categories. There is undoubtedly some relationship to social class since the different agreement patterns generate, to varying
degrees, stigmatized forms, but this could not be investigated in the
present sample.

As mentioned earlier, the absence of concord in AE occurs typically
where a plural subject is present. This contrasts with a variety such as
Vernacular Black English, which has extensive *-s* absence in the third person singular verb forms. There are some instances of this type of nonconcord in this sample of AE but they are primarily of three well-defined
types. The first appears to be restricted to the lexical item *seem* as in:

(16) a. It just *seem* like it does something for you. 160:6
      b. *Seem* like they just don't care about one another. 22:18
      c. He can tell it seriously and *seem* like it's real. 164:22

The total number of instances were not tabulated, but this feature appears
to be fairly common--particularly in older speakers.

A second kind of differing concord relationship is used with what
has been called the "historical present," a fairly common feature found
in many non-mainstream varieties. It is most characteristically found in
narratives where first person singular subjects are paired with verbs with
the third person singular ending, but further comments on patterns of its
usage would require more investigation. It is illustrated in a sentence
like: "I *says*, you should start dating. I *says*, you're too young, and,
I *says*, man is made to be with woman..." (30:27).

Finally, there is a common form that is characteristic of many non-
mainstream varieties, the use of *don't* with third person singular subjects:

(17) a. Well, a whippin' *don't* do no good. 35:8
      b. He *don't* beat her now. 151:33

As Wolfram and Fasold (1974:155) note, this form seems to favor *-s* absence in many varieties where *-s* absence is otherwise never or very sel-
dom found, which seems to be the case here. The frequency of the usage
of *don't* where the standard form would be *doesn't* is 76.5 percent for
this sample. This compares with a variety of Vernacular Black English
investigated by Fasold (1972:124) where *don't* occurred in 87.5 percent
of the cases with third person singular subjects. Although the overall
frequency levels may vary, the pattern for *don't* in AE does not appear
to differ from that found for other non-mainstream varieties.

Irregular Verbs

The verb system in English as it has evolved currently has a single
productive suffix to signal past tense.[4] This is the ending that is
usually spelled *-ed* and it is added to most verbs for the preterit and
the past participle. The preterit is the simple past form in English
(They *dropped* it.) while the past participle is used with the auxiliary

have and in passive sentences. (They *had dropped* it; It *was dropped* by
them.) This past ending has three phonologically conditioned variants
([t], [d], and [Id]) and represents the maintenance of the suffix used
for these tenses on verbs in Old English, which in turn came from a Ger-
manic process.

The formation of verb past tenses in English has evolved from a
more complex system of inflectional endings (including at one point, for
example, a distinction between singular and plural in the preterit, which
survives today only in the *was* and *were* forms of *to be*). Language change
is a continuous process and the English verb system is part of this ongoing change. One way of determining change that is in progress is
through the observation of variability in a given feature. This variability exists in the use of certain of the irregular verbs, in terms of
a fluctuation between what can be considered the current standard English
form and one or more others.[5] The examples in (18) and (19) below illustrate some of the other forms. As an indicator of change, the period of
variability falls between two nonvariable periods, one with only the
older forms before change begins, and one with only the new forms after
change is complete. During this in-between time, both the old and new
forms are in use. Geographical and/or social factors are often closely
related to the distribution of variants during this period.

In the case of the past tense system for verb forms in English, the
overall variability has apparently existed since the earliest varieties
of English and still continues. Old English had seven morphologically-
defined classes of irregular or "strong" verbs which by the Middle
English period had begun to break down. Pyles (1964:162) notes that in
Middle English, many of these irregular forms acquired regularized (i.e.
-*ed* suffixed) counterparts and then disappeared, leaving the regularized
form. He cites examples such as *helpen* (infinitive), 'to help', which
in Old English had the preterit singular *healp*, the preterit plural
hulpon, and the past participle *holpen*; in Middle English they became
halp, *hulpen*, and *holpen*. During the Middle English period leveling to
the current form *helped* in all past uses also began. Some of the fluctu-
ations mentioned in connection with Early Modern English (17th and 18th
centuries) are still found in current non-mainstream varieties of English.
For example, certain participles occurred which lacked the -*en* ending,
as in *bit* or which were identical with the preterit, as in *rode* and
drove (Pyles, 1964:196). Both of these processes provide alternant forms
for the participle in the sample being considered here.

In addition, there are a number of verbs in present day English
which typically undergo different processes in forming the preterit and
past participle. These verbs are referred to as "irregular," a term which
is used in the present discussion for any verb which does not follow the
productive pattern for forming both its preterit and past participle,
such as *kept*, *thought*, or *grew/grown*. In most cases, such verbs are related to verbs which were also "irregular" in earlier forms of English,
although the patterns involved and the distribution among classes has
changed considerably (Pyles, 1964).

In some varieties of English, these irregular verbs have alternant
past forms which differ from what is typically considered the standard.
Our sample of AE contains many examples of such forms; of the 52 informants whose speech was analyzed, only one showed no instances of nonstandard usage in this area. The others, as might be expected, ranged
from extensive to fairly minimal amounts of such usage, regardless of the
age group. Examples from the sample which illustrate this phenomenon
include:

Preterit: (18)   a.   I told her I *done* it.   1:14

                        b.   We *throwed* them a birthday party. 36:3

                        c.   Finally the state *come* by and they pushed it
                             all out. 46:7

                        d.   She *give* him a dose of the castor oil. 153:5

Past Participle: (19)   a.   Her home *had went*, I guess, 50 yards or more
                             from its foundation. 37:8

                        b.   And they *hadn't* never *saw* a ghost before.
                             77:4

                        c.   Well, he *had begin* to improve. 157:34

                        d.   When I brung it back out, my rod *was broke*.
                             10:15

As shown in these examples, there seems to be a variety of ways in which "leveling" of irregular verb forms takes place in AE.

The sample of AE under discussion here exhibits quite extensive variability in the past forms of the irregular (with respect to present day English) verbs showing degrees of nonstandard variants from 100 percent nonstandard to 100 percent standard. To illustrate the size of the data base, Table 22 presents the 10 most frequently occurring irregular verbs, with a preterit/past participle breakdown and the respective percentages of nonstandard variants used. (See p. 83.)

The figures illustrate certain characteristics of the entire data base. In general, preterit forms are far more frequent in occurrence than past participles. There appears to be no obvious effect of raw frequency on the probability that a nonstandard variant is used, since some of the verbs (i.e. *say*) are used standardly all of the time, while others have fairly high rates of nonstandard usage in either the preterit (*come*) or the past participle (*get*). This also points to the lack of any direct connection between the use of a nonstandard variant in the preterit and in the participle in those cases where the standard forms differ (*go*). Where the standard forms are identical (*hear*), the frequencies seem fairly even.

In terms of the group of verbs as a whole, there were 106 different irregular verbs used in a past form in the corpus. Fifty-five of these had only standard realizations and the remaining 51 had one or more instances of a nonstandard variant. There are, of course, other irregular verbs in English, but only those that actually occurred in our sample will be considered. It is unlikely that a verb in very common use in AE would not have appeared, given the extensive amount of data collected.

The wide variety of nonstandard variants for the irregular verbs of English observed in this set of data indicates that, although the change in language may be moving ultimately toward complete use of the productive past tense suffix on all verbs, the present situation is far from this. While some of the verb forms were found to conform to this regular pattern, a large number did not. By considering how the nonstandard alternants differ from the standard forms, we can characterize these usages and extract several patterns that are operating. This will also serve to indicate that, although the variation may seem quite diverse, it is not unsystematic.

Three processes emerge which apply to both preterits and past participles. For regularized forms, the productive past suffix *-ed*, in the appropriate phonological shape, is added for the past tense, giving, for example, *knowed* instead of *knew* or *known*. In some cases, what may be considered a different irregular form is used, but this is rare. This applies both to verbs which already have an irregular past tense, as in *brung* for *brought* (probably an analogy with patterns like *sting/stung*), and a few cases where the standard past variant follows the regular pattern, as in *drug* for *dragged*. Finally, some verbs are represented in the past by the uninflected basic word form (or the infinitive without the *to*), as, for example, in *eat* and *give*. Illustrations of these processes are given in (20):

(20) a. David *throwed* him in the creek and jumped in after him. 1:27
      b. And the rest of us was *borned* in the hospital. 35:3
      c. It's *drug* on for so long that I've got sick of it. 65:17
      d. And the water was real deep and we *swim* for about two or three
          hours. 124:16
      e. ...then the man that had *give* it to them *come* back. 80:2

Two other processes occur in which one form is extended for both pre-terit and participial uses of the verb. In one case, the participial form is extended to the preterit, the most common examples being *seen*, which has *saw* as its counterpart in standard English and *done* for *did*. In the other case, the preterit form is extended to the participle, as in *got*, where standard English uses *gotten*, *wrote* for *written*, and *went* for *gone*. These two processes commonly result in identical AE surface forms of pre-terit and past participle. In standard English they are not.

(21) a. That's all I *seen* of it, cause I had to go back up in the
          woods. 49:3
      b. He shoulda known better in the first place than to do what he
          done. 65:17
      c. Every year I've *went* to camp and regional meetings. 151:40

A complete list of the irregular verbs whose past forms have nonstandard variants in this sample of AE is given in Table 23. The list is separated into classes based on the types of forms described here. The number of times each form occurs is given in parentheses following the particular verb. (See p. 84.)

Another way of looking at this data involves how the individual speakers display patterning with respect to this feature. By assessing the extent of nonstandard usage for each speaker according to the various forms possible, certain inferences can be made concerning the way this feature is evaluated within the community. The usage of a particular type of nonstandard form may always take place, fluctuate with a standard variant, or never take place. When viewed in this light, certain relation-ships between these types emerge. For example, a class of forms that is always standard for the majority of speakers would seem to be more stig-matized if used nonstandardly than one which is always nonstandard for many speakers. When these verb types are considered in this way, it turns out that the use of a preterit for the past participle function is the most acceptable of the group, with regularized and different strong forms the least acceptable. This observation coincides with some evidence from British English with respect to the past participle of *get*. The use of the preterit form *got* is apparently nonstandard only within varieties of American English, since as Pyles (1964:200) reports, *got* is the stand-ard past participle in British English. In terms of language change, this aspect of irregular verb participles is more advanced for British English than for standard American English. AE, with its extensive, but not categorical use of participial *got*, falls somewhere in-between.

In addition to the verbs listed in Table 23, there is another set of forms of a different sort that seem to be nonstandard. For these, the standard form of the regular past tense suffix, [d], is changed to [t], as in:

Table 21

	Past *be*		Present *be*		Other Verbs		Total	
	No. NS / Total	%	No. NS / Total	%	No. NS / Total	%	No. NS / Total	%
Expletive *There*	107/115	93.0	163/170	95.9	-	-	270/285	94.7
Conjoined NP	60/67	89.6	11/16	68.8	14/23	60.9	85/106	80.2
Collective NP	6/9	66.7	10/24	41.7	32/94	34.0	48/127	37.8
Other NP	103/160	64.2	52/178	29.2	50/173	28.9	205/511	40.1
Subtotal	276/351	78.3	236/388	60.8	96/290	33.1	608/1029	59.1
Pronoun	659/826	79.8	5/762	0.7	4/2927	0.1	668/4515	14.8
Total	935/1177	79.4	241/1150	21.0	100/3217	3.1	1276/5544	23.0

Incidence of Nonstandard Concord in AE by Type of Verb and Subject (NS=Nonstandard)

Table 22

	Occurrences			Percentage of Non-standard Variants	
Verb	Total	Preterit	Participle	Preterit	Participle
have (main verb)	1,422	1,355	67	0	0
get	1,296	1,208	88	0	89.8
go	1,237	1,114	123	0	51.2
say	996	991	5	0	0
come	609	579	30	71.2	3.3
take	386	369	17	22.5	58.8
see	354	243	111	72.9	5.4
tell	327	299	28	0	0
think	259	248	11	0	0
hear	208	120	88	20.0	27.3

Most Frequently Occurring Irregular Verbs in AE

Table 23

Regularization of Productive Suffix	Preterit as Participle	Participle as Preterit
knowed (45)	got (72)	seen (169)
heared (31)	went (66)	done (80)
borned (17)	bit (22)	taken (10)
throwed (13)	broke (16)	broken (2)
growed (12)	tore (12)	sunk (2)
blowed (11)	took (11)	drunk (2)
drinked (6)	wore (8)	grown (1)
drawed (4)	saw (6)	mistaken (1)
bursted (2)	froze (6)	
runned (2)	hid (5)	
shedded (2)	wrote (5)	
betted (1)	fell (4)	
lighted (1)	rode (3)	
eated (1)	forgot (3)	
gived (1)	woke (3)	
hanged (1)	beat (3)	
stinged (1)	did (3)	
spreaded (1)	ran (2)	
	ate (2)	
	stole (2)	
	drove (2)	
	gorgave (1)	
	flew (1)	
	drank (1)	
	swam (1)	
	gave (1)	
	grew (1)	
	came (1)	
	redid (1)	
	spoke (1)	

Base Word Form Unchanged	Different Irregular Form
come (381)	set (75)
run (80)	tuck (73)
give (64)	brung (11)
eat (22)	drug (8)
begin (7)	hearn (7)
become (3)	het [heated] (1)
swim (2)	
hear (2)	
sing (1)	

Patterns of Nonstandard Use of Irregular Verbs in AE

(22) a. Every time I *boilt* water, I burnt it. 36:23
      b. I got so sick at my stomach, when I *smelt* them green beans.
          29:13
      c. ...and we *fount* some money. 1:18

This process, which can be considered as devoicing the [d] to [t], is also
found in the alternations of *learned/learnt, held/helt, ruined/ruint,
spilled/spillt,* and *spoiled/spoilt*. This appears to be an extension of
what happens in standard English *burnt* and (perhaps) *dwelt*. Generally,
the voiced consonantal suffix [d] is added when the verb ends in a voiced
segment (other than [d] or [t]), with the voiceless variant [t] for those
ending in a voiceless sound. In these cases a verb which has a voiced
final segment such as [n] or [l] may take the voiceless consonantal suffix, broadening the class of items that can differ from the regular pattern in AE.

One final case to consider is the verb *sit*, with its standard
English past form *sat*. In this sample of AE, however, the standard
variant for the past never occurred. In both the preterit and past participle, the form used is *set*, as in:

(23) a. We *set* there one day for three hours straight. 6:11
      b. One night they had *set* up and listened to actual ghost
          stories. 28:33

Although it cannot be claimed that this usage is categorical beyond this
particular corpus, there is reason to conclude that it is quite extensive
and perhaps the predominant form of the area. At least some instances
of *sit* in other tenses were realized as *set*. This could mean that the
verbs *sit* and *set* are coalescing into one surface shape--*set*--with no
difference between past and present forms. This extension of *set* to include *sit* is attested by the dialect studies in other areas as well as
in West Virginia, as reported in Atwood (1953:21).

Despite the apparent wide variety of usage for irregular verb past
forms in AE, there is a systematic patterning which emerges. The patterning and the variability point to a potential situation of language
change in progress and historical evidence about the development of the
irregular verb system in English tends to confirm this. As previously
mentioned, the area where nonstandard usage is most acceptable is in
the participial forms and this would seem to indicate that they will be
the first part of the system to advance to completion, or the situation
where participles are no longer differentiated from preterit forms. However, it is not possible to predict how social factors, such as the degree
of stigmatization of various forms, will affect the course of this change
or what the role of education will be in inhibiting the change.

Perfective *Done*

The use of *done* as a kind of *perfective* marker has been noticed in
analyses of a number of varieties originally derived from the South.
This feature also occurs in AE, and though there may be some differences
between varieties in the details of its operation, this marker generally
seems to be a part of many non-mainstream English systems.

The feature in question is the use of *done* in constructions like the
following:

(24) a. I *done* forgot when it opened. 159:22
      b. And the doctor *done* give him up, said he's got pneumonia.
          22:12

c.   ...because the one that was in there had *done* rotted.   35:21
d.   If she had, she woulda *done* left me a long time ago.   30:29
e.   We thought he was *done* gone.   51:11

The pattern which the usage of *done* typically follows can be seen in the
examples cited in (24). It can occur alone with a past form of the verb,
as in (24a,b) or it can intervene in a complex verb phrase which consists
of an auxiliary and a main verb, and may also include a modal, as in
(24c-e).

A more restricted context for the distribution of this marker might
be considered, for example, that it is only followed by the past participle form of the verb. However, in this data from AE, the existence of
pairs like the utterances in (25) would seem to make such a restriction
unsuitable since both the preterit and past participle forms of *take* are
found in construction with *done*.

(25)   a.   ...and then she *done taken* two courses again.   83:7
       b.   ...she *done took* the baby away from her.   159:38

Even if a restriction like this was not contradicted in the data, it
could only be made with reference to the irregular verbs in English,
since for regular verbs, the two past forms are identical. It seems then
that the appropriate generalization is simply that *done* is normally associated with a past form of the main verb which may have a preterit or a
past participial function.

As Labov (1972c:56) observes, *done* has "lost its status as a verb"
in the usage described above. It does not change in form to show tense
marking or agreement and occurs within the same clause with an inflected
verb. Various other grammatical classifications have been suggested for
done, including "quasi-modal" (Labov, 1968) and adverb. It does not
appear, however, that either label is particularly suitable due to differences in syntactic behavior. For example, adverbs typically can be
moved away from the verb phrase to another part of the sentence, as in
(26):

(26)   a.   They *quickly* put out the fire.
       b.   They put out the fire *quickly*.
       c.   *Quickly,* they put out the fire.

This type of movement is not allowable for *done* since it can only occur
in a position relative to the verb phrase as in the sentences in (24)
and (25) above.

Since other classifications do not seem to work very well for *done*,
we will simply consider it to be an aspect market, specifically marking
the past completion of an action or event. As Wolfram and Fasold (1974:
152) observe, *done* is "an additional perfective construction in some nonstandard dialects, not a substitute for present perfect tense in standard
English but in addition to it." The fact that it is not a substitute
for any tense in standard English can be seen in the following *done* sentences where it interacts with each of the possible tenses where a past
verb form is involved:

(27)   a.   She (*done*) sold it at noon yesterday.
       b.   She has (*done*) sold it by now.
       c.   She had (*done*) sold it by the time I got there.

Since *done* can accompany any one of these tenses, it would not appear to function as a substitute for any of them. Furthermore, it does not share the co-occurrence restrictions of any tense. It does, of course, impose some of its own restrictions on various co-occurrences due to its completive meaning which we shall discuss.

There are certain syntactic limitations on the occurrence of *done* in addition to its position with respect to the verb phrase. As previously mentioned, *done* is an aspect marker which can only be used in the presence of a past verb. However, there may also be cases where a past verb can occur and *done* cannot. These cases are syntactically determined. One such situation appears to exist with reduced embedded clauses; that is, sentences which are reduced in some way when subordinately joined to another sentence. Thus, we do not find sentences like those in (28) despite the fact that the clause with *done* contains a past verb:

(28)   a. *They seem to have *done* left.
       b. *John's having *done* left surprised me.

We see in (28) that *done* is restricted to unreduced clauses, since for such sentences it is not ruled out because of meaning, as we see in (29):

(29)   a. It seems $\begin{Bmatrix} \text{like} \\ \text{that} \end{Bmatrix}$ they('ve) *done* left.
       b. It surprised me that John *done* left.

We mentioned above that *done* is essentially "completive" in nature, referring to a characteristic of its meaning. Other proposals concerning the meaning of this form have been made and many simply suggest a close synonym, like the perfective auxiliary *have* or the adverb *already*. Although these both have aspects which show a similarity to *done*, neither is actually equivalent in meaning. Although there are contexts where substituting *already* for *done* would lead to much the same meaning as in (30), there are also a large number of examples where this is not the case, as in (31):

(30)   If I'd do the laundry, she'd do the laundry, you know, go back
       and do the same thing again that I *done* ironed and put away. 36:15
(31)   a. He said, "My God, you *done* killed that man's horse!" 146:8
       b. We thought well we can sit back and enjoy our labor of the
          years gone by since the children had *done* left home. 37:16

Both of the proposed synonyms seem to center on the aspect of pastness that enters into *done*'s use. The distinctiveness of *done*, however, appears to lie instead in its "completive" aspect. That is, it signals the completion of the activity described by the verb, which is already in a past form. This claim can be supported by evidence which comes from sentences that are unacceptable when *done* is included because they contain some feature that prevents a completive interpretation. For example, a progressive as in (32) usually signals continuity which is contradictory to completion:

(32)   I didn't know it then but I was (*done*) stepping on a snake.

Even though the verb indicates past time, the progressive is incompatible with *done*. Otherwise semantically, the sentence is acceptable as seen when the progressive is replaced as in (33):

(33)   I didn't know it then but I (had) *done* stepped on a snake.

Other factors which can force an incompletive sense include certain adverbials and verbs. Adverbs which imply some sort of continuity or repetition cannot modify a verb phrase containing *done*, although the sentence without *done* is perfectly acceptable, as we see in (34):

(34)   a.   They *often* (**done*) forgot their lunch.
        b.   They had *generally* (**done*) paid their bills on time.

Other adverbs which overtly signify incompletion seem more acceptable, and it may be that the completeness associated with *done* can be qualified.

(35) He (**done*) *almost* fell down two flights of stairs.

In addition, verbs which are noncompletive in nature generally cannot be combined with *done*, as in (36):

(36)   a.   She (**done*) *was* happy to hear the news.
        b.   They had (**done*) *seemed* upset.

From this type of evidence, it seems that the major characteristic of *done*'s meaning is the completive component. The requirements for a past main verb form and the associated semantic pastness would appear to be derivative of that aspect.

A further consideration in describing any language phenomenon involves viewing it from a functional perspective. Why would a speaker choose to use it in a particular utterance (over and above syntactic and semantic aspects that may limit the choice), and what job does it accomplish there? In order to do this, such factors as the role of speaker intentions and assumptions are given attention. A pragmatic characteristic of this type that appears to be associated with *done* is the emphasis that it carries with it when a speaker uses it.

The use of emphasis is most obvious in narratives where such devices are frequent, as in example (37), where the speaker was relating a story about the accidental baking of a cat:

(37)   She opened the oven door to put her bread in to bake it and there
        set the cat. Hide *done* busted off his skull and fell down and his
        meat just come off'n his bones. 31:23

The emphatic effect is also present in some non-narrative contexts, as in (38), which was uttered as part of a discussion of what happens to certain kinds of women:

(38)   ...and then the next thing you know, she's *done* throwed herself
        plumb to the dogs. Well, oncet when she puts herself to the
        dogs, it's harder for a woman to pull herself back than it is
        a man. 30:29

This last example is further strengthened by the inclusion of the intensifying adverb *plumb*, a feature of AE which is treated later.

The notion of emphasis is somewhat difficult to discuss precisely since very little is known about it, in terms of how it is accomplished (i.e. its correlation with stress, intonation, etc.) and how it functions. One characteristic that has been proposed is that it relates to the speaker's intentions and assumptions, particularly with respect to certainty about or agreement with the proposition involved. In other words, it is unlikely that speakers would use a device to make a proposition

more emphatic if they are uncertain about its validity. This characteristic seems to fit the instances of *done* observed in the present corpus. A
substantial number of propositions containing *done* are clear-cut assertions
(non-interrogative, non-negative, non-subordinate clauses), and the use
of an assertion is an obvious way for speakers to indicate certainty.
Some instances of embedded clauses also appear to be assertive. The examples in (39) are of this type, illustrating both non-embedded (39a,b)
and embedded (39c,d) assertives:

(39) a. When I was a boy, if you seen a woman's knee, you had *done*
          seen something. 31:15
      b. And they *done* bought their home up there so they can't, you
          know, just up and leave it. 36:19
      c. I reckon she's *done* sold it. 153:32
      d. She asked us if we turned in the assignment. We said we
          done turned it in. 46:15

Another reason for looking at *done* with respect to emphasis comes from
the fact that our data contain no instances in which it occurs in questions
or in negative utterances. This is a further argument for the emphatic
use of *done* although its use may not be limited to fulfilling an emphatic function; it may have other functions as well. This pragmatic
aspect of *done* may be optional--the speaker may choose to use *done* em-
phatically or not, depending on what assumptions are held about the proposition being expressed.
   When we speak of *done* as a feature of AE, this does not mean that
it is used by all speakers or to the same extent by its users. Instead,
it is present variably and a major factor in our sample appears to be
age. Table 24 shows the number of occurrences of the feature by sex and
age group. From these figures, it seems that being a male speaker may

Table 24

Age Group	Male	Female	Total
8-11	3	3	6
12-14	5	2	7
15-18	4	1	5
20-40	5	9	14
40+	26	7	33
TOTAL	43	22	65

Number of Occurrences of Perfective Done *by Sex and Age Group*

increase the chances of *done*'s occurrence but this cannot be clearly established. What is *more* significant is the much greater use of *done*
found by speakers in the older age groups. This type of distribution
may be an indication that the phenomenon is dying out in this area. The
factors causally related to its disappearance are at this point not at
all clear. It is undoubtedly a stigmatized form in this variety. In
fact, many individuals in the present sample show no instances of *done*
in this usage at all (only about 25 percent do), but it is not possible
to determine whether they never used it or simply did not have occasion
to include it while being taped. There are probably individuals of both
types represented--with social class interacting since it is a stigmatized
form.

Finally, a note on the history of this form is of interest. *Done*
in this usage was apparently present in earlier stages in the development
of English but has disappeared in most varieties. Traugott (1972:146)
observes that Middle English "saw the development of a further segmentali-
zation of the perfective, as in *I have done gone*," surviving only in
northern English after the fifteenth century. In addition, at this time,
done did not seem to require a past participle following it. Traugott
(1972:193) speaks of the past participle "spreading" to the main verb
in late Middle English, and speculates that "an emphasis on the completion" may have been involved.

Such historical facts may provide evidence for the source of *done*
in AE. If *done* originated as an additional component of the perfective
aspect as it was developing in the English language, it may have retained
its status as an added aspect marker while modifying its privileges of
occurrence somewhat in those varieties where it was preserved. Traugott
(1972:193) gives its initial environment as *have + Past Participle + do
(+Past Participle)*, indicating that, at first, *have done finish* was the
acceptable form. Later, the "spreading" of the past participle to the
main verb gave the form *have done finished*. Once the past participle
spread to the main verb, *done* may have attained some degree of inde-
pendence from the *have* construction, its distribution privileges broadening to include simple past verbs and the *be* auxiliary, while keeping
its function to mark a completive aspect. This is only speculation
based on the facts we have gathered on current usage of *done* in AE, and
the historical evidence available on its possible origins.

Double Modals, *liketa*, *supposeta*

Many investigators of southern White English and Vernacular Black
English have noticed the presence of constructions which commonly have
been termed "double modals" (Atwood, 1953; Labov, 1968, 1972c; Feagin,
forthcoming). These include such phrases as *might could*, *might should*,
useta could, etc. As Labov (1972c:57) observes, these are not considered
part of standard English since they do not conform to the rule that prohibits one modal from following another. There is no one-to-one relationship evident between these forms and corresponding ones in standard
English. Although some of the double modal constructions may have a
close "translation," as in substituting *might be able to* for *might could*,
there are others, such as *might should*, where no apparent equivalent
exists.

It is interesting that the variety of AE we consider in this study
exhibits many other characteristics of other southern varieties, but it
does not appear to share in the usage of double modals to any significant degree. The data contain infrequent examples of such usage, as in
(40):

(40) a. I looked around, couldn't find him nowhere. Boy, I hollered
          for him, couldn't, he *musta didn't* hear me. 17:16
      b. You know what? I *useta couldn't*, I *useta couldn't*, couldn't
          count. Why, I *useta couldn't* count anything 'til I, 'til I
          got me some work up here. 85:21
      c. People *useta didn't* have frigidaires or nothing. We just had
          a big old milk house. 85:25
      d. I *might could* make up one, but I don't know. 74:8

It would be difficult to identify any constraints on this feature for
this variety, either social or linguistic, based on such occasional cases.

The scarcity of the examples might indicate that the usage is receding in this area, but the evidence is uncertain.

Labov (1972c:59) considers double modals to be part of a wider phenomenon affecting certain items which resemble auxiliary verb forms. This group includes not only the first member of a double modal (*must, may, useta,* etc.) but also forms like *liketa, supposeta,* and *better.* He concludes that they all function formally like adverbs, due to their lack of tense marking and other syntactic behavior which is unlike that normally found with the first member of an auxiliary (inversion for questions, etc.).

Although the present AE sample contains relatively few occurrences of constructions generally classed as double modals, there are a greater number of instances of other members of the set discussed by Labov, in particular, *liketa* and *supposeta.* This fact about the data could constitute evidence against Labov's (1972:59) claim that these structures are "examples of a single ongoing process." It seems more likely that in the variety under consideration, the productivity of the process is fading, but to a lesser extent with some of the members of the set than with others. This could account for the imbalance in numbers of examples and also for the difference in numbers of speakers who use the forms.

Liketa occurs in both positive and negative contexts as in (41):

(41)   a.   And I knew what I'd done and boy it *liketa* scared me to
            death.   152:28
       b.   That thing looked exactly like a real mouse and I *liketa* went
            through the roof.   64:19
       c.   When we got there, we *liketa* never got waited on.   151:2
       d.   I *liketa* never went to sleep that night.   2:5

A past form of the main verb of the clause always follows it. This is the place where the tense marking is carried, since it is absent from *liketa.* There are no cases of the form occurring in questions or embedded clauses, and the only negative environment represented is *never.*

Labov (1972c), in describing the form in Vernacular Black English, concludes that *liketa* is equivalent to "almost." In addition, he mentions a further characteristic, referred to as "intensive significance." While Labov's account appears to be essentially accurate when applied to the data from AE, a few additional comments can be made.

From the instances found here, the equivalence of *almost* seems to be too general. *Liketa* can apply in a wider variety of contexts than *almost.* Furthermore, *almost* does not seem to relate directly to the aspect of exaggeration that accompanies the use of *liketa.* A closer approximation would be "on the verge of," or, at more length--"came so close that I really thought x would" where x is the subject of the *liketa* clause. This aspect may be what Labov meant by the "intensive" part of its meaning. The latter paraphrase also expresses the fact that the intensiveness represents the attitude of the speaker, in that it is the speaker's opinion that the action of the main clause just missed happening, whether the subject is *I* (that is, the speaker) or not. For example, (42) is a case where the subject of the *liketa* clause is not *I*:

(42)   Oh, he *liketa* had a fit. He said, "My God, you done killed that
       man's horse!" 146:8

Here, it seems fairly clear that the narrator's perception of the situation is such that the man in question came close to having a real fit over what had happened, perhaps even so close that the speaker really thought he would.

A related characteristic of *liketa* is the counter factuality it imposes on the clause in which it appears. The use of *liketa* signals that,
although the situation came very close to happening, it in fact did *not*
happen, and the proposition contained in the clause is admittedly untrue
(or exaggerated). This is apparent in a case like (43), where in order
to allow for the possibility that the situation did actually occur, the
speaker must separately assert it:

(43) Well, she's *liketa* threw me, thrown me through a wall before.
      Matter of fact, she did one time. 149:13

A sentence like (43) also points out that scope of the adverb must be
taken into consideration in positing synonymy between *liketa* and *almost*.
Almost bears a resemblance to *liketa* when its scope is the entire proposition and there is no degree of or "partial" truth possible--the content of the proposition *almost* happened *but did not*. Other uses of
almost indicate the degree to which something happened or was true in
some way. *Liketa* could not be used in these situations:

(44) They *almost* made it to the top of the mountain.
(45) *They *liketa* made it to the top of the mountain.

In this case, *almost* signifies that they made it some of the way,
but not all of the way to the top. The difference is also clear in sentences which have both a metaphorical and a literal interpretation possible:

(46) a. They *almost* went through the roof when they saw the mess.
      b. They *almost* went through the roof, but the drill they were
          using wasn't powerful enough.
(47) a. They *liketa* went through the roof when they saw the mess.
      b. *They *liketa* went through the roof, but the drill they were
          using wasn't powerful enough.

These comments apply equally well to the occurrences of *liketa* in
negative contexts and might in fact shed light on why *never* is strongly
favored, if not the only possibility for such an environment. In cases
like (41c,d), the speaker claims that the situation "came close" to
never happening, but it finally did. This latter aspect is again the
counterfactual component. The truth value of an utterance without *liketa*
is the opposite of one with the form, whether it is positive or negative,
as seen in the comparison of (48) and (49):

(48) I got lost there and I *liketa* never found my mommy. 75:5
(49) I never found my mommy.

Never may simply be favored for syntactic reasons in that it can be followed by a past form of the main verb whereas the negative particle *not*,
for example, requires the auxiliary form of *do*, with *do* carrying the
tense marking. However, these factors of meaning and truth values may
also contribute to its favored status.
        Another member of the set mentioned by Labov that is also found in
the data being considered here is *supposeta* (with variants *sposeta* and
'poseta). While less frequent than *liketa*, it is found to a considerable
extent. Again, the construction involves a past form of the verb following it, and most instances are preceded by the auxiliary *was*. Sentences
such as (50) are representative of the sample:

(50) a. He was *supposeta* went up in this big two story house. 35:12
  b. And a bunch of guys jumped on him, something he was *sposeta* done, and killed him. 66:6
  c. And so they *poseta* met on one side of the ridge, you know, in so many hours. 156:19

Labov (1972c:59) maintains that *supposeta*, like *liketa* and *useta*, has become a fixed form, related to *supposed to* but with the past tense ending no longer operative. Instead, tense marking is included on the following element (with, in addition, the past tense on the auxiliary *was* when it is present). Labov (1972c:56) also notes that the auxiliary *do* is needed when *supposeta* is negated as in *don't supposeta*, but only rare cases of *do* with *supposeta* were found in this sample of AE.
Unlike the form *liketa*, however, *supposeta* seems to have retained much the same meaning as its related verb *supposed to*. In fact, it looks very much like a form of *have* deletion has simply taken place in what in standard English would be the embedded clause. Sentence (51) points toward this possibility:

(51) Different things that was *supposeta been done* personally I don't think they *been done*. 37:19

Here there is clearly a case of *have*-deletion in the second part and this seems to be a direct parallel of what happened in the relative clause. This is not so clear in cases like, "We *sposeta went* to the gymnasium." (88:(199), which are less frequent. The differences may represent in some way stages relating to the distance of the form from its standard English correspondence as it becomes more independent.
There is one further example that seems to involve the same process discussed by Labov but is not included in his list, namely *boundta*. Like *supposeta*, this form also seems to retain much the same significance as its standard English counterpart.

(52) I don't know but she was just a little bit of a girl, 'cause Rass was a baby, you know, she *boundta been* little. 153:35

It appears that an item such as this may represent an extension of the process, although we have too few examples to make such a claim without qualification.

Table 25

Age	Double Modals		Liketa		Supposeta	
	Male	Female	Male	Female	Male	Female
8-11	0	1	0	3	2	2
12-14	0	0	3	2	0	0
15-18	1	0	2	4	0	4
20-40	0	0	0	3	0	6
40+	0	2	4	12	0	5
TOTALS	1	3	9	24	2	17

Number of Occurrences of Double Modals,
Liketa *and* Supposeta *by Age and Sex*

Table 25 gives the distribution of the forms discussed above with respect to age and sex. While the figures are not substantial enough to warrant any definitive statements, certain tendencies may be indicated for the forms *liketa* and *supposeta*. Both seem to be favored by female speakers rather than males. In addition, *liketa* may be receding given the relatively greater frequency of its occurrence in the older groups, while *supposeta* appears to have a fairly even distribution across age. The implication from these figures that *liketa* may be disappearing seems to correlate with its greater degree of difference from standard usage when compared with the other forms. This could correspond to a more general movement toward the standard language in which the more nonstandard forms would not be maintained.

Verb Subclasses

Many of the AE rules dealt with in the preceding sections are relatively general in nature. That is, they affect a broad class of items that meet the conditions for the operation of the rule. In those cases where the rule affected a restricted set of items, we discussed the feature in some detail because of the important structural consequences of the small class of items. There are, however, rules that are more restricted and not as significant structurally in terms of the class of items affected by the rule, applying to small subsets of items or even an individual item within a general class. Some of these processes affect subclasses of verbs as AE is compared with other varieties of English.

One of the categories of verb classification that may be found to be different across dialects relates to the distinction between *transitive* (the verb takes an overt object) and *intransitive* (the verb does not take an overt object) verbs. While the great majority of verbs may be expected to coincide in their classification across varieties of English, there are occasional instances where verbs may differ. One example of such a difference, as found in AE, concerns the verb *beat*. In most mainstream varieties of English, an overt object is required to appear with *beat* so that we typically get sentences like *The Phillies beat the Pirates*. In these varieties, *beat* cannot be used as an intransitive verb. In AE, however, as in some other non-mainstream varieties of English, *beat* can be used as an intransitive verb, so that we observe sentences like (53):

(53)   a.   Like if we *beat*, they cause trouble.   150:4
       b.   Sometimes I *beat*.   41:(70)
       c.   And Willie just passes 'em up and *beats*.   52:(294)

In such cases, the intransitive counterpart required in most varieties of standard English would be *win*, so that a sentence such as *Sometimes I win* would be the correspondence for AE *Sometimes I beat*. This particular feature seems more characteristic of younger speakers than older ones, so that it is age-graded to some extent.

Further differences in the subclassification of transitive or intransitive verbs may also be found across dialects. For example, standard varieties of English permit the verb learn to take an object as long as it is nonhuman. This, however, is not the case in AE, where the verb *learn* may take a human object as in:

(54)   a.   But it still didn't *learn him* anything.   164:9
       b.   She *learnt me* how to count.   85:21
       c.   They *learnt him* how to run.   16:(151)

The verb form corresponding to this in standard English would be *teach*. AE, like a number of other non-mainstream varieties of English simply extends the structural context in which *learn* can occur. This particular item has become one of the stereotyped features relating to verb subclassification, and many teachers make a special effort to teach the standard English correspondence.

In many cases, as we have seen above, the different subclassification of verbs involves the extension of the semantic territory covered by a particular verb form. We thus have a case like *set*, which is extended in AE to cover the semantic areas usually reserved for *sit* or *stay* in other varieties of English. Sentences like (55) illustrate this pattern, which turns out to be fairly widespread among varieties of southern origin:

(55) a. We *set* there a while and we seen 'im. 121:(430)
       b. Everybody *sets* wherever they want. 46:15
       c. Well, I *set* here. 83:15

While *set* is usually used as a transitive verb in standard English, it is clearly used as an intransitive one in the sentences illustrated. Because of the similarities in the pronunciation of *set* and *sit*, it has sometimes been suggested that the close phonetic resemblance caused them to merge.

One of the fairly well known cases where verbs are used to cover different semantic areas across dialects involves the uses of *take* and *carry* in many varieties of southern origin. In most northern varieties of standard English, *carry* cannot be used with reference to escorting or accompanying; this usage is reserved for the verb *take*. In southern varieties, including AE, we get sentences such as *He carried her to the movie* or *He carried her to the store* corresponding to northern *He took her to the movies* or *He took her to the store*.

While the usage of *carry* is semantically extended in AE to cover areas reserved for *take* in other varieties of English, it is interesting to observe that *take* may be expanded in a different direction. We thus find *take* being extended in this variety to cover items which would typically correspond to *catch* or *get* as used with reference to acquisition of sickness or disease.

(56) a. I *took a virus*. 35:5
       b. My kids *taken the chicken pox*. 40:15
       c. I *take weak spells*. 85:7

And, with the addition of the particle *up*, *take up* is observed to cover the semantic reference usually covered by *live* or *stay* in other varieties of English, as illustrated in (57):

(57) a. Did ever a stray animal come to y'all's house and *take up*?
         [Fieldworker] 2:7
       b. ...come and *take up* with us. 5:(nc)

In this case, *take up* may be used as an intransitive verb form, which is different from its usual function in varieties of standard English.

There are a number of other verb forms that simply have to be treated as different lexical items in AE. Most of these would have to be discussed individually. An illustrative inventory of some of these lexical verb differences is given in Table 26, where some AE verb forms and their approximate correspondences in standard English are given.

Table 26 is intended to be illustrative rather than exhaustive. These items primarily involve individual vocabulary differences and would

have to be discussed as such. Our major concern is the more general
phonological and grammatical rules. (See p. 97.)

    Need + Verb + -ed. One of the restricted grammatical patterns
affecting verbal phrases in AE involves the verb *need* and its complements.
In most mainstream varieties of standard English, there are at least
several alternant forms of the complement. Among the complements *need*
may take is an infinitive form of *to be*, as in *The house needs to be
painted* or simply a participial *-ing* form without the infinitive *be*, as
in *The house needs painting.* Although the form *be* does not occur with
the *-ing* participial form, it is required to be present with the *-ed*
participial form in standard English. In AE, as in other regional
varieties of English surrounding this general area, the *-ed* participial
can occur without *be*.

(58) a. It *needs remodeled* all over it. 35:21
      b. I like my hair, except it *needs trimmed* right now. 155:7
      c. ...just about everything that *needs done.* 122:(353)

In this case, there is an option for forming the complement structure
that is not present in some other regional varieties of English, where
-ed participles require the infinitive *to be.*

    There is an extension of this general pattern involving verbs other
than *need* and non-participial (*-ing*) complement forms. The verbs *like*
and *make out* apparently fit this class when the predicate constructions
following them are nominatives or locatives. We find:

(59) a. It *liked around people.* 77:2
      b. They all *made* him *out the liar,* but I believe the man was a-
          tellin' the truth. 83:15

    Since there are so few instances of this type of construction, it
is difficult to give a detailed descriptive account, but it appears
that these are specialized lexical cases in which the form *be* (either
in its infinitival or participial forms) may be absent in a complement
sentence.

    To + Verb + ing. In standard varieties of English, there are sev-
eral ways in which complement sentences can be embedded within another
sentence (in a sentence like *I believe that the world is round, The world
is round* is the complement sentence to *I believe [something]*). One of
these alternatives involves the formation of an infinitive with the
verb of the complement sentence. Thus, we have a sentence like *He
started to mess around* where *to mess* is the infinitivized form of the
verb in the complement sentence. Another way in which complement sentences may be embedded involves the use of a participial *ing* form on the
verb, giving us an alternant like *He started messing around.* In most
standard varieties of English, these alternant processes involve mutually exclusive forms; that is, either the infinitive form WITH *to* is
chosen or the *-ing* form WITHOUT *to* is chosen. In AE, as in some other
varieties of southern origin, there is another alternant in which the
to complementizer may co-occur with the *ing* participial form. This
gives us sentences like:

(60) a. Boy, I *started to runnin'.* 10:21
      b. They *started to messin'* around. 2:3
      c. Chickens *started to peckin'* them. 16:(2240

    In cases such as these, we simply have another alternant formation
for complement sentences. It is interesting to note, however, that this

Table 26

AE Verb	Standard English Correspondence	Illustrative Sentence
aim	intend, plan	I been *aimin'* to go down and see 'im. 87:5
bless out	scold severely	I got *blessed out.* 28:17
doctor	treat	If I taken the cold, they just *doctored* it themselves the way they thought it sposeta been *doctored.* 160:13
fixin'	prepare, plan	It was just *fixin'* to bite me and I taken off a-runnin'. 160:25
fuss at	scold, yell at	She'll probably give me a whippin' or I'll get *fussed at.* 126:(87)
get	become	My older sister, she used to have these birfday parties when she *got* sixteen. 17:6
go	travel	Half the time, in '17, you couldn't *go* the road. 31:6
happin in	come, arrive	They sometime *happen in* at the same time. 31:3
hear tell	listen to, heard	I've *heared tell* of some that happened years ago. 36:6
reckon	suppose, guess	I *reckon* she's done sold it. 153:32
reckon to	acknowledge, defer	I *reckon to* my age and the way I've had to work hard all my life. 85:14
whup	whip	...'cause if they heard you say it, they'd *whup* you. 10:(386)
set out	start	We *set out* to teach them to be able to take care of theirselves. 40:3
tree	chase up a tree, corner	Our dog *treed* one under the chicken house. 40:40

Some Illustrative Lexical Differences in AE Verbs

alternant formation is apparently restricted to verbs denoting inception or commencement. Most predominantly, this involves *start* but there are other cases, such as the inceptive functions of *got* and *went*.

(61) a. A vein in his nose bursted and he *went to hemorragin'*. 40:16
     b. She practically raised 'im 'til he *got up to walkin'*. 36:38
     c. Dad really *went to drivin'* fast. 30:22
     d. We got over there and we *got to messin'* around in this old tree and there was something on top of it. 49:2

For these verbs, the *to* particle may have to be considered an integral part of the verb form (i.e. the verb is *got to* or *went to*) which is necessary for the verb to be used with an inceptive reference.

    Have + Noun Phrase + to + Verb. Whereas many complement sentences in English can be formed through the formation of an infinitive, including the complementizer *to*, there are occasional complement sentences in standard English where *to* is not included. One of these constructions involves the verb *have* as it is used with reference to causation or procurement. Thus, a sentence like *They had the machine do the work* or *He had him come home* is formed without *to*. In these cases, the noun phrase which is the object of *have* is also the subject of the complement sentence. Unlike many other complement constructions, *to* does not occur. In AE these constructions may include the form *to*, giving us sentences like (62):

(62) a. Just recently, I *had an aunt to come* from Texas. 3:(554)
     b. *He had the blacksmith to make* him a pair of forceps. 31:9
     c. They'd *have a thrashing machine to come* in and thrash it. 85:2
     d. Usually, I hafta *have somebody else to do it*. 3:(765)

Such constructions do not appear to be especially stigmatized socially, and there is some evidence that forms such as these are spreading into more mainstream varieties of English.[6]

ADVERBS

    Another general class where a number of differences can be observed cross-dialectally is adverbs. While some of these differences may not have the significant structural consequences of certain verb differences, there are some general grammatical rules which set apart different varieties of English.

Time Adverb Placement

    In English, there is a class of time adverbs that commonly occur after the verb phrase, often taking the end position in a sentence. In sentences like *We go to the store all the time* or *We write home once and a while*, the adverbial phrases *all the time* and *once and a while* occupy this end position. These adverbs may be moved to the front of the sentence in some instances giving us alternant sentences *All the time, we go to the store* and *Once in a while we write home*. In many varieties of English, these are the only positions in a sentence that adverbial phrases may occupy. In AE, however, adverbial phrases of time (typically referring to frequency) may be moved within the verb phrase (usually before the main verb, but they may in some cases precede the auxiliary). We thus get sentences like the following:

(63)   a.   We'd *all the time* get in fights.   10:15
       b.   We's *all the way* talkin'.   10:20
       c.   We *once and a while* will have pretty bad floods.   38:(nc)
       d.   She's *all the time* wantin' to watch something.   15:(745)

The placement of these types of adverbial phrases within the verb phrase
simply generalizes a pattern in which single adverbs of frequency (e.g.
always, usually, rarely, etc.) may occur in this position within the verb
phrase.
        While adverbs of frequency such as *ever, rarely, always,* etc. typi-
cally are placed within the verb phrase, there are special conditions
found in AE under which they may be moved out of the verb phrase. Consider, for example:

(64)   a.   That was the brightest light that *ever* I seen.   157:31
       b.   That's the biggest rattlesnake *ever* I seen.   157:27
       c.   Did *ever* a stray animal come to y'all's house and take up?   2:7

In examples such as (64a,b) the frequency adverb *ever* is moved to the
front of an embedded sentence. In a sentence like (64c) the frequency
adverb is moved with the auxiliary to the front of a question sentence.
We thus see that an embedded sentence and a question sentence may allow
the frequency adverb to be moved to the front of a sentence. The extent
to which this process affects the general class of frequency adverbs in
AE is not known at this point since most of our citations involve the adverb *ever*.
        In connection with the placement of the adverb *ever*, it is note-
worthy to mention how *ever* combines with pronoun forms, particularly *what*.
The standard English formation of these items is typically *whatever*, but
in AE it is observed that the *ever* may precede *what*, giving us *everwhat*.

(65)   a.   ...so *everwhat* you planted.   22:9
       b.   ...*everwhat* it is.   22:26
       c.   ...*everwhat* the case may be.   32:(200)

Although *ever* most frequently combines with *what* in this way, occasional
instances are also found with other pronoun forms as well. This is seen
in utterances like (66):

(66)   a.   Say five or six of us boys, *everhow* many was in the..., you
            know, lived close to us.   30:1
       b.   And they said "*Everwho* gets bloodied first won."   51:3
       c.   *Everwho* bloodied the person.   51:3

At this point, we do not know the extent to which this process can apply
to other forms, but it appears to be quite restricted.
        Finally, there is one extension of the lexical item *ever* which should
be mentioned: the coalescence of *ever* and *every*, so that *ever* may be
used in contexts that would correspond to *every* in standard English.

(67)   a.   Boy that thing was jerkin' me *ever* which way.   9:(637)
       b.   And *ever* time I say something to her, she act like she's
            gonna kill me.   15:(30)
       c.   They go just *ever* change of the moon.   85:(330)
       d.   We had *everthing* to eat.   163:(67)

        The merger of *every* into *ever* is obviously due to the close phonetic
similarity of these items to begin with. In fact, it is sometimes diffi-

cult to perceive the phonetic difference between a reduced form of
and *ever* in rapid casual speech, so that this merger is not as socially
obtrusive as might be expected. Some items which may, on first glance,
seem to be related to the order of *ever* and the *wh* pronoun (e.g. *ever
which* as in (67a) or *ever where* for *every where*) seem related to this
phonetically-based merger rather than the actual movement of the form
ever seen in the examples in (65) and (66).

Comparatives and Superlatives

     In standard English, there are several different forms which com-
parative and superlative constructions can take. One way of forming
these constructions is through the addition of a comparative *-er* or superlative *-est* suffix. For the most part, the comparative *-er* and superlative *-est* suffixes are used on words of one syllable, as in items like
taller and *tallest* or *fatter* and *fattest* and two syllable words that end
in a vowel, such as *prettier* and *prettiest* and *easier* and *easiest*. In
words of two syllables that end in a consonant and those of more than
two syllables, standard English shows a preference for the comparative
adverb *more* and the superlative adverb *most* rather than the addition of
a suffix. This results in items like *more beautiful* and *most beautiful*
or *more awful* and *most awful*. In addition to these patterns for forming
comparatives, there are certain irregular items where a different item
is used in the comparative and superlative form. For example, the following items are irregular in their comparative and superlative formation.

Item	Comparative	Superlative
good, well	better	best
bad	worse	worst
much, many	more	most

     In AE, as in most non-mainstream varieties of English, the pattern
for forming comparative and superlative constructions may differ. One
difference involves an extension of the *-er* and *-est* suffixes to words
of more than one syllable that end in a consonant. We thus get the following formations:

(68) a.   It was the *awfulest* mess. 34:(36)
      b.   ...one of the *beautifulest* pieces. 30:(156)
      c.   ...the *awfulest* stuff. 31:(113)

In cases such as these, the conditions for adding the suffixial forms of
the comparative and superlative are different from standard English.
     Another pattern that differs from most standard English varieties
involves the use of both the comparative adverb before the item as well
as the addition of the suffixial form. This pleonastic or redundant comparative formation may occur on items that would only take the suffix in
standard English as well as items that typically take the comparative or
superlative word, although it appears more common in the former case.
We thus get items such as (69):

(69) a.   ...a little bit *more older*. 52:(162)
      b.   ...it's *more easier* to prepare food. 37:(53)
      c.   ...got *more closer* and *more closer*. 151:(404)
      d.   ...*more stricter* than my father. 37:(53)
      e.   ...*most stupidest* thing. 64:(267)

Pleonastic comparative and superlative forms such as these appear to

be more socially stigmatized than the cases where the suffixes are extended to certain polysyllabic words. This is probably due to the fact that
there is some flexibility in the standard English rule for the addition of
the suffix (in some instances, it simply being a stylistic preference)
while there is a general prohibition against marking comparatives and
superlatives with both the comparative word and the suffix in standard
English.

Finally, there is a regularization of some of the irregular comparatives in AE. This may involve simply the addition of the suffixial comparative or superlative on the base word or the redundant addition of the
suffix to the irregular form. The result of this regularization tendency is constructions such as the following:

(70) a. ...the *baddest* dream. 5:(986)
      b. She got *worser*. 108:(413)
      c. ...the *mostest* people. 73:(539)
      d. Things are getting *worser* anymore. 108:(413)

This type of regularization process seems more characteristic of
younger AE speakers than older ones, so that it is age-graded to some
extent. The comparative and superlative constructions found in AE do
not appear to be any different from those found for other northern and
southern non-mainstream varieties of English. In most cases, these forms
are variable, fluctuating with forms that would be considered characteristic of standard varieties of English.

Intensifying Adverbs

In AE, as in a number of English varieties of southern origin, there
are adverbs which function to intensify a particular attribute or activity.
These adverbs are a well known characteristic of AE and often become stereotypes of speakers from this region. Despite recognition of these forms
by many speakers of English, they often carry nuances of meaning that
sometimes make them difficult to describe precisely. Even apart from
their meaning, the exact syntactic privileges are sometimes difficult to
pin down, since there are overlapping syntactic contexts as well as contexts in which only certain submembers of this class can be used.

One of the most common of these intensifiers is the item *right*. In
standard English *right* is limited to indicating precise direction and
location in space or time with select adverbs, as in sentences like *It's
right near here* or *He's right over there*. AE is among those varieties
of English where *right* can also be used with adjectives. Bolinger (1972:
51) notes that:

> ...it is normally used with adjectives whose meanings
> suggest concentration rather than diffuseness, a point
> rather than a spread, something that hits the senses
> rather than something with little effect. A fairly
> close synonym is *keenly*.

Its usage with adjectives in AE is found in the following types of sentences:

(71) a. It was *right* cool. 84:(296)
      b. It'd be *right* soupy wet. 31:9
      c. It was *right* large. 161:(321)
      d. It was *right* amusing. 22:14
      e. Makes you feel *right* foolish. 152:17

In addition to its use with adjectives, it can also be paired with adverbs other than those with which it occurs in standard English. We thus
find it being used with adverbs of manner and time.

(72)   a.   I hollered *right* loud for help. 152:31
       b.   You can take it and grind it up *right* fine. 22:14
       c.   ...she'd nudge me *right* hard. 28:20
       d.   Well, back years ago, whiskey was used *right* often for medi-
            cinal reasons. 32:30
       e.   ...and they found it and *right* quick they seen him with it.
            42:10

     As compared with standard varieties of English, AE allows a general-
ization of the intensifier *right* from a restricted set of adverbs to a
wider set of adverbs and to adjectives. Although it is very difficult
to choose a synonym, it appears to correspond closest to the intensifiers
very or *really* (He's *really/very* nice) in standard varieties of English.
     The intensifier *right* can also function as an intensifier in com-
bination with the item *smart*. While *right* by itself occurs preceding
adjectives, *right smart* typically is used with nouns, as indicated in
the following examples:

(73)   a.   I don't know how long they would leave it, but for a *right
            smart* while. 31:12
       b.   Yeah, we could keep it a *right smart* while in there. 23:(331)
       c.   Yeah, he had a *right smart* temper, but he never got mad at
            me. 153:4
       d.   I've sold *right smart* butter. 23:(338)

The most common usage for *right smart* is with reference to time, half of
the examples in our sample occurring with the item *while*, as in (73a,b).
Although it is difficult to specify precisely what the meaning of this
item is, the closest synonym seems to be "considerable" or "a good amount
of," with the intensification of *right* adding to the intensification of
smart. Thus, sentences like (73a,b) refer to a considerable amount of
time while (73d) refers to a considerable amount of butter. Sentence
(73c) is a little more difficult to interpret with respect to quantity,
although it appears to refer to a great amount of volatility in temper.
With certain subclasses of nouns, an alternant for *right smart* would be
right much as in sentences like (74):

(74)   a.   I can remember being exceptionally quiet and having *right much*
            fever. 25:(nc)
       c.   There has been *right much*,...er...a lot of publicity. 25:(nc)

With reference to time nouns, the alternant would have to be *right long*
as in "We had a lily pond for a *right long* while." (25:(nc).
     There are also cases of *right smart* which are used with verbs and
adverbs rather than nouns:

(75)   a.   ...and I've lived around *right smart* too. 85:8
       b.   I like to draw *right smart*. 124:19
       c.   ...traveling with him *right smart* and he was a-workin'. 24:(140)

In a number of these instances, the meaning seems to refer to a considerable amount of time, the most frequent type of context observed in connection with nouns, although this is not an exclusive meaning in such
contexts.

There is an interesting correspondence between the use of *right* in
AE and some historical facts about the form discussed by Stoffel (1901).
Right apparently was formerly used as an intensifier before both adjectives and adverbs in much the same way as it is currently used in AE.
Instances of this usage, with the sense of *completely* or *very*, can be
found from writings of the 15th century, and Stoffel cites examples like
right rich, right much, right worthy, right cruelly (1901:35-36).   It
frequently occurred in the writings of Shakespeare but appears to have
since disappeared in most varieties of English.   Stoffel (1901:37-38)
notes an interesting retention in standard English for certain titles,
such as Right Honorable and Right Reverend, but observes that "In other
cases, the intensive *right* usually figures as a conscious archaism."
Based on evidence of its frequent occurrence in AE the use of *right* before both adjectives and adverbs has survived in at least one variety of
English, with a sense like that of *very*.   The other sense--*completely*--
that Stoffel found in his research to be associated with *right* is no
longer current.   The restrictions on the distribution of *right* in most
English varieties which developed apparently have not yet affected AE
and the intensifier remains quite common.

   Another adverb sometimes considered as a part of this class of intensification words is the item *plumb* (sometimes spelled *plum*).   *Plumb*
most typically occurs with other adverbs and verbs as in sentences like
the following:

(76) a. And the house burnt *plumb* down.   Nothin' left but the chimney.
          10:18
      b. If he'd shot hisself, man, he'da blowed his head *plumb* off.
          17:17
      c. And me and him jumped from the window *plumb* over the porch,
          from the porch, *plumb* up on the roof.   20:(986)
      d. He shot him *plumb* through like this.   22:24
      e. It would scare you *plumb* to death.   34:(400)

Unlike the items *right* and *right smart*, which refer to relative degrees
of an attribute, *plumb* refers to something carried through to completeness.   It seems most synonymous with "completely" or "all the way."   The
notion of completeness must be viewed metaphorically in some instances
since phrases such as "scare you *plumb* to death"--a relatively common
context for *plumb*--does not refer to death literally but to the completeness of the state of fright.

   It is also possible to find *plumb* with adjectives:

(77) a. That was *plumb* foolish.   34:(100)
      b. I didn't hear him 'cause I'm *plumb* asleep.   4:3

Some adjectives may be used with either *right* or *plumb*, as in a phrase
like *right foolish* or *plumb foolish*.   The use of *plumb* is stronger than
right in such cases, so that *plumb foolish* refers to a complete state of
foolishness whereas *right foolish* refers to a degree of foolishness not
quite as strong.   In these contexts, it is observed that *right* is used
with both positive (e.g. *good, pretty*) and negative (*foolish, nasty*) at-
tributes, whereas *plumb* is largely restricted to the latter.

   It is also noted that there are some adjectives with which only
plumb may be used, such as *asleep* in (77).   In a case such as this, it
appears that the state of sleeping is something that is conceived of as
categorical in nature.   We thus get phrases like *plumb asleep* but not
right asleep.   On the other hand, it is possible to form a phrase like

right sleepy but not *plumb sleepy* since the state of sleepiness is something which is viewed only in terms of relative degrees, the categorical state being sleep itself.

Finally, we should mention something about phrases like *big old*, *great big old* (or *great old big*), *little old*, or just *old* (sometimes spelled *ole* because of the frequent absence of the final *d*). While there is a degree of literalness which is part of the uses of *big* and *little*, their usage goes beyond that.

(78) a. It's a *great old big* wide piece on top. 10:273
      b. There was a *big old* block of wood. 9:(166)
      c. Them *old* midwives, you can't beat 'em. 31:(123)
      d. This was just a *little old* harmless chicken. 13:(785)
      e. Mother packed me a lunch in a *little old* half gallon syrup bucket. 31:19

The term *old* by itself may be used as a term of endearment, in some instances referring to traditional institutions in a somewhat positive light. *Little old* may also be used with some of the same endearing qualities as *old*. There are, however, instances in which there is connotation of harmlessness as it is used with reference to animate objects. Thus, a phrase like *little old snake* would not necessarily mean that the snake is viewed fondly, but simply that it is viewed as harmless. We do not have any examples in our sample in which *great* is used with *little*, but it occurs quite frequently with *big* or *big old*, as in sentences like (78a). Objects which are described as *great big old* or *big old* differ from those qualified with *little old* in that there may be either a positive or negative connotation. For example, in a sentence such as *Paul Bunyan was a great old big guy* (12:536), it appears to be used with a positive connotation, whereas in a sentence like *I told him to stay away from it cause big old rocks is up above it* (10:1109), *big old* is used with reference to a condition which holds some potential for harm. In examples such as these, the qualified object must be considered literally to be relatively large, but it is intensified to some degree. Although there are undoubtedly more subtle connotations added when phrases such as these are used, they are somewhat difficult to define specifically at this point.

-*ly* Absence

In English, there is a class of items that may function either adverbially or adjectivally in terms of their usage within a sentence. For some of the items in this class, the form of the item is the same, regardless of whether it ultimately functions as an adverb or an adjective. An item like *fast*, for example, takes the same form in its adverbial (e.g. *He ran fast*) and its adjectival (e.g. *the fast train*) function. There are other items in this class where the adverbial form may, but is not required to take an -*ly* suffix when it functions as an adverb. Thus, an item like *wrong* may or may not take the -*ly* suffix in a sentence such as *He answered wrong(ly)*. In most cases, items like this do not take the -*ly* suffix in the casual speech style of most standard English speakers. There are other cases in standard English, however, where the -*ly* suffix must be present when the item is used in its adverbial function, so that -*ly* would be be required when an item like *original* is used adverbially (e.g. *He comes from Virginia originally*). It is quite difficult to specify a formal basis which determines which of these classes an item falls into, although it seems that the frequency with which an item occurs may have something to do with its subclassification in these terms.

While it is difficult to specify the exact basis for the different subclasses, it is quite apparent that there are differences across English dialects. A number of the items that are required to take the *-ly* suffix in standard English fall into the optional class for AE. The following examples illustrate some of these optional *-ly* forms.

(79) a. I come from Virginia original__. 96:(26)
      b. I'm frightful__ scared of spiders. 28:(285)
      c. It certain__ was some reason. 37:(321)
      d. ...if they pray sincere__. 160:(1101)
      e. An organ player's terrible__ hard to follow. 155:(55)
      f. ...enjoyed life awful__ well. 31:(34)

In the above list, the *-ly* absence on some of the forms seems much more socially obtrusive than others. For some items like *awful* and *terrible* it would not be unusual to find speakers of mainstream varieties using them without the *-ly* suffix in their most casual styles of speech, while items like *original* and *certain* would always be expected to have the *-ly*. It appears that the social stigmatization of *-ly* absence is more of a continuum related to particular items than a clear-cut distinction between an obvious standard form and its socially stigmatized non-mainstream counterpart.

Positive *Anymore*

One of the interesting divergences in English syntax involves the use of the adverb *anymore*. All varieties of English can apparently use the adverb *anymore* in negative sentences of the type given below.

(80) a. I don't like T.V. *anymore*.
      b. He didn't live there *anymore*.
      c. Why wasn't he there *anymore*?

In sentences like (80), *anymore* is used in a negative context with reference to something which took place or was characteristic of past time but is no longer the case. As mentioned above, this particular usage of *anymore* is common in most varieties of English. There are, however, cases in which *anymore* is used in positive sentences, with a meaning of "nowadays." In positive sentences like *I like T.V. anymore* or *He lives there anymore, anymore* refers to a situation or activity which was not true in the past, but is characteristic of the present. The relationship between the use of *anymore* in negative and positive sentences has been diagrammed by Labov (1973:72) as follows:

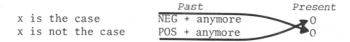

		Past	*Present*
x is the case		NEG + anymore	0
x is not the case		POS + anymore	0

While speakers who come from regions where *anymore* is only used in negative contexts may find the use of positive *anymore* rather obtrusive, native speakers of varieties where positive *anymore* is current tend not to view it as a socially diagnostic linguistic feature.

Current studies of *anymore* in positive sentences have identified it as characteristic of regions within the Midland settlement area of the United States. Its usage in regions of Appalachia is fully attested by the following types of sentences from our sample.

(81) a. She's more northern than she is southern *anymore*. 149:(1094)
      b. I mean things are getting worser *anymore* 'n what they used to
          be. 108:(413)
      c. Even in the small towns *anymore* it's getting like that.
          155:(199)
      c. *Anymore*, all the guys you get ahold of just don't think that
          way. 66:(63)
      e. What it is *anymore*, people have wrote so much music, it's diffi-
          cult to find a tune that hadn't been written already. 155:(1114)

The above examples show that *anymore* may be placed at the end of the
clause or at the beginning, including the phrase *what it is anymore*. This
use of *anymore* is found to be fairly extensive in the speech of some AE
speakers. While it has been noted (see Labov, 1973:66) that this form is
used frequently in parts of "western Pennsylvania, Ohio, Indiana, and parts
of Illinois, Kansas, Missouri, Utah and other western states, and is apparently spreading to other parts of the United States," it is apparent
that its use in AE is fairly stable and has been for some time. A number
of our examples from AE come from older residents of Appalachia who have
had limited contact with outsiders.

Adverbial *But*

When combined with a negativized verb phrase, *but* can be used in AE
to refer to a single fact or instance. Consider, for example, the use of
but in the following types of sentences:

(82) a. He *don't* come to see me *but* oncet a month. 66:(65)
      b. I *ain't* never seen him for *but* one time since he went in the
          army. 77:(998)
      c. He *ain't but* thirteen. 121:(96)
      d. I *didn't* attend *but* one of them. 32:(100)
      e. In the whole thing, it *wouldn't* be *but* forty people. 34:(300)

In contexts such as those cited in (82), *but* is observed to have an
exclusive or single reference which corresponds to adverbs such as "only"
or "merely" in other varieties of English. In this usage, *but* is quite
different from its use as a conjunction introducing a dependent clause,
as in a sentence like *I wanted to go, but I couldn't* or *It's not red, but
blue*. In sentences such as these, *but* operates as a conjunction outside
the clause with the negativized verb phrase, while for sentences like
those in (82) the negativized verb phrase and *but* are co-occurring items
within the same clause.
     The usage of *but* with the negativized verb phrases in AE seems to
parallel an adverbial usage of *but* with positive verb phrases in some
varieties of English, as in a sentence like *He's but a child*. A sentence
like this would be used only for elegant emphasis and is relatively rare
in most varieties of standard English. In AE--as in other varieties of
southern origin--the negativized verb phrase with *but* is certainly not
socially prestigious, although it does not seem to be particularly stigmatized either. It does, however, appear to occur in more emphatic contexts than the contexts in which adverbs such as *only* or *merely* are used.
There also appear to be subtle differences between the use of adverbial
but in negative sentences by AE speakers and the corresponding usage of
adverbial *but* in positive sentences. In positive sentences, it is found
almost exclusively with the copula *be*, while the use of *but* with the negativized verb phrase occurs in less restricted types of contexts. *But*

in positive sentences also seems to suggest a characterization that exceeds the expectation of the subject. Thus, it is most appropriate in a context like *He's but a child, although he plays the guitar like a man.* We would not typically expect it to occur in a context such as *He's but a child so we didn't expect him to play the guitar very well.* But with a negativized verb phrase does not necessarily carry this attitudinal aspect.

Druther

It seems farily obvious that the use of the form *druther* by AE speakers originally derived from *would rather*, where the contraction of the modal resulted in *'d rather* and eventually became simply *druther*. There are ample examples of this form in AE:

(83) a. In some ways I *druther* have a good bicycle. 2:(1241)
     b. *Druther* than seein' him lose his crop, why they would come right there to help him do all this kinda work. 30:(562)
     c. Would you *druther* I did something I didn't want to do? 155:(1019)

Although *druther* was apparently derived historically through the described contraction process, it has become lexicalized as a separate word. Thus, it can occur in contexts other than those where it might be related to the contraction of *would* and even occurs with a form of *would* as in (83c). AE speakers now treat it as a simple correspondence for *rather* instead of a correspondence for *would rather* or *d'rather*.

Adverbial Lexical Differences

In addition to the adverbial differences discussed above, there are a number of other differences which simply involve single lexical items or

Table 27

yet, still yet	still	I *yet* eat a lot of honey. 32:(500)
subject	likely	If you use Ajax or Comet, it's *subject* to kill 'em. 40:(403)
some of these days	one of these days	It'll get better *some of these days.* 31:11
along about (with reference to time)	about	We tromped through the woods 'til *along about* six o'clock in the morning. 31:(27)
this day and time	nowadays	...that the girls *this day and time* cook so much better. 31:17
dang	darn	You're *dang* tootin'. 31:28
to boot	as well	They can see every direction and straight up *to boot* at the same time. 31:28
yonder	there (considerable distance)	I've got an old horse way back up *yonder.* 146:8
pert 'near	nearly, almost	...need trees that're *pert 'near* square. 45:(17)
t'all	at all	I wasn't sure that nothing wasn't gonna come up *t'all.* 35:23
for sure	sure, certain	I'm not *for sure.* 149:(347)

Some Illustrative Lexical Differences in AE Adverbs

phrases and which will not be treated in any detail here. An illustrative
list of some of these lexical differences found for AE is given in Table
27 on the preceding page. Many of these are simply southern in origin
and not peculiar to AE, although others appear to be used only by AE
speakers (see Kurath, 1949).

A number of the items in Table 27 are obviously due to phonological
changes which have lexicalized as different forms (e.g. *t'all, pert 'near*)
while others involve differences in the semantic territory covered by a
particular lexical item (e.g. *yet, subject*). Some of these items occur
fairly commonly within AE while others are used more infrequently, although
we have not systematically studied the distribution of these forms among
AE speakers.

NEGATION

Several of the most widely-known socially diagnostic features of
American English concern aspects of negation. One of these concerns the
formation of negative sentences with indefinite forms and the other the
use of the lexical item *ain't*.

Multiple Negation

One of the stereotyped features of social dialects throughout American English concerns the use of what has traditionally been termed "double
negation" or multiple negation. Sentences like *He didn't do nothin'* come
to mind immediately in connection with the speech of most non-mainstream
varieties. As pointed out by Wolfram and Fasold (1974:163-166), the rules
that govern such constructions in non-mainstream varieties are completely
regular and somewhat complex. While both standard and non-mainstream
varieties share certain rules governing negation, there are also differences
in some of the rules. We shall not attempt to give in detail the types of
rules needed to govern the various types of negation in English, but it is
necessary to summarize some of the main points in order to understand the
rules governing multiple negation in AE.

To begin with, we note that negation typically ranges over an entire
sentence as the notion of sentence is defined by most modern grammarians.
Because of this, it has been suggested that, in an abstract representation
of the sentence, a negative element is generated separately from the main
constituents of the sentence and then placed in the appropriate place within the sentence through the series of rules that eventually lead to the
spoken form. In this abstract formulation of the sentence, for example,
a negative element (usually represented simply as NOT) might be placed before the main constituents of the sentence such as a Noun Phrase and a
Verb Phrase (i.e. have a representation such as S →(NOT) NP + VP where
the parentheses indicate that a negative element may optionally be chosen
for a sentence in addition to the constituents Noun Phrase and Verb Phrase
which are found in every sentence).

From this abstract formulation we then incorporate the negative into
the sentence in the appropriate places. The first rule which governs the
incorporation of the negative within the sentence places it within the
Verb Phrase. This rule is given by Wolfram and Fasold (1974:163) as:

Rule 1. *In a negative sentence, place NOT in the main verb phrase.*

This rule places the negative element NOT (with its various forms to
be accounted for later by the pronunciation rules of English) after an

auxiliary or *be*, as in *He didn't do it*, *He couldn't help the man*, or
He was not there.   In other words, this rule places NOT at the proper
place within the Verb Phrase.   This rule, of course, is found in all varieties of English.

The second rule is related to indefinite items such as *any*, *anything*, *anybody*, etc. when they precede the main verb in a sentence.   This
rule is stated by Wolfram and Fasold (1974:163) as follows:

Rule 2.   *In a negative sentence, if there is an indefinite element preceding the main verb, remove NOT from the main verb phrase and
incorporate it into the indefinite element.*

This rule accounts for the fact that a preverbal indefinite such as
anything takes the negative element from the main verb phrase when it precedes it.   Thus a sentence like *Nobody did the work* comes from a sentence
like *Anybody + do + NOT + the + work*.   Rule 2 takes the NOT from the main
phrase and places it within the preverbal indefinite *anybody*, leading to
the sentence *Nobody did the work*.   This again is a rule needed in all
varieties of English since we do not get sentences like *Anybody doesn't
do the work* in any variety.

The third rule concerns indefinite elements that follow the main
verb of a sentence.   The rule(s) governing this have both standard and
non-mainstream versions of the rule.   Again following Wolfram and Fasold
(1974:163), we state Rule 3a as follows:

Rule 3a.   (Standard English Version).   *For elegant emphasis, remove NOT
from the main verb phrase and incorporate it in the first indefinite after the main verb phrase.*

This rule accounts for the fact that we have sentences like *He did
nothing* which may alternate with forms like *He didn't do anything* in
standard English.[7]   Whereas Rules 1 and 2 *must* apply in order to account
for grammatical English sentences, Rule 3a is *optional*--it may or may not
apply.   Rule 3a takes the negative element from the main verb phrase and
moves it to the first indefinite following the main verb phrase.   Whereas
it has been argued that some non-mainstream varieties never apply Rule 3a,
it seems that AE speakers can apply this rule, although they may not apply
it as frequently as some standard English speakers.

The second version of Rule 3 is one which applies to many non-mainstream varieties of English.   Wolfram and Fasold (1974:164) state this
rule as follows:

Rule 3b.   (First Nonstandard Version).   *For emphasis, incorporate a
copy of the NOT which is in the main verb phrase in all indefinites after the main verb phrase, but leave the original
NOT intact.*

This rule produces the traditional cases of double or multiple negatives that are illustrated by the sentences in (84) from our AE speakers:

(84)   a.   They *don't* have *no* work in the winter.   35:16
       b.   I didn't have *nothin'* to do for these stitches.   36:9
       c.   I *ain't* goin' back *no more*.   36:27
       d.   They *didn't* see *no* baby, you know, *didn't* see *none nowhere*.
            37:29

Since Rule 3b can affect as many indefinites as follow the main verb
in a sentence, it appears more accurate to refer to this copying of the

negative on the indefinites as multiple rather than simply "double" negation.

At this point, we should parenthetically note that multiple negation
can also be expressed with the negative adverbs *hardly* and *never*, as well
as its incorporation into ANY. Multiple negation can be expressed by a
negative adverb and by another negative element within the same sentence.
The result is sentences like *He can't hardly see his face* or *He hardly
never comes to see us*. It has been noted that standard English speakers
who avoid other types of multiple negation may sometimes use multiple
negatives of this type.

One of the questions that arises with respect to Rule 3b is the extent of its application in a given non-mainstream variety of English.
For some non-mainstream varieties, it appears that this rule *must* operate
and there is virtually no fluctuation between forms like *He didn't do
nothin'* and *He didn't do anything*. AE, however, does not appear to be
one of these varieties and most speakers do show fluctuation between multiple negation and its singly negated counterpart. To examine the extent of multiple negation following Rule 3b in AE, we have examined the
frequency levels at which various speakers are shown to apply the multiple
negation rule. These frequencies have been tabulated for 25 speakers
representing 5 speakers of the age levels examined in this study. The
graph given below indicates the frequency range of multiple negation for
these speakers. Frequencies are based on the number of actually realized
multiple negatives in relation to the cases where multiple negation might
have potentially applied. That is, a sentence like *He didn't do nothin'*
would be considered as an actual case of multiple negation while a sentence
like *He didn't do anything* would be considered as a potential instance of
multiple negation which was not realized. The distribution of these 25
speakers is given in terms of five arbitrarily delimited frequency ranges:
80-100 percent, 60-79 percent, 40-59 percent, and 0-19 percent multiple
negation.

Figure 5

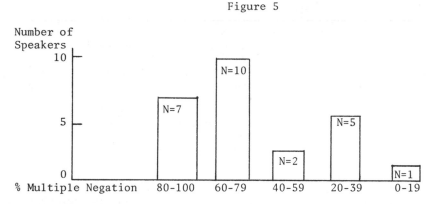

*Distribution of AE Speakers with Respect to the Extent of Multiple
Negation*

We see in Figure 5 that all of the speakers in this subsample use
the multiple negation rule to some extent, and that the majority of them
use it in well over half of all the instances where they might have. Only
one speaker in this sample, however, uses it in all the cases. There
are only a few speakers who use multiple negation in the middle ranges

of frequency usage; the majority use a predominance of multiple negation
while a minority use a predominance of its singly negated counterpart.
    At this point, we may ask how the relative frequency of multiple
negation in AE compares with the frequency of multiple negation found in
studies of other non-mainstream varieties. In Table 28 (see p. 115), we
present the extent of multiple negation found in other studies as compared with the figures for AE. The figures for the other mainstream varieties included in this comparison are given for each of the groups. First,
we give the percentage of multiple negation found in each of the groups.
For our AE speakers, the percentage represents the mean percentage for
the group of five speakers representing each of the age groups. In addition to this statistic, we present, where available, the number of speakers in each sample where multiple negation is used categorically--the
number of speakers out of the total sample who apply the multiple negation
rule (Rule 3b) in all cases where it might have been applied.
    The extent of multiple negation related to post-verbal indefinites
in AE appears to compare more favorably with the figures found for other
non-mainstream White varieties of English than a variety like Vernacular
Black English, the frequency levels falling within the figures based on
a group of White teen-aged peers in New York City and a cross-section of
the working class White population in Detroit. While the younger speakers of AE show a slightly greater degree of multiple negation than do
the older speakers (see for example the 7-11 and 40+ age groups), we do
not find a consistent decrease in multiple negation with progressively
increasing age level delimitations. Multiple negation following Rule 3b
is fairly well distributed among all age groups of AE speakers.
    It is interesting to note that multiple negation as we have dis-
cussed it in the preceding paragraphs is a rule which is well documented
in the history of the English language. Citations from Old and Middle
English abound where the multiple negation copying rule can be shown to
be the predominant if not the exclusive pattern for forming negatives
with indefinites. For example, Williams (1975:280) notes the following
types of sentences from Early Middle English:

(85) a. *There nas no man nowhere so vertuous.*
      b. *Ne taketh nothing to hold of no men ne of no womman.*
      c. *Ne mon nule don hum no good.* (No man ne-will do him no
          good.)

Quite clearly, allowing only one negative element to appear in a sentence
was a relatively recent change in the dialect of Early Modern English that
became recognized as the standard English norm. Williams (1975:280-281)
observes:

> The change requiring that only one NEG appear in a sentence
> is a relatively recent rule in the dialect of Early ModE
> that has become standard. In fact, it is one of the few
> instances where prescriptive grammarians may have encour-
> aged a tendency already at work. Standard Early ModE had
> already begun to favor single negation before the prescrip-
> tion against multiple negatives appeared in usage books of
> the eighteenth century. When prescriptive grammars like
> Lowth's extremely influential *Short Introduction to English
> Grammar* stated that...*two Negatives in English destroy one
> another, or are equivalent to an affirmative,* the tendency
> was simply defined as the logically prescriptive norm for
> standard speakers. His advice has been repeated so often
> and so strongly that few English speakers who have endured

our educational system can fail to recognize that *No one
didn't have no money* is not a favored construction among
educated speakers, despite the weight of respectable
English history behind it and the testimony of numerous
other languages in which multiple negation is not factored
out like an algebraic formula, languages in which the
more negatives there are in a sentence, the more negative
it is.

Whereas a multiple negation rule copying the negative element on indefinites following the verb was once a general pattern of English, a
change to a pattern which allowed only one negative element became the
norm associated with standard English. The effect of the older multiple
negation rule (i.e. Rule 3b), however, is still quite characteristic of
all non-mainstream varieties of English to some extent. Although this
is true, there is another version of this rule which is somewhat more
limited in its scope. This rule is stated by Wolfram and Fasold (1974:
164) as follows:

Rule 3c.   (Second Nonstandard English version). *For emphasis, incor-
           porate a copy of the NOT which is in the main verb phrase or
           the pre-verbal indefinite into the main verb phrase (if it is
           not there already) and all indefinites after the main verb
           phrase, but leave the original NOT intact.*

This rule allows (or places) the negative element on the indefinite before
the verb phrase to be copied into the main verb phrase and any additional
indefinites that may follow the verb phrase. The effect of this rule produces sentences like *Nobody don't like it*, meaning "Nobody likes it." In
standard English it is possible to interpret this sentence something like
"Everybody likes it" because of the tendency to interpret the two negatives as cancelling each other.
     Sentences in which Rule 3c applies can be found among various speak-
ers of AE:

(86) a.   *Nobody didn't* see him. 152:(625)
      b.   *Nobody couldn't* handle him. 36:(463)
      c.   *Nothin' hadn't* come up. 35:23
      d.   *Nobody* else *won't* move in it, I know I ain't. 36:18
      e.   *Nobody wouldn't* say nothin' about it. 17:21

AE is like some other southern varieties of English and Vernacular Black
English in its application of Rule 3c. It is different from some northern
non-mainstream varieties which do not appear to have a rule like 3c.
     Apparently related to Rule 3c is another rule that is found in some
southern varieties of English and Vernacular Black English. This is a
rule which moves an auxiliary verb which has been negativized to a position before a pre-verbal indefinite. This rule may be given as follows:

Rule 4.   *A negativized auxiliary in the main verb phrase which follows
          an indefinite may be placed immediately preceding the pre-verbal
          indefinite in a declarative sentence.*

The application of this rule means that a sentence such as *Nobody didn't do
it* may be transposed to *Didn't nobody do it*. The negativized auxiliary
didn't is simply moved to a position in front of the indefinite *nobody*.
It is important to note that this is a *declarative* rather than a question

sentence. The difference between this declarative and a question sentence
(since questions also involve an inversion of this type) may be impossible
to determine in writing, but it is quite clear in spoken language since
question or declarative intonational patterns will be followed depending
on the intended usage.[9] We get negative inversion in sentences such as
the following:

(87) a. *Didn't nobody* get hurt or nothin'. 18:(493)
      b. It had this room that *wouldn't nobody* stay in. 45:(175)
      c. *Hain't nobody* hardly believed it. 85:13
      d. *Wasn't nothin'* but acorns on the ground...and *wasn't nobody*
          there. 22:26

Typically, this inversion affects auxiliaries such as *don't* or *didn't*,
won't or *wouldn't*, *can't* or *couldn't*, and *ain't* or *wasn't*. While most
cases of this type also involve multiple negation, it is possible to apply
this rule without multiple negation applying, giving sentences such as
Won't anybody do it or *Can't anybody do it*. The single negative version
is more characteristic of middle class speakers, who would be more prone
to avoid the application of this rule. It is, however, occasionally
found in this form.

In some cases involving the forms *ain't* and *wasn't*, it appears that
the expletive *there* (which may also be *they* or *it* in AE as discussed) is
deleted from the actual sentence so that a sentence such as *Ain't nobody
there* may come from *There ain't nobody there*. If there is an actual expletive *there* which has been deleted, the ordering of the negativized
auxiliary before the indefinite may be due to a process different from
that described in Rule 4. (Note, for example, the identical order of
the analogous standard English sentence *There isn't anybody there*.)

One final aspect of multiple negation should be noted here, although
it apparently is quite infrequent even in those varieties of English
where it has been found. This is the special case of multiple negation
which applies across clauses, negativizing the auxiliary in the second
clause. It has been noted that a sentence like *There wasn't much I
couldn't do* may mean something like "There wasn't much I could do" in
some varieties of English. The same sentence interpreted by a standard
English speaker would usually have the opposite meaning, since the negatives across clauses would be expected to cancel each other. This pattern of multiple negation described by Labov (1972c:193), appears to
occur in the sentence "I *wasn't* sure that *nothin' wasn't* gonna come up
a'tall. (35:23)" The meaning of this sentence, as indicated by the context in which it was uttered, is that the speaker wasn't sure that anything was going to come up. Sentences of this type, as noted above,
are actually quite rare even in those varieties of English which do allow
this type of construction. It has been claimed by Labov (1972c:193)
that these constructions are unique to Vernacular Black English among
non-mainstream varieties of English, but they are also found in AE (although admittedly quite rarely), just as in Vernacular Black English.

We may conclude our discussion of multiple negation by looking at
where AE fits into the continuum of English varieties with respect to
the use of multiple negation. This can be done through a table which
shows the relationship of various dialects of English to each other.
Four main aspects of multiple negation are delimited to the chart: (1)
copying of the negative element on post-verbal indefinites in addition
to the negative element in the main verb phrase (i.e. sentences like
He didn't do nothin'), (2) the copying of the negative on a pre-verbal
indefinite and the main verb phrase (i.e. sentences like *Nobody can't
do it*), (3) inversion of the negativized auxiliary and the pre-verbal

indefinite (i.e. sentences like *Can't nobody do it*), and (4) application
of the negative to an auxiliary in another clause. In Table 29, three
different symbols are used to represent the operation of the rules; *1*
is used to indicate the categorical operation of multiple negation (i.e.
it is used in all cases where it might be used), *X* is used to indicate
that it is used variably (i.e. it sometimes applies but not in all cases),
and a *0* is used to indicate that it is never used (i.e. it categorically
does not apply). See Table 29, p. 115.

As indicated in Table 29, AE is more distant from standard
English than most northern varieties of English and is more like southern
varieties of English, including Vernacular Black English. The one main
difference between Vernacular Black English and AE is the extent of multiple negation with post-verbal indefinites--Vernacular Black English reveals categorical and AE shows variable application of multiple negation.

The Use of *Ain't*

One of the shibboleths of social dialects in American English concerns the form *ain't*. It has become a popular stereotype of non-mainstream English. There is evidence to indicate that it was used freely
by many upper middle class educated speakers of the southern part of
England as late as the turn of the century (Williams, 1975:277). Despite
attempts to eradicate this form, it still persists in many non-mainstream
varieties of English.

Originally, there were two sources from which the form *ain't* was derived. First, it was derived from a contraction of *have* + *not*, where
have or *has* + *not* became *han't*, which became *hain't*, and eventually *ain't*.
As we saw previously, the *hain't* form still persists as a form in AE along
with the form *ain't*. The second source of *ain't* comes from a contraction
of *am* + *not*, where *am* + *not* became *amn't*, then changed to *aan't* and eventually *ain't*. In most non-mainstream varieties of English, the correspondence for *am* + *not* became generalized to include *isn't* and *aren't* as well.
And, by analogy with the form derived from *have* + *not*, the *hain't* alternant was used for the *be* + *not* forms. In some varieties, such as Vernacular Black English, a third correspondence developed--the use of *ain't* for
didn't, so that we have constructions such as *He ain't go to the store*
in this variety (Wolfram and Fasold, 1974:162).

AE appears to be much like other non-mainstream varieties of English
in its use of *ain't*. Along with the alternant pronunciation as *hain't*
discussed previously, it can be used as a contracted form for negative perfect constructions.

(88)   a.   I *ain't* been 'ere. 49:(24)
       b.   I've walked by there in the night, but I *ain't heared* nothin'
            so I *ain't* scared. 18:(365)
       c.   Tell 'em I *ain't* never believed in 'em. 46:(212)

Likewise, it can be used for the present tense negative contracted
forms of *be* + *not*, corresponding to *am* + *not*, *isn't* or *aren't* as seen in
example (89):

(89)   a.   No, it *ain't* no speed a'tall. 47:(38)
       b.   Well, *hain't* that awful? 83:(1266)
       c.   They *hain't* any higher now accordin' that they was. 83:(1139)
       d.   That's the reason I *ain't* a-goin'. 85:(447)
       e.   I *hain't* scared. 134:(329)

While we see that *ain't* is used for the *have/has* + *not* contracted

Table 28

Varieties of English	% Multiple Negation	Number of Categorical Multiple Negation Users Out of Total Number of Subjects[8]
Puerto Rican English		
East Harlem (NYC)	87.4	12/27
Vernacular Black English		
Jets (NYC)	97.9	11/13
Detroit	77.8	4/12
East Harlem (NYC)	97.8	7/10
White Northern Nonstandard English		
Inwood (NYC)	81.0	2/8
Detroit	56.3	No Data
Appalachian English		
Age 7-11	72.8	1/5
Age 12-14	62.5	0/5
Age 15-18	61.8	0/5
Age 20-40	68.2	0/5
Age 40+	53.1	0/5

Comparison of Multiple Negation as Indicated in Various Social Dialects of American English

Table 29

English Dialect(s)	*Post-Verbal Indefinites*	*Pre-Verbal Ind/Neg. Aux.*	*Negative Inversion*	*Neg. Aux. Across Clauses*
Standard English	0	0	0	0
Some Northern White Varieties	X	0	0	0
Other Northern White Varieties	X	X	0	0
Some Southern White Varieties	X	X	X	0
Appalachian English	X	X	X	X
Vernacular Black English	1	X	X	X

Comparison of Various Dialects of English with Respect to Different Types of Multiple Negation

forms and the present tense forms of *be + ing*, we do not observe its usage
for *didn't* in AE (i.e. there are no cases such as *He ain't go to the store*.)
In this regard, its use in AE appears to be more like other non-mainstream
White varieties spoken in the North and South than it is like Vernacular
Black English.

The usage of *ain't* is fairly extensive in AE, perhaps moreso than
some other non-mainstream varieties of English. Table 30 tabulates the
extent of *ain't* usage for 25 AE speakers, the same sample chosen for the
tabulation of multiple negation in the last section. In the table, the
frequency of *ain't* is tabulated in relation to its corresponding standard
English form (i.e. *aren't/isn't* or *haven't/hasn't*.) Figures are not given
for *am + not* since a contracted standard English form corresponding to
ain't does not exist (i.e. We don't get *amn't*).[10]

Table 30

Age	Number ain't	Number aren't/isn't	% ain't	Number ain't	Number haven't/hasn't	% ain't
7-11	17	1	94.4	18	1	94.7
12-14	16	0	100.0	4	6	40.0
15-18	9	1	90.0	4	5	44.4
20-40	15	0	100.0	18	9	66.7
40+	24	3	88.9	5	2	71.4
TOTAL	81	5	94.2	49	23	68.1

Extent of ain't *for Five Age Levels of AE Speakers*

Several observations can be made on the basis of Table 30. We see
that there are very few instances of the form *isn't* and *aren't*; in fact,
there are only four cases of *isn't* and one case of *aren't*. For most AE
speakers, we can therefore conclude that *ain't* is almost categorically
used instead of the standard English correspondences *isn't* and *aren't*.
We note, by contrast, that the negativized contractions *haven't/hasn't*
are more variable in the speech of most of the AE speakers in our sample,
although *ain't* tends to be used more frequently than *haven't/hasn't*.
Finally, we note that there does not appear to be any significant difference in the extent of *ain't* usage by all five different age groups represented here. This is quite unlike a number of other linguistic features found in AE, which apparently are in the process of fairly rapid
change. Despite attempts by many teachers to eradicate the use of *ain't*,
it is found to be quite alive and well in the spontaneous speech of most
AE speakers. While *ain't* usage is socially diagnostic to some extent in
AE, its usage does not appear to be as socially stigmatized as it may be
in some northern contexts.

NOMINALS

Another main category which exhibits a number of cross-dialectal
differences is that of the nominals. This includes various aspects of
the noun phrase, including pronominal forms.

Plurals

Studies of some non-mainstream varieties of English have indicated
there is a pattern in which the plural form typically represented by

-s (or *-es*) in spelling, is occasionally absent. This pattern is well
documented for various regional areas (e.g. Allen, 1971:91). In AE,
plurals may be absent, but the pattern is limited almost exclusively to
nouns of weight and measure when preceded by a quantifier. For nouns of
this type, the pattern of *-s* or *-es* absence is quite extensive for some
speakers. Following are examples of nouns typically affected by this
pattern and instances from our sample.

(90) *Pound:*   a. Ten hundred pound_ of nails. 4:(343)
                  b. ...75 or 80 pound_. 22:(243)
                  c. ...two pound_ of butter. 28:(130)
(91) *Gallon:*   a. ...two gallon_ of moonshine. 20:(462)
                  b. ...three, four gallon_ of that. 31:(246)
                  c. ...so many gallon_. 32:(500)
(92) *Bushel:*   a. ...18, 19 bushel load_. 36:(38)
                  b. I don't know how many bushel_. 70:(74)
                  c. We had eleven bushel_. 160:(304)
(93) *Inch:*   a. It's 41 inch__. 85:(107)
                  b. It's just 36 inch__. 85:(180)
(94) *Feet:*   a. ...a thousand *foot* off the road. 30:(319)
                  b. ...four *foot* through the stump. 31:(408)
                  c. ...three *foot* of them. 31:(466)
(95) *Mile:*   a. ...about two mile_ to the store. 23:(131)
                  b. ...three mile_, maybe two mile_. 23:(145)
                  c. ...ten mile_ to one another's house. 22:(93)
(96) *Year:*   a. ...20 year_ ago. 30:(26)
                  b. She stayed single for 14 year_. 83:(268)
                  c. ...for about some 20 year_. 83:(268)
(97) *Month:*   a. He was about three month_ old. 83:(108)
                  b. ...for three month_. 83:(126)
                  c. ...a couple of month_. 83:(229)
(98) *Hour:*   a. ...eight, nine hour_. 23:10
                  b. ...in three hour_. 22:(253)
                  c. ...in about three hour_. 22:(253)

The pattern of plural absence for nouns of weight and measure is predominant when the noun is preceded by a numeral such as *ten pound* or *two
mile*. It is much more sporadic with non-numeral quantifiers such as *many
pound* or *few bushel*, and some speakers restrict this rule exclusively to
items with preceding numerals. The absence of *-s* also appears to be less
frequent on nouns of time (e.g. *month*, *year*) and is relatively rare on
monetary nouns (such as *dollar*). (Absence does, however, appear to be
more frequent on the item *cent* as in *50 cent*.) There are occasional instances in which plural *-s* is absent following other nouns (e.g. *he had
two pillow* 9:(163), *he heard two shot* 14:(815), but these are so infrequent (less than 1 percent out of all instances in which they might be
absent) that no regular pattern for other types of plural absence has
been found.
In addition to the pattern of *-s* absence with nouns of weight and
measure, some AE speakers have a tendency to regularize those plural forms
which are formed by irregular changes in English. In mainstream varieties
of English, for example, the plural of *man* is formed by an internal
change within the word (*men*) rather than by the addition of *-s*. And some
items such as *sheep* or *deer* have the same form in the plural as in the
singular (*four deer, four sheep*). In AE, items such as these may be regularized. The following types of examples illustrate this process.

(99) a. snowmans 129:(159)

b.   watermelons 121:(250)
c.   aspirins 138:(214)
d.   firemans 157:(1046)
e.   squashes 35:(2)
f.   deers 162:(853)

In some cases involving irregular forms the internal change may be made in addition to the regular -*s* plural suffix, as indicated by the examples in (100):

(100) a.   oxens 85:(790)
       b.   policemens 44:(84)
       c.   peoples 108:(97)
       d.   mens 56:(223)

The regularization process noted above does not appear to occur as frequently in AE as it does in Vernacular Black English. It is much more typical of younger speakers of AE, and seems to be a phenomenon which is age-graded.

We should further note the use of what has been labeled the "associative plural" construction *and them*. In constructions such as *Holly and 'em was goin' down through the river* (52:270) or *Becky and 'em ain't comin'*, the construction *and 'em* is used to indicate those who are associated with the specific person named in the first part of the coordinate construction. This pattern in AE has also been found in several other non-mainstream varieties.

In addition to the grammatical aspects of plural formation which we have discussed, we should mention one pattern of regularization which actually involves the phonological shape of the word. There is, in English, a small set of nouns in which the final voiceless fricative sound becomes voiced when the plural is added. Once the final sound becomes voiced, the *z* form is added instead of the usual *s* form which is added to voiceless forms. Items which typify this set are *wife* and *leaf* which become *wives* and *leaves*. In AE, as in some other non-mainstream varieties of English, these forms may be regularized so that *s* is added to the final voiceless segment of the base word. This results in pronunciations of *leaves* and *wives* as *leafs* and *wifes*.

Definite Articles with Terms for Illness and Disease

Among the various uses of the definite article *the* in English is its function before some non-technical names of diseases. We thus find that *the* is permissible before diseases such as *the measles*, *the flu*, or *the mumps*. While the definite article may be used with these disease nouns in most varieties of English, it is typically not found when the noun refers to a more general condition of illness, such as *toothache*, *stomachache*, or *cold*. In these cases, only the indefinite article is used, giving us *a toothache*, *a stomachache*, or *a cold*. There are also other cases where neither a definite nor indefinite article can be used with an illness or disease, such as *colic* or *cramps*. In AE, the class of illness and disease nouns taking the article *the* is considerably broader than is found in some other varieties of English. We thus encounter the following types of examples:

(101) a.   ...if you had *the toothache*. 163:(235)
       b.   What about *the earache*? 164:(908)
       c.   ...if I taken *the cold*. 160:(421)
       d.   ...when she had *the colic* or *the stomachache*. 156:(375)

e. You kinda got *the chills* or something, that's when you start takin' *the cramps*. 156:(409)

In the above examples it is observed that *the* is found with nouns that take neither the definite nor indefinite article in other varieties of English as well as those that may only take an indefinite article. At one period in the English language, it was much more common to use the definite article with diseases, but a gradual change eliminated it with many types of illness or disease. The article was completely eliminated from some diseases and became optional with others, so that the article before *measles* or *mumps* is now optional in many varieties of English (i.e. *the measles* or *measles*; *the mumps* or *mumps*). AE is simply one of those varieties of English where the older, more expansive pattern of article usage before diseases has been retained to some degree.

Pronouns

There are few, if any, pronominal forms found among AE speakers that are unique to this variety among American English dialects. Some of the forms found in AE are common to most non-mainstream varieties of English; others are found only in English varieties of southern origin.
Reflexive Pronouns. Like most varieties of non-mainstream English in both the North and South, AE may add the form *self* to all personal pronouns. This is different from standard English, where first and second person are formed with the possessive pronoun (i.e. *myself, yourself, ourselves, yourselves*), but the third person reflexives are with the accusative form (i.e. *himself, herself, itself, themselves*). In AE, the possessive form is simply extended to third person reflexive forms resulting in forms such as *hisself* (e.g. *A man hung hisself* 28:(44), *If he'd shot hisself* 17:(699) and *theirselves* or *theirself* (e.g. *They doctored them theirself* 35:(46); *out in the wild theirself* 163:(751). It is noted that *theirself* is preferred over *theirselves*, so that a distinction between the singular form *self* and the plural form *selves* may not be operative with reflexives. (By the same token, forms like *ourselves* and *yourselves* may be *ourself* and *yourself*.) AE is unlike some other varieties of southern origin in that *theyself* does not typically occur as an alternant for *theirself*.
Object Pronoun Forms. AE is also similar to most other non-mainstream varieties of English in its use of the subject and object forms of pronouns. Forms such as *me, him, her, us*, and *them*, in addition to their function as objective forms, may function as subjects in coordinate constructions, giving us sentences such as *Me and him and the rest of the boys gets out there and plays football* (52:(217) or *Me and my baby goes back and sleeps the day* (36:(6). These same forms cannot occur in non-coordinate constructions, so that we do not observe forms such as *Me plays football* or *Me sleeps the day*, as a part of AE. In this regard, AE is quite like most non-mainstream varieties of English. The reference to forms such as *me* or *them* as objective forms is, of course, somewhat of a misnomer in terms of their current function, since their usage has clearly expanded to certain non-objective functions.
We also find demonstrative forms such as *them* in AE corresponding to *those* in standard varieties of English, in sentences such as *Them boys got killed up there at Morgan* (121:(665), *Was that one about them guys* (49:(93). AE is also among those varieties of English that can add *here* and *there* to the demonstrative, giving us phrases such as *this here one* (47:(605) or *this here bonded stuff* (85:(117). In several cases, it was

observed that *this here* became a fixed phrase occurring with both single
and plural noun forms (e.g. *this here guys* 49:(36). The use of demonstratives in AE is similar to that found generally among non-mainstream varieties of American English.

   Possessive Pronouns with -n. One type of pronoun sometimes associated
with AE is the possessive in which -n is added to the pronoun, giving forms
such as *yourn, hisn, hern, ourn,* and *theirn* (see McDavid, 1971:471). This
particular possessive formation is historically derived from the older
English possessive formation *-en* which developed originally in the south
and midland of England. It is still retained in other dialects of English
in items such as *mine* and *thine* from *my* and *thy.* The *-n* possessive formation is found only when the pronoun form occurs in an absolute position
(e.g. *It's yourn, Yourn is nice*), but not when modifying a following noun
phrase. (It is not found in constructions such as **It's yourn house* or
*Yourn house is nice.) Although we do find occasional instances of *-n*
possessive formation in AE (*It's yourn after you done checked it in* 22:22),
it appears to be dying out fairly rapidly, being replaced by the more
current possessive formation with *-s.*

   As a part of the trend toward acquiring the more current *-s* possessive formation with pronouns in absolute position, we find instances in
which the *-s* possessive is extended to *mine* resulting in a sentence like
Most of mines are carnation baby (34:(233). This formation is created
by the analogy of *mines* with possessives such as *yours, his, hers, its,
ours,* and *theirs.* Parenthetically we should note that AE does not appear
to be among those varieties of English that has possessive *-s* absence in
items such as *the boy hat* for *the boy's hat* or *John car* for *John's car.*
Possessive *-s* is present in such an overwhelming number of instances
where we would expect it to be present in standard English, that no case
can be made for possessive *-s* absence from the rare examples in which it
is not found.

   Plural y'all. Like most English varieties of southern origin, the
plural form of *you* may be *y'all* in AE. This is, of course, different
from many northern varieties where *you* is used for both single and plural
second person pronouns.

(102)   a.   One of *y'all* has to go in.   49:(3)
        b.   *Y'all* eat before you go -- eat you something.   84:(115)
        c.   Fonda wants to know if *y'all* want to help *y'all.*   87:(255)

Although earlier records of dialect geographers (Kurath, 1949:Figure 114)
indicate that *you'ns* may be used as an alternant form for *y'all* in this
general area of Appalachia, we do not have any attestations for this form
in our sample. If *you'ns* was used as an alternant form during earlier
periods, it has apparently been replaced by *y'all.*

   Relative Pronouns. There are several aspects of relative pronoun
usage in AE which distinguish it from the use of relative pronouns in
most varieties of standard English. One aspect of this difference concerns the contexts in which relative pronouns can be deleted. In standard English, the relative pronoun such as *who, which, that,* etc., may
be absent if the noun phrase it replaces is the object of the subordinate
clause. According to this rule, a sentence such as *That's the boat that/
which I built* may also be realized without the presence of the pronoun,
giving us *That's the boat I built.* In a sentence such as this, the noun
phrase *the boat* is the object of the subordinate or embedded clause (i.e.
I built the boat). If, however, the relative pronoun represents the
subject of the subordinate clause, the pronoun is usually present in
standard English, as in a sentence like *That's the snake that/which bit*

me. In this sentence, the noun phrase which the pronoun replaces (viz. *the snake*) is the subject of the subordinate clause (i.e. *The snake bit me*). AE is among those non-mainstream varieties of English (usually those of southern origin) where relative pronoun deletion is permissible whether it functions as a subject or object of the subordinate clause.

(103) a. I got some kin people ___ lived up there. 2:(998)
       b. He's the funny lookin' character ___ plays baseball. 114:(199)
       c. 'Cause they was this vampire that killed people ___ come in it. 14:(190)
       d. My grandma's got this thing ___ tells me about when to plant. 16:(191)

As we have seen with many other aspects of AE, we find the regularization of a pattern which is observed to some extent in standard varieties of English.

Hackenberg (1972:114) has noted that the deletion of the relative pronouns is considerably more frequent when the main clause of the sentence is introduced by the expletive *there* (or its AE alternants *it* and *they*). That is, deletion would be more frequent in a sentence like *There was a snake come down the road* than in a sentence like *I ran over the snake come down the road*. In fact, the deletion of relative pronouns in sentences introduced by expletive *there* appears to be coming into some varieties of spoken standard English and is apparently becoming less socially stigmatized.

Another usage of relative pronouns which is becoming more characteristic of standard varieties of English involves the "associative" or "conjunctive" use of *which*. The traditional standard usage of *which* allows it to replace inanimate noun phrases or whole sentences or phrases. Thus, in a sentence like *He goes to the school which is only two blocks from here, which is fine with me*, the first *which* replaces the noun phrase *the school* while the second one replaces the entire sentence up to the comma. There is, however, another use of *which* which does not fit this general analysis. In sentences such as *I went to Cleveland which my cousin lives there* 66:(78) or *I remember the doctor comin' and deliverin' the baby which we were in the other room* 163:(247), it does not appear that there is an identifiable referent in the preceding clause. Instead, *which* seems to function more as a general conjunction such as *and*. The conjunctive use of *which* is characteristic of a number of varieties of standard English, often found in more careful styles as well as the more informal styles of spoken standard English.

Finally, we should mention the use of *what* as a relative pronoun. In sentences such as *It was these two what lives back in the country* 132:(70) or *Anybody what didn't want butter* 85:(90), *what* functions as a relative pronoun corresponding to standard English *who* (or *that* in informal speech styles). While the use of *what* as a relative pronoun is a stereotypical characteristic of a number of non-mainstream varieties, we have actually found very few instances of it in AE, and these occasional instances are limited to older residents of the area.

Personal Datives

In English, when the same referent is mentioned twice within a clause, the second occurrence typically takes on a reflexive form, that is, a form with *-self*, as in *myself, themselves*. This happens not only when both references show up in the same clause in the utterance, but also when they both are part of the underlying structure, with one deleted at some prior point. Some examples are:

(104)   a.   Did you hurt *yourself?*
        b.   They fixed *themselves* some soup for lunch.
        c.   I went to New York to find *myself* a job.

In some varieties of English, including AE, it is possible to use a non-reflexive pronoun in certain cases for the second occurrence of a single referent within the same clause. This usage, illustrated in (105), appears to be fairly common and is often represented in stereotypical characterizations of the speech of these varieties.

(105)   a.   I'd go out and cut *me* a limb off of a tree, get *me* a good
             straight one.   7:(803)
        b.   It was about these people moved out on the prairie and they
             built *'em* a house.   58:(42)
        c.   We had *us* a cabin, built *us* a log cabin back over there.
             146:(333)
        d.   And then you'd get *you* a bowl of ice water.   160(696)

There are certain general observations which can be made about this construction, which will be referred to here as the "personal dative," although its exact distribution is somewhat difficult to pin down. It apparently always occurs as an indirect object where the direct object is also present. There are no cases like *I hurt me* or *We could see us in the mirror.* Personal datives are restricted to animate referents. Although there were no instances observed of nonhuman animates being referred to in this type of construction, it seems unlikely that the distribution is limited to human subjects. Rather it would appear that as long as a pronoun other than *it* (generally used for nonhuman referents) is supplied, the usage is acceptable. For example, *The dog dug him up a bone* might be found, but not *The dog dug it up a bone* (where the pronoun is co-referential with the subject). With the exception of *it*, however, the full range of pronouns was observed.

There is a fairly strong resemblance between this usage and the dative construction involving *for* in English (for those datives where the subject and indirect object are co-referential). The dative relationship is expressed by either *to* or *for* phrases as in (106a,c) and many of these have counterparts which involve what may be called "internal" indirect objects, as in (106b,d):

(106)   a.   We gave the book *to our teacher.*
        b.   We gave *our teacher* the book.
        c.   They bought a new car *for me.*
        d.   They bought *me* a new car.
        e.   I knitted a sweater *for myself.*
        f.   I knitted *myself* a sweater.

The form of personal datives has been linked to sentences like (106f), with the suggestion that the non-reflexive constructions follow the same derivation as the internal *for*-dative, and simply lack the requirement that the pronoun be reflexivized. For example, Green (1974:190) gives a lengthy discussion of the verbs which take datives, and at one point notes that:

> All of the *for*-dative verbs, in contrast to the *to*-datives, may occur with non-reflexive co-referential indirect object pronouns, but only in certain colloquial, rural, or sub-standard types of speech, and for no apparent reason, only if the indirect object is internal.

This observation may be accurate to some extent, but the facts from AE indicate that a one-to-one correspondence between this non-reflexive pronoun usage and its proposed counterpart in standard English does not exist.

The first problem arises from the fact that a number of verbs occur with personal datives in the sample which do not appear to be derivable from *for*-datives in this way. Many, but still not all, could be paired with a phrase of the form *for + reflexive pronoun*, but it is not clear whether these would all be considered datives. If they could be, the reflexive pronoun could not be placed in the internal position to provide the proposed standard English counterpart for the AE utterance. This is illustrated by the sentences in (107):

(107) a. Well, I take *me* a pick and a shovel. 8 :(261)
       b. He done had *him* a way figured out to get out. 146:(303)
       c. She wanted *her* some liver pudding. 152:(60)
       d. ...just put *you* a little flour in it. 85:(70)

The context surrounding the above personal datives might allow the use of a *for*-phrase, for example, in (107c): *She wanted some liver pudding for herself*. The use of the internal indirect object counterpart appears unacceptable: **She wanted herself some liver pudding*. Thus, if the AE personal datives are to be related to the *for*-dative construction in standard English, some extension to include other verbs like those in (107) would need to be allowed.

Another problem with this proposal centers on the actual relationship between these personal datives and the other dative constructions. It is necessary to determine if the two types of structures are sufficiently similar to suggest that their derivations are alike. One aspect of this involves how close the meanings of the proposed counterparts are. For most of the examples found where a reflexive pronoun counterpart was acceptable, the two variants seem to be close paraphrases, as in (108):

(108) a. I finally did buy *me* a coffee pot. 31:32
       b. I finally did buy *myself* a coffee pot.
       c. He wanted some straw to build *him* a house out of. 14:(1382)
       d. He wanted some straw to build *himself* a house out of.

There do appear to be at least some subtle differences in meaning, but these are somewhat difficult to pinpoint. They may be more evident in the example in (109):

(109) a. I shot *me* a pheasant. 2:(540)
       b. I shot *myself* a pheasant.

The personal dative in (109a) seems to vary in meaning from the dative phrase *for myself* in that the *me* seems less the benefactor of the action than the *for*-phrase would indicate. It is possible, though, that this is a more widespread difference between the construction with the overt *for*-phrase and the one with the internal indirect object. Further investigation is needed to resolve this issue of meaning differences.

Certain structural differences show up when the two forms are compared as they combine with other dative phrases and these might have implications for the meaning relationships. For example, the personal dative can be found in some instances with a verb that takes *to*-datives, such as *write*:

(110)   a.   I'm gonna write *me* a letter to the President.
        b.   *I'm gonna write myself a letter to the President.

(This example was provided by Richard Smaby, personal communication.)
The alternant form with a reflexive pronoun is strange and would not appear derivable from a *for*-dative, since, although *I'm gonna write a letter to the President for Fred* is acceptable, the only internal indirect
object possible is *the President*, not *Fred*, as in (111):

(111)   a.   I'm gonna write the President a letter for Fred.
        b.   *I'm gonna write Fred a letter to the President.

Other *to*-dative verbs, such as *read* or *sell*, also seem potentially acceptable with personal datives, as in *I only need to sell me a dozen more
toothbrushes*, although none were observed in this sample. There is, in
addition, the possibility of a personal dative co-occurring with an overt
for-dative phrase. In these cases, the *for*-phrase clearly specifies the
benefactor of the action, and its inclusion serves to reduce, if not eliminate the benefactor aspect of the personal dative. For example:

(112)   a.   He went to the store to buy *him* a present *for his friend*.
        b.   I need to find *me* a place to live for my *family*.

Here, the presence of the personal dative blocks the possibility of the
for-dative occurring as an internal indirect object, though it could
otherwise, as in *buy his friend a present*. This fact makes it look like
the personal dative fills the indirect object function although it doesn't
seem comparable to the reflexive form.
    From the observations that have been made, it seems that there is a
degree of similarity but also some definite differences between the AE
personal dative and the *for*-dative construction in English. These differences may make it inappropriate to argue for a common *for*-dative source
for both the reflexive and non-reflexive indirect objects. They would
at least make it necessary to qualify any correspondence proposed to
account for them. It may be simply the case that the personal datives
were derived from the *for*-datives originally and have had their usage
generalized to a wider variety of contexts with a concurrent shift in
meaning. Further investigation is needed to determine how substantial
the differences are and how best to account for this usage.

Expletive *there*

    There are several different functions for the item *there* as it is
typically used in many varieties of English. One of the common uses in
standard English is what has sometimes been referred to as "expletive"
or "existential" *there*. In this function, *there* fills a slot in a sentence while it contributes little or nothing to the basic meaning of the
sentence. The form *there* is simply used to anticipate the words or phrase
that contribute the basic meaning to the sentence. Thus, a sentence like
There were four students who flunked English is quite similar to a sentence like *Four students flunked English*. In the former sentence, *there*
is used to anticipate the parts of the sentence that carry its central
meaning. This function is quite different from the locational usage of
there, where it functions adverbially, as in a sentence like *He found
the books over there*. The item *they* may correspond to the expletive
there in AE. We therefore observe the following types of sentences:

(113)   a.   They say if *they's* a lotta woolly worms, you know, dark woolly

worms, it'll be a bad winter. 28:5
b. Now *they's* a difference in sayin' a fun ghost story and what
they used to tell back years ago. 28:33
c. Are *they* stories about snakes? 131:(336)
d. *They's* copperheads around here. 28:26
e. *They's* nothin' to keep 'em from turnin'. 30:151

Given the contexts in which these sentences were uttered, it is apparent
that *they* is being used in AE as a correspondence for the standard English expletive *there*.

As noted above, there are several different functions for items that
are pronounced identical to *there*. In addition to the expletive and locative functions described, it may also be used as a possessive. Although
spelled differently, the possessive form *their* in sentences like *It's
their house* and *Their clothes are nice* is pronounced the same as the form
spelled *there*, and the contracted form of *they are*, *they're*. In sentences like *They're nice* or *They're home* is also pronounced the same as
there.

One of the questions that has arisen in the study of various non-
mainstream varieties of English concerns the extent to which the form
they may correspond to the various functions of the form *there* or its
identically pronounced forms *their* or *they're*. In Table 31 (see p. 128)
we present a comparison of different non-mainstream varieties in their
use of *they* for these forms, delimiting four different functions: (1)
locational *there*, (2) possessive *their*, (3) contracted *they're*, and (4)
expletive *there*. In the table, an *X* denotes that *they* can be used as a
correspondence and *O* indicates that it cannot. Parentheses are used to
indicate that the form *they* can be used but to a very limited extent.

Table 31 indicates different ranges for the *they* correspondence in
the various non-mainstream varieties. For most northern White non-mainstream varieties, the correspondence *they* cannot be used at all. AE is
like most other southern White varieties in that *they* can be used for
contracted forms *they're* and existential *there*. The correspondence *they*,
however, is not typically used for possessive *their* in these varieties.
Studies of Vernacular Black English indicate the extensive use of *they*
for contracted *they're* as a part of the general process of copula deletion and the correspondence of *they* for possessive *their*. Vernacular
Black English is not reported to use *they* for either locational or expletive *there*.

It has sometimes been suggested (Labov, 1969:756) that the correspondence of *they* for the various standard English counterparts is due
to a phonological process related ultimately to the general process of
deletion found in these varieties. This process takes place in several
steps, including the initial change of final *r* to a schwa (phonetically
[ðeə]), a loss of the schwa (phonetically [ðæ]), and an eventual raising
of the vowel to become like the form of the pronoun *they* (phonetically
[ðei]). While this appears to be a reasonable explanation, we might
expect a general phonological process to affect the various grammatical
functions of this identically pronounced form, but we have observed that
it does not. If this process was the historical reason that the *they*
correspondence arose, it was clearly restricted in terms of the grammatical forms to which it applied.

In addition to the correspondence *they* for expletive *there*, there is
another correspondence which is found to some extent in AE--*it*. We therefore observe the following types of sentences, where *it* is interpreted to

correspond to its standard English counterpart, expletive *there*.

(114) a. King Cobra 'posed to be 'bout the deadliest snake *it* is.
           17:(1070)
       b. *It's* too much murder. 11:(907)
       c. *It's* a lotta them does that. 10:(178)
       d. *It's* rapids down there. 5:(268)
       e. *It* was a fly in it. 16:10

The use of *it* as a correspondence for expletive *there* is a pattern that
appears to be fairly extensive. In fact, it may be hypothesized that one
of the reasons that expletive *they* does not occur in Vernacular Black
English (see Table 31) is due to the fact that *it* is used so extensively.
It is also found in White non-mainstream varieties spoken in the North
and South. Wolfram and Fasold (1974:171) have noted the extent to which
the choice of this one word potentially affects the interpretation of a
sentence:

> ...This difference in the choice of one word in a single
> construction affects the understanding of a considerable
> number of sentences in normal conversation. For example,
> if a speaker of a dialect with expletive *it* were waiting
> for water in ice cube trays to freeze, he could ask *Is it
> ice yet?* To him, this would mean *"Is there (any) ice yet?"*
> To speakers of most standard dialects, it means *"Has it
> become ice yet?"*

Both expletive *it* and *they* are used to a considerable extent in
AE; however, most speakers show a clear preference for one or the other
as the correspondence for expletive *there* in standard English. Younger
speakers tend to prefer the *it* correspondence while older speakers show
a preference for *they*.

PREPOSITIONS

Although there are a number of differences in the uses of prepositions in AE as compared with other varieties of English, the majority of
these concern limited subsets of items or even individual lexical items.
One of the common patterns of prepositional usage in AE which differs
from most mainstream varieties of English concerns the use of the preposition *of* with times of day or seasons of the year. We thus find many examples of the following type, where *of* typically corresponds to *in*:

(115) a. ...get up *of* the morning. 6:(64)
       b. If you plant *of the winter*, frost'll get it. 56:(94)
       c. We play rummy *of the nights*. 83:(532)
       d. ...favorite places to go fish -- *of the morning* or late
           of the evening. 21:(448)

This particular pattern for forming prepositional phrases with *of* is
quite pervasive among AE speakers of different age levels and different
social classes.
   A number of the differences in the use of prepositions are actually
related to particles which occur as an integral part of verb plus particle combination rather than the prepositional phrase as such. For example, the use of *out of* with *leave* as in *She finally left out of there*
(36:(188) or *We leave out of there* (149:(150) is actually part of the

verb plus particle sequence instead of a difference in the use of a preposition in a prepositional phrase. Likewise, a phrase such as *met up
on* as in *We met up on a snake* (4:(469) consists of a sequence of a verb
and its particles rather than a prepositional phrase difference. Similar
situations may involve the types of particles occurring with certain nouns
as in *I don't know what's the matter of him* (83:(690) where *matter* co-
occurs with *of* rather than *with* or even adjectives as with *enough of*
in a sentence such as *I ain't got enough of breath* (31:(507).

Since most prepositional differences consist of particular lexical
items rather than patterns involving more general syntactic rules, we
shall not detail the lexical differences here. It is sufficient to give
an illustrative list of some of the types of prepositional differences
found between AE and other English varieties. (See Table 32, p. 128.)

Some of the items in the list, such as *agin* and *off'n*, are
characteristic of older speakers only; others such as *upside* or *at* for
to are characteristic of the more general population. Many of these differences simply seem to be regional characteristics which carry little
social diagnosticity among the various classes of speakers living within the Appalachian region. An illustrative list such as Table 32 may be
extended considerably by adding more of the individual lexical differences
found in propositional usage.

There are also other cases where the correspondence between AE and
standard English does not involve different preopositions as such, but
relates to a preposition in some contexts which may be absent in AE.
Thus, an example such as *I lived Coal City* (85:248), which occurs with
a verb like *live* and a following place of location, may be equivalent to
I lived at/in Coal City in other varieties of English.

While many of the differences between AE and other English varieties
concern individual prepositions, there also may be differences in the
formation of phrases rather than in the prepositions. One such difference concerns the type of fixed phrase typically used with reference to
year dates. In many varieties of English, the alternant phrases for a
century date such as 1925 would be *nineteen hundred twenty-five* or simply
nineteen twenty-five. In AE, however, such phrases may be realized as
nineteen and twenty-five. This pattern is indicated in the following
types of examples.

(116)   a.   ...from *nineteen and twenty-five* 'til about thirty-one.   11:(91)
        b.   I believe it was *nineteen and fifty-six*.   31:(84)
        c.   ...somewhere along *eighteen and seventy-one*.   11:(10)

In this case, we simply have the conjunction *and* as a part of the phrase
for specifying century dates.

INDIRECT QUESTIONS

The typical pattern for forming direct questions in standard English
involves the movement of the auxiliary to the front of the sentence.
Given a declarative sentence such as *He was going home*, the direct question counterpart would be *Was he going home?*, in which the auxiliary *was*
is moved to the beginning of the sentence. If there is also a question
word involved (i.e. one of the so-called *wh* words such as *who*, *where*,
when, *how*, etc.), it is also moved to the front of the sentence, thus resulting in a sentence such as *Where was he going?* as a direct question
counterpart of a declarative sentence such as *He was going home*.

In indirect questions, the movement of the auxiliary and question
word does not take place; instead, the conjunction *if* or *whether* is used
while the declarative word order is retained. We thus get the indirect

Table 31

	Locative *there*	Possessive *their*	Contracted *they're*	Existential *there*
White Northern Non-Mainstream Varieties	0	0	0	0
Appalachian English	0	0	(X)	X
White Southern Non-Mainstream Varieties	0	0	X	X
Vernacular Black English	0	X	X	0

Non-Mainstream they *Correspondence, by Grammatical Function*

Table 32

AE Preposition	Standard English Correspondence	Illustrative Sentence
agin	against	I got up *agin* it. 47:(90) ...clear over *agin* the garden fence. 85:(848)
beside of	beside	The river was right *beside of* the railroad. 157:(400) ...a real old guy that lived *beside of* us. 21:(187)
at (with times of the day or seasons of the year)	in	...*at the wintertime*. 30:(74) ...go to church *at the night*. 28:(10)
at (with movement verbs)	to	I just go *at* my uncles and fool around.
by	with	She's like that *by all the guys* that come in here. 149:(1514)
off'n	off of, off	They give us apple *off'n their* apple tree. 73:(494) Take the rim *off'n of the* barrel. 162:(36)
upside	on the side of, on, in	...hit him *upside the head*. 44:(325) ...*upside the jaw* or something. 2:(513)
on account of	because, because of	You should wear bright clothes *on account of* they could be another hunter. I'd say it wouldn't be as safe as it used to be *on account of* so much poison in the air. 163:(159)

Illustrative List of Prepositional Differences in AE

question form *He asked if (whether) he was going home* or *He wondered if (whether) he was going home* where the auxiliary *was* retains its original position in the verb phrase.

In AE, the rule for forming indirect questions may follow the direct question rule. This means that the auxiliary and question word is moved to the front of the clause and the conjunction *if* and *whether* is not used. We thus observe the following types of indirect question sentences in AE:

(117) a. Momma asked me *where have I been.* 1:(379)
       b. I asked him *could I come downstairs.* 9:(473)
       c. We stopped down at my aunt's to ask her *did she want some cucumbers.* 80:(478)
       d. I asked her the first year *was I gonna pass.* 1:(871)
       e. We asked him *would he make us big.* 19:(197)

The formation of indirect questions in this manner involves a regularization of the rules for forming questions, so that the same rules apply whether it is a direct or indirect question. This regularization in question formation actually seems to be coming into standard varieties of English. It can be observed in the casual speech of some standard English speakers, although not to the extent that it is found in AE or other non-mainstream varieties. Butters (1975) cites evidence that indirect questions of this type have been used in certain British dialects (particularly Anglo-Irish) for some time, and suggests that the Irish settlers in the South might have been the source of this dialect form in American English.

It has been suggested (Gordon and Lakoff, 1971:76) that there are some non-mainstream varieties of English in which the difference between the inverted order of the indirect question may differ in meaning from that of the uninverted order. Wolfram and Fasold (1974:170) have summarized the possible meaning difference:

> ...there is a distinction between *I wonder how did he finish the job* and *I wonder how he finished the job.* The first question counts as a request for information and requires an answer such as *I don't know* or *He did it by convincing his friends that whitewashing a fence was a privilege.* To answer *I wonder how did he finish the job* from a speaker of such a dialect by saying *Yeah* or *It would be nice to know* would be rude. But because *I wonder how he finished the job* can count as a statement about something the speaker is curious about and need not be interpreted as a request for information, these latter two answers would not be out of place. In this dialect, it would not be possible to say *I wondered how did he finish the job but I found out later* because one would not request information he already has.

At this point, it is not known if such a meaning difference is operative in AE.

Notes
1. Due to the regular realization of *-ing* participial forms as [In] rather than [Iŋ], we have adopted the popular convention in which these forms are indicated as *in'* orthographically.
2. It is interesting to note that there are some speakers of AE who still use the prepositions *on* and *at* in a broader range of contexts

than is found in other varieties of English. We therefore have the
following sorts of examples from our AE speakers:

(i)   a.   How do you avoid drugs if you were a parent *at rearing* a child
           in an environment that had a lot of that sort of thing?
           (Fieldworker 61:20)
      b.   I'm trying to get him back *on huntin'* again. 159:22
      c.   ...cause there's some things that just really no use *on
           fussin'* about. 148:7

The syntactic range for the prepositions *on* and *at* apparently was
much broader at one point in the development of the history of the English language than it is currently.

3. Morgan (1972) points out that it is possible for certain conjoined
    subjects to act as singular subjects when interpreted as a combina-
    tion, as in *Cookies and milk is Sam's favorite snack.*
4. By "productive," we mean that this is the suffix that would be used
    if a new verb (new as a lexical item) came into the language. This
    can be demonstrated by giving a word that is made up like "crub" to
    speakers of English and asking for the past tense. Typically, they
    will supply the form "crubbed."
5. In most cases, the distinction between a standard and a nonstandard
    form is fairly clearcut, as in *blowed* vs. *blew/blown*. There are, how-
    ever, instances where alternation between regularized and non-regu-
    larized forms exist with no obvious difference in acceptability. In
    such cases, the verbs were excluded from consideration here. These
    include *dived* vs. *dove*, *shined* vs. *shone*, and *sneaked* vs. *snuck*.
6. It should be noted that forms like these, where the subject of the
    complement sentence is the object of the matrix sentence, function
    differently from those where the subject is the same in both sen-
    tences, such as *I have to go* (typically *hafta*). The meaning of *hafta*
    with reference to obligation is also somewhat different from the
    have + Noun Phrase + *to* + Verb construction.
7. In a recent paper, Bolinger (1976) observes that the assignment of
    this rule as a simple case of elegant emphasis is inadequate and
    that there are structural and pragmatic constraints on this type of
    negative usage.
8. Both Labov et al (1968:278) and Wolfram (1974a:168) note that the
    extent of multiple negation must be based on only those items which
    are part of a distinction between post-verbal indefinites within and
    outside the main clause (as in sentences such as *He ain't good look-
    ing either* and *He don't get a second try or anything*) do not appear
    subject to the categorical application of multiple negation even when
    it applies to indefinites within the main clause. Figures on the
    categoricality of multiple negation therefore do not include such
    items that are outside the same main clause.
9. Depending on the placement of stress, it is possible to emphasize the
    predicate (e.g. *Dón't nobody like him*) or the indefinite element (e.g.
    Don't nobódy like him) in constructions of this type.
10. The contracted negative forms such as *isn't* or *aren't* are not the
    only alternative forms for speakers. It is also possible to use a
    non-contracted negative, as in *He's not* or *They're not*. Instances
    of this type are not tabulated here, since it is apparent that this
    variation exists for all speakers. It is not as certain, however,
    if forms such as *isn't* or *aren't* are used to any extent within some
    non-mainstream varieties (see Wolfram, 1974a:152-155).

Chapter Five: Educational Implications of Dialect Diversity

All these years of talking about "meeting the child where he is" have come back to us with interest, for it has become clear that language research is finally catching up with educational precept and, quite simply, it is time to practice what we preach.

— **Roger W. Shuy, *"Teacher Training and Urban Language Problems"***

LANGUAGE ATTITUDES

It seems appropriate that any discussion of the educational implications of dialect diversity begin with a consideration of language attitudes. Subjective reactions to language differences appear to be inevitable. It is a well-attested fact that individuals respond to language
patterns evaluatively based on their reactions to social characteristics
that various language forms may imply for them. When individuals react
subjectively to the speech of a particular group, they are expressing
their attitudinal reactions toward the behavioral patterns of that group
on the basis of the manifestations of language. It is not simply coin-
cidence that the language of socially stigmatized groups is typically
stigmatized and that of socially prestigous groups has a prestige value.
The fact that individuals tend to correlate linguistic differences
with social and/or regional differences is well attested and, in itself,
is not a problem. The problem, instead, arises because the stereotype
interpretations of such differences often have no basis in reality. The
following sorts of characterizations of non-mainstream varieties and
their speakers are commonly found: (1) Non-mainstream varieties are
simply incomplete attempts to master the standard variety; (2) Speakers
of non-mainstream varieties use their language in an unpatterned, unsystematic way; (3) Speakers of non-mainstream varieties learn their
language at a slower rate than children who speak standard dialects; and
(4) Speakers of non-mainstream varieties are handicapped cognitively by
their language system.
Each of these interpretations of language differences can be thoroughly refuted. If nothing else, the account of the linguistic features
given in Chapters Three and Four should demonstrate the systematic nature

of AE. There are often intricate and detailed rules which account for the
forms of AE--just as there are for any dialect or language. While systematic relations exist between standard English and AE, the AE system can
in no way be viewed as an incomplete mastery of the rules of standard English. At various points we have shown the historical relation of the forms
of AE and other varieties of English, and how the language forms have systematically developed. In some cases, AE may have retained forms which
have changed in more standard varieties of English, but in other cases
changes in AE may have progressed beyond those found in standard varieties
of English. In neither case, however, is the development related to mastery of learning the language system or any linguistic superiority of one
form over another.

The claim that the language acquisition of speakers of non-mainstream
varieties progresses at a slower rate than that of their mainstream counterparts is an illusion which, in many cases, is created by the norms set
up for language acquisition. All cross-cultural studies of language acquisition point to the fact that the rate of language development is roughly
parallel for children of different social groups. The difference is simply that non-mainstream speakers learn the language of their community
which is different from that of the mainstream dialect. In many cases,
this difference is interpreted as a deficit. This is true not only on
the level of informal observation, but also in terms of many of the standardized instruments utilized for assessing language development. All
evidence points to the fact that AE speakers acquire the AE system at
approximately the same rate as standard English speakers acquire their
system.

Sometimes cited in conjunction with language acquisition is the
notion that nonstandard English imposes certain cognitive handicaps on a
speaker; however, there is nothing inherent in any given language variety
that will interfere with the development of the ability to reason. All
languages adequately provide for the conceptualization and expression of
logical propositions, but the particular grammar for encoding conceptualization may differ among language systems. This does not necessarily
exclude the possibility that particular language categories may predis-
pose particular conceptions of the external world, or that a particular
cultural conceptualization may influence language categories. There is
no evidence that different language categories will impede the fundamental
processes that are the basis of human thought.

Our insistence upon the linguistic integrity of non-mainstream dialects should not be taken to mean that we deny the reality of social class
distinctions found in language. It is obvious that there is a correlation
between social class and language differences, and non-mainstream varieties
will be socially stigmatized. This social fact exists independent of the
inherent linguistic structure. The important aspect of social class distinctions in language is related to who uses certain forms, not the particular linguistic organization of the forms. Thus, for example, if the
use of multiple negation were predominant among the middle classes and
the singly negated equivalent were predominant among the working classes,
then single negation, not multiple negation, would be socially stigmatized.
In fact, we noted in our earlier description of multiple negation that it
was the standard formation of negation with indefinites at one point in
the history of the English language. Similar cases could be cited for a
number of the features we have described in Chapters Three and Four, demon-
strating the arbitrariness of the features which become socially diagnostic
in language. It is the social class structure, not the linguistic structure, which determines which forms will be socially stigmatized and which
ones are socially prestigious.

The basis for attitudinal changes concerning non-mainstream varieties of English lies in developing an authentic respect for the linguistic
integrity of these systems. We are not calling for a paternalistic toler-
ance of such a language variety because its speakers are "incapable of
doing better," but a consideration of the systematic nature of the detailed
rules governing the system and the historical development of the English
language which has led to such diversity.

Our experience has indicated that the most crucial contribution that
the study of social dialects can make to education is in the area of attitudes. An educator who considers non-mainstream varieties to be legitimate
linguistic systems rather than simply distorted English will be a more effective teacher. Such a person will be slower to make judgments of intelligence based on the usage of nonstandard English, and will be skeptical
of the results of standardized tests which contain aspects presuming the
mastery of a mainstream variety of English. This educator will further
refrain from concluding that a child has a language disorder simply because
his language is not standard. Finally, such an educator will be prone to
spend more time on essential educational skills themselves as opposed to
expending a great deal of effort on correcting phonological and grammatical manifestations that differ from standard varieties.

Given the effect that teacher attitudes can have on student performance, the role of teacher attitudes toward non-mainstream varieties can
hardly be underestimated. Unfortunately, it is an arduous task to realis-
tically bring about such attitudinal changes, given the popular miscon-
ceptions of dialect diversity which have become so widespread. Ultimately, attitudinal change must rest in an understanding that intricate
and detailed linguistic rules govern language regardless of social connotations.[1]

DIALECT DIVERSITY AND TESTING

The importance that mainstream society places on standardized tests
is fairly obvious to most educators. Crucial decisions in the diagnosis
of educational abilities are often based on standardized test scores of
one type or another--decisions that affect children's current and future
lives in our society. Admittedly, test scores are difficult to resist,
given their widespread use by all types of agencies. Standardized tests
are used as instruments that produce objectified, quantitative information of one type or another. Quantifiable scores do show significant
distinctions between various groups of individuals, so that their use as
an objectifiable parameter of measurement can become a highly valued
basis for evaluating a group or an individual's performance. Obviously,
when a test reveals significant differences between various groups in
the population, we have demonstrated something. But the uneasy question
which arises is whether the instrument actually measures what it is designed to measure. Do the scores faithfully represent the domain set
forth by the tests? And, we may take this one step farther and ask what
can be inferred about other behavior on the basis of a test. This would
involve assessing the usefulness of the measurement as an indicator of
some other variable or as a predictor of behavior. These questions deal
with the test *validity* (the former case being a matter of *content validity*
and the latter *criterion-related validity*).

Although there are various aspects of validity that have at times
become controversial issues with respect to standardized testing, one of
the recurrent themes relates to the appropriateness of such measurements
for different cultural groups. Included in the concern for cross-cultural
applicability is consideration for some of the rural, relatively isolated

groups found in regions of Appalachia. In many instances, we find that the distribution of scores among these groups is disproportionate when compared with mainstream populations. These findings have raised several different questions concerning the tests. One of the questions posed has been whether higher test scores from high socio-economic groups reflect genuine superiority of one type or another. Or, do high scores result from an environmental setting which provides certain advantages? Or, do the differential scores reflect a bias in the test materials and not important differences in capabilities at all? Recent research in testing (Roberts, 1970; Meier, 1973; Cicourel et al, 1974) indicates the last question is becoming increasingly important in the consideration of test application across different social and cultural groups in American society. It is also the area in which linguistics can play a significant role in suggesting ways of examining specific tests and the testing process in general.

Although we might look at the general question of test bias from several different approaches, our central concern here is that of a sociolinguistic perspective. From this perspective, we are interested in how language diversity in the context of society may be used to the advantage of certain groups as opposed to others. Our research into language diversity in American English has shown that there are considerable differences in language systems, such as those which we demonstrated for AE in the preceding chapters. Our knowledge of those differences may serve as a basis for understanding certain types of potential sociolinguistic interference in testing. Although we shall examine in some detail the affects of these types of dialect differences on testing language skills, the crucial nature of the testing question shall carry us somewhat farther[2] than the differences in linguistic form which we have discussed there.

Differences in Linguistic Form

One aspect of test interference involves the differences in linguistic items which speakers may have as a part of their linguistic system. The background of this sort of investigation is found in the descriptive accounts of various linguistic systems as they contrast with responses to linguistic items considered correct by tests. In a sense, this is what is done in *contrastive linguistics* where the descriptive accounts of linguistic systems are placed side by side in order to observe where the patterns of a language are similar and where they are different. In contrastive studies as they are applied to different language or dialects, these comparisons often serve as a basis for predicting where a speaker of Language Variety *A* will encounter difficulty when confronted with Language Variety *B*. Although all predicted interference will not, of course, be realized for one reason or another, the comparison can anticipate many of the patterns or items which will, in fact, interfere. On the basis of a contrastive analysis of standard English and a non-mainstream variety such as AE, we may therefore predict what types of interference we would expect a test to potentially hold for the speaker of AE.[3]

Language tests may be used for a wide range of purposes, including the assessment of language development, auditory discrimination, the diagnosis of learning disabilities, reading assessment, and achievement in language arts. In all these cases, the norms called for in the test may systematically conflict with the language system of a non-mainstream speaker. Although each of these language tests might be dealt with in detail, we may most efficiently discuss our perspective by illustration. For this purpose, we shall focus on the Illinois Test of Psycholinguistic Abilities (henceforth ITPA), a widely used test in several different disciplines, particularly in speech pathology and learning disabilities assessment.

The ITPA consists of a battery of tests to measure various facts of cognitive abilities. It is essentially a diagnostic tool in which specific abilities and disabilities in children may be delineated in order for remediation to be undertaken when needed (ITPA Examiner's Manual, 1968:5). Among the various subtests is one entitled "grammatical closure," which was designed to "assess the child's ability to make use of the redundancies of oral language in acquiring automatic habits for handling syntax and grammatic inflections" (ITPA Examiner's Manual, 1968:11). While the manual mentions that the test elicits the ability to respond in terms of standard American English, no warning is given about the use of this test with children who may speak non-mainstream varieties of English. The test is, in fact, routinely administered to quite different dialect and social groups. In the grammatic closure subtest, the child is asked to produce a missing word as the tester points to a picture. For example, the examiner shows a plate with two pictures on it, one with one bed and the other with two beds. The examiner points to the first picture as he says, "Here is a *bed*."; he then points to the second picture and says "Here are two ____.", with the child supplying the missing word. The focus is on a particular grammatical form, such as the plural *-s* in this case. All of the responses must be in standard English in order to be considered correct.

With this background information in mind, let us consider the specific items of the grammatic closure test in terms of the grammatical description of AE presented in Chapter Four. Based on our contrastive analysis of the items considered to be correct responses according to the test manual and the different grammatical rules of AE, we may predict those cases of possible divergence accounted for by the grammatical rules of AE. According to the manual for scoring, all these items would have to be considered "incorrect," even though they are governed by legitimate linguistic rules which simply differ from dialect to dialect. Table 33 on p. 136 gives each of the stimulus items in the test, the responses considered to be "correct" according to the test manual and, where applicable, the corresponding dialect form which would be an appropriate response for AE speakers. In all the cases cited in the table, the legitimate AE form would have to be considered incorrect according to the scoring procedures in test manuals. In each case where the dialect form of AE would be different from the expected correct response, we have cited the section in Chapter Four where this form has been discussed.

We see, in Table 33, that 25 of the 33 items in the test have alternant forms in AE, following the grammatical rules we described in Chapter Four. These are forms which are a legitimate part of the AE grammatical system, but, according to the instructions for scoring the test, they would have to be considered incorrect responses. To understand what the implication of such divergence may be for diagnosis of language abilities, consider the hypothetical case of a ten-year-old AE speaker. Suppose that such a speaker obtains correct responses for all of the other items in the test, but his appropriate AE responses are considered to be incorrect according to the guidelines given for scoring this section. When the raw score of eight correct responses is checked with the psycholinguistic age norms for this test, we find his abilities to be equivalent to those of a child of four years and five months. This, of course, may be somewhat exaggerated, given the fact that most of the features of AE are variable and a particular speaker may not use all of these features as a part of his system. Instead we may arbitrarily say that the AE speaker only realizes approximately half of the potential AE alternants in his actual performance on such a test. This would give him a raw score of 20 correct responses, and his psycholinguistic age level

Table 33

Stimulus with "Correct" Item According to Test Manual	AE Alternant	Section in Chapter Four Where Discussed
1. Here is a dog. Here are two *dogs/doggies*.		
2. This cat is under the chair. Where is the cat? She is on/(any preposition--other than *under*-- indicating location).		
3. Each child has a ball. This is hers; and this is *his*.	*his'n*	Possessive Pronouns with *-n*.
4. This dog likes to bark. Here he is *barking*.		
5. Here is a dress. Here are two *dresses*.		
6. The boy is opening the gate. Here the gate has been *opened*.		
7. There is milk in this glass. It is a glass *of/ with/for/o'/lots of* milk	No Preposition	Prepositions
8. This bicycle belongs to John. Whose bicycle is it? It is *John's*.		
9. This boy is writing something. This is what he *wrote/has written/did write*.	*writed/writ, has wrote*	Irregular Verbs
10. This is the man's home, and this is where he works. Here he is going to work, and here he is going *home/back home/to his home*.	*at home*	Prepositions
11. Here it is night, and here it is morning. He goes to work first thing in the morning, and he goes home first thing *at night*.	*of the night*	Prepositions
12. This man is painting. He is a *painter/fence painter*.	*a-paintin'*	A-Verb-*ing*
13. The boy is going to eat all the cookies. Now all the cookies have been *eaten*.	*eat, ate, eated*	Irregular Verbs
14. He wanted another cookie; but there weren't *any/any more*.	*none/no more*	Negation
15. This horse is not big. This horse is big. This horse is even *bigger*.	*more bigger*	Comparatives & Superlatives
16. And this horse is the very *biggest*.	*most biggest*	Comparatives & Superlatives
17. Here is a man. Here are *two men/gentlemen*.	*mans/mens*	Plurals
18. This man is planting a tree. Here the tree has been *planted*.		
19. This is soap and these are *soap/bars of soap/ more soap*.	*soaps*	Plurals
20. This child has lots of blocks. This child has even *more*.		
21. And this child has the *most*.	*mostest*	Comparatives & Superlatives
22. Here is a foot. Here are two *feet*.	*foots/feets*	Plurals
23. Here is a sheep. Here are lots of *sheep*.	*sheeps*	Plurals
24. This cookie is not very good. This cookie is good. This cookie is even *better*.	*gooder*	Comparatives & Superlatives
25. And this cookie is the very *best*.	*bestest*	Comparatives & Superlatives
26. This man is hanging the picture. Here the picture has been *hung*.	*hanged*	Irregular Verbs
27. The thief is stealing the jewels. These are the jewels that he *stole*.	*stoled/stealed*	Irregular Verbs
28. Here is a woman. Here are two *women*.	*womans/womens*	Plurals
29. The boy had two bananas. He gave one away; and he kept one for *himself*.	*hisself*	Reflexive Pronouns
30. Here is a leaf. Here are two *leaves*.	*leafs*	Plurals
31. Here is a child. Here are three *children*.	*childrens*	Plurals
32. Here is a mouse. Here are two *mice*.	*mouses*	Plurals
33. These children all fell down. He hurt himself; she hurt herself. They all hurt *themselves*.	*theirselves/ theirself*	Reflexive Pronouns

ITPA Grammatical Closure Subtest with Comparison of "Correct" Responses and Appalachian English Alternant Forms

according to this measurement would be that of a child six years and eight
months of age. This is still over three years below his actual age, and
would, in many cases, be sufficient to recommend such a child for remedial
language training. The implications for using such a test to assess the
language capabilities of the AE-speaking child appear quite obvious given
the norms of the test and the legitimate differences found in the AE system. On the basis of a test such as this, it would be quite possible to
misdiagnose a child's language abilities and penalize him for having
learned the language of his community.

Testing as a Social Occasion

Although a primary focus in this study has been the linguistic form
of AE, the extent of sociolinguistic considerations in tests is not restricted to different linguistic items. There are other matters which
take us beyond the limitations of systematic differences between linguistic items *per se* as discussed above. One of the important considerations in any test is the context of the testing situation. Testing, like
other types of behavior, necessarily involves the existence of a social
occasion. The testing process is not devoid of cultural context regardless of how standardized the testing procedure may actually be. Testing
is "social" in several ways. First of all, it is social in the sense
that it involves interaction between the test administrator and the test
taker. Second, it involves a particular division of labor that distin-
guishes the testing situation from other aspects of behavior. And finally,
it is social in the sense that it operates on the output of socialization
that has taken place prior to the actual situation.
     Test construction involves elaborate plans for the manipulation of
the subject's behavior. These plans are first based on the assumption
that the test designer has a viable (though perhaps implicit) model
which can serve as a guide for his own actions in constructing the test.
It is further assumed that the researcher knows the ways in which the
properties of situations might influence the behavior of the subjects,
and how to place these properties under control in the standardization
of procedures.
     In order to promote the orderly interpretation of data that are
derived from the test situation, the researcher has no other alternative
but to presume that the subject can enter and remain in the experimental
frame constructed for the test. In other words, he must assume that the
subject can play the researcher's game. And, if he cannot bring the subject into the experimental frame, then there is no objectifiable way in
which the abilities of the subject which the tester wants to measure can
be tapped.
     The basic issue here, then, concerns the assumption of the "sameness"
of the environment and the irrelevance of potentially different socialization processes which may lead to this test situation. From a sociolinguistic viewpoint, the question at this point is determining the extent to which potentially different historical backgrounds may be in-
dividualistic or cultural. We cannot completely dismiss the individual
aspects which may result in different perceptions of the social occasion
since there seems to be some evidence that certain individuals from all
socio-economic groups may be adversely affected by the judgmental and
competitive conditions that characterize the testing situation. But we
must go one step farther and look at the systematic cross-cultural aspects of the testing situation. For a number of reasons, we are led to
believe that the testing situation is culturally biased in favor of particular classes. The regulation of the testing situation, the social
style of the test administration, the expectations of the experimental

frame, and the expected behavior of the test takers while engaged in the
testing activity all point to a particular class orientation. Those individuals who are not members of this class, then, are likely to be at
some disadvantage when in this situation.

The importance of the social occasion in testing can be illustrated
best by citing the instructions from a fairly typical test guide. The
"hints" for successful test taking given below are taken from a brochure
on taking aptitude tests, published by the U. S. Department of Labor
(1968), but they could have come from any number of test instructions.

(1) Get ready for the test by taking other tests on your
     own.
(2) Don't let the thought of taking a test throw you, but
     being a little nervous won't hurt you.
(3) Arrive early, rested, and prepared to take the test.
(4) Ask questions until you understand what you are sup-
     posed to do.
(5) Some parts of the test may be easier than others.
     Don't let the hard parts keep you from doing well
     on the easier parts.
(6) Keep time limits in mind when you take a test.
(7) Don't be afraid to answer when you aren't sure you
     are right, but don't guess wildly.
(8) Work as fast as you can but try not to make mistakes.
     Some tests have short time limits.

All of the above "hints" are really concerned with the socialization
process involved in test taking. For example, hint (1) deals with the
development of test-taking as a type of social activity into which one
should become enculturated by exposure to the process of test-taking itself. Chances of success on any given test are enhanced by having been
exposed to previous test-type activities, whether they be other tests,
preparatory test activities, or other socialization processes that
simulate the types of activities called for in tests. Or, for example,
hints (5), (7), and (8) deal with particular types of orientation procedures which tell how we are to assess different variables in the test.
Hint (5) deals with a "coping" task in which the test-taker should know
he can compensate for the difficult parts by concentrating on the easier
sections. Hint (7) deals with an assessment of the role of guessing as
opposed to only answering questions of which the test-taker is certain.
And hint (8) deals with an understanding of how the relation of time
should be dealt with in respect to accuracy. Now the interesting paradox
found in the hints for test-taking is that a number of them are theoretically part of the assumptions about the neutrality of the testing situation at the same time that they are admitted as contributing factors to
success or failure in a test. If it is admitted that these hints may
change how a person scores in a test, then the assumption about neutrality
or control of the social occasion cannot be entirely valid.

The importance that the social occasion may have in testing has, in
fact, led some educators to endorse the teaching of test-taking as a distinct, important and learnable skill in itself. While this may not be a
completely satisfactory answer to the problem for other reasons, efforts
to equalize the orientation to the testing occasion do deserve consideration.

Task Bias

In addition to the aspects of the social occasion discussed above, testing makes certain types of assumptions concerning the specific tasks involved in test-taking. The standardization process of testing requires not only that the test be uniformly administered, but that the test materials be understood and interpreted uniformly by the subjects taking the test. The assumption that there is one correct answer is based on the constructor's faith that he and the test taker share a common symbolic background in which objects have only one meaning which is apparent to all. From this perspective, meaning is not negotiated and built up over the course of the interaction, but it is assumed to share a commonness by the way in which the task is arranged.

All tests, no matter what the focus of the particular subject matter, must start with the assumption that the test taker comprehends the instructions (whether written or oral). These instructions are dependent upon linguistic comprehension of some type, so that even tests which do not seek to measure language skills at all still involve language and certain assumptions about it. From a linguistic standpoint, this involves the comprehension of sentence meanings, including the presuppositions and implications of questioning.

The obviousness of the instructions and questions becomes a point at which we must investigate the possible discrepancy between the interpretations of the test designer and testee. The first observation is that not all presumed obvious information is in fact necessarily obvious. In some cases, the appeal to obviousness comes from an inability to design the task clearly enough so that only the intended interpretation is possible. However straightforward the task may appear to the test designer, we can never exclude the possibility of ambiguity in the task. Although psychometric means of "validating" procedures may exist, there is no assurance that this is sufficient. We know, of course, that there are a number of reasons why an individual may not obtain the "correct" response. From our vantage point, it becomes crucial to know exactly why a subject or group of subjects did not come up with the correct response. A subject may give an incorrect response because he is unfamiliar with the vocabulary; or he may obtain the incorrect answer because he interpreted the question in terms of his own common sense; or because his presuppositions did not match those of the test designer. In terms of potential task interference, it becomes important to identify exactly why the answer is considered inappropriate by the test designer but not by certain test-takers. One type of investigation of this is an analysis of errors using patterns that correlate with membership in socially and linguistically-defined groups. However, another investigative approach is available that makes use of the test material itself as data (see Cicourel et al, 1974 for important studies of test material as data). From a sociolinguistic perspective, it becomes essential to identify some of the potential ways in which the task as presented may interfere with the identification of correct responses. We are here concerned not so much with the stated protocol in test administration, but with the subtleties of the task which may interfere with the assumption of "obviousness."

Different groups may share a desire to succeed in their performance on a test, but simply interpret the protocol of "obvious" instructions differently. Take, for example, the simple instruction to repeat something. The first problem we must recognize is that the instructions to repeat allow for more than one interpretation. One interpretation calls for verbatim repetition, whereas another allows for similarity in com-

municative content through paraphrase. The second problem lies in the
assumption that the test-taker can extract from his real life uses of
repetition (which are drastically different) and remain in the experimental frame where repetition is an end in itself. Interestingly enough,
an informal survey of lower class children's performance on a sentence
repetition task showed two types of departures in the performance of the
task (King, 1972). One was a tendency to respond in terms of language
use outside the context of the specified experimental frame which called
for verbatim repetition. Thus, asked to repeat a sentence like "Is the
car in the garage?" while being shown a picture of a car in the garage,
many children chose to answer by giving the information relevant to the
question rather than simply repeating the question. This, of course, is
a reasonable way to respond to a question--outside the specialized testing
situation. The other problem involved a tendency to give more detail
than the verbatim repetition called for in the response. In essence,
many of the stimuli were paraphrased rather than repeated verbatim. From
the children's perspective, the paraphrase had to be interpreted as an
attempt to succeed at the task, but from the test designer's perspective,
the task was not followed as prescribed. Strict verbatim was the avenue
for success in this task, not detailed recapitulation. But suppose the
child's experience suggests that positive value should be placed on those
types of language use which might involve a paraphrase or caricature of
what a first party has said rather than verbatim recall. One can see
how interpretations of this sort would lead to serious misunderstandings
of the "simple" instructions to repeat.

     Quite obviously, task interference may be reflected in the choice of
a general method for obtaining the desired information. The information
which the test taker has to give back is relatively constant, but one
method may tap this information to a much greater extent than another.
Consider, for example, the notion of "word knowledge" as an illustration.
Word knowledge may be obtained in a number of different ways, one of
which is synonymy. The notion of synonymy as such involves a task which
is fairly well restricted to the testing situation and fairly educated
writing styles. This, however, is not to say that the notion of "word
knowledge" is not found outside of these situations. There is ample
evidence that all individuals can give approximate definitions or uses
of words, but it does not necessarily involve the notions of "word re-
placeability" which is a part of synonymy. As Meier (1973:10) puts it:

> A synonym is only one approach to "word definition" and
> involves a quite abstract notion about the replaceability
> of one word for another. If pressed for a "meaning,"
> children (and adults) generally give a story example
> that describes the word or context which uses it appro-
> priately.

     Similarly, antonymy is another method commonly used to get at the
notion of word meaning or relationship. However, the notion of opposition
may in fact imply different relationships than those which the test designer intends when he illustrates the notion with an "obvious" example of antonymy. Meier points out that the notion of opposite may
in fact quite legitimately be interpreted as something which is "very
different." By this interpretation items like "tall" and "far" might
be considered opposites, just as surely as "tall" and "short." Failure
to obtain the "correct" notion of antonymy might then be interpreted
not as a result of an inability to get the right answer, but as a result
of focus on a different relationship. The assumed neutrality of tasks

must indeed be questioned as it relates to different individuals and different social groups. Middle class children, because of their familiarity with specific tasks as they are employed to get certain types of information, would appear to hold a serious advantage over their working class counterparts in playing the test game. Given the fact that testing tasks involve a particular type of extraction from real life language tasks, the only way an equal chance for success can be assured for all social groups is to ensure similar familiarities with the tasks.

Principles to Guide the Test User

In the previous sections we have presented a sociolinguistic perspective on testing. We have also provided examples of the types of potential sociolinguistic interference that may be found in tests. At this point, we may summarize our discussion by setting forth some principles to guide the test user in the consideration of tests.[4] Although some of the principles relate specifically to a sociolinguistic perspective on testing, others are more general in nature. In terms of general standards and guidelines for tests, we would strongly recommend that all test users become familiar with the principles set forth in *Standards for Educational and Psychological Tests*, which gives a much more extended set of guidelines.

Principle 1: *The test user must compare what the test claims to be testing with what it actually tests*. It cannot always be assumed that a test actually assesses what it claims to. With respect to language, we must ask what aspects of a language are actually being tested as compared to what the test claims to tap. All tests which consistently differentiate groups of individuals measure something, but not necessarily what they set out to measure. For example, the Peabody Picture Vocabulary Test, which is widely used in a number of different disciplines, may be an effective measure of a person's receptive ability to recognize the pictorial referents of dialectally-specific lexical items. This, however, is quite different from the general claims about assessing vocabulary acquisition it makes, let alone any indications of intelligence which may be a derivative of the test. The initial question of content validity is the touchstone for evaluating any testing instrument.

Principle 2: *The test user must consider the types of assumptions which underline the testing task*. Tests which involve participation of some type involve certain assumptions about the nature of this participation. The range of assumed abilities may, of course, vary greatly from test to test. For example, one test of language may require only that a child show recognition of a pictorial reference through the activity of pointing. Others may involve the assumption of reading ability and an orientation of a particular multiple choice format. If the assumptions necessary for performance on the test cannot be met satisfactorily by all the test takers, then the test will prohibit the collection of adequate data on the actual test items.

Principle 3: *The test user must ask what specific problems may be encountered by the speaker of a non-mainstream variety of English*. Given the current faddishness of ridiculing tests, it is imperative for the test user to give an account of the specific ways in which a test may hold potential for bias. For example, we have given specific cases where the speaker of AE may be expected to give alternant forms according to the grammatical rules for AE. The demand for specific information naturally requires a knowledge of the dialect in question and available reference works. In cases where descriptive reference works may not be available, the observant test user may pay attention to the linguistic form of an

individual and check his usage against that of the speaker's peers to see
if test performance can be attributed to a legitimate dialect difference
or not.

Principle 4: *The test user should consider the accessibility of
information on individual items in the test from the scoring.* In some
cases, recurrent patterns in the answers of test takers may give important clues as to the nature of sociolinguistic interference. In order
to perform the type of item analysis necessary to discover such patterns,
however, it is necessary to be able to retrieve not only information on
specific test items, including the categories of "wrong" answers. Unfortunately, there are a number of standardized tests where the results
are available only in terms of total scores. This means that there is no
potential for looking at the distribution of specific responses. On one
level, test scores must be considered as important sociolinguistic data,
and there are a number of ways in which the data can be analyzed if the
test user has access to information on specific items. Without such specific information, however, the sociolinguistic usefulness of test results
is minimal.

Principle 5: *The test user should know how to interpret the results
of a test for non-mainstream speakers.* Given the possible ways in which
a test may systematically favor certain groups, it becomes essential to
know how the results from a given test must be interpreted. For example,
it is important to know what a raw score of 8 out of 33 correct responses
on the ITPA grammatic closure subtest may mean for the AE speaker who
systematically uses legitimate AE alternants for many of the items which
would have to be scored incorrect according to the directions for scoring
in the test manual. The language capabilities of such a speaker may be
very different from that of the speaker of the mainstream variety who
obtains a score of 8 or the AE speaker who obtains a low score not because
of the AE alternants but because he has a genuine language disability.

Principle 6: *The test user must know what justifiable classifications
and assessments can be made in light of the test's potential for sociolinguistic bias.* Ultimately, the use of test results in the decision-making
process is the most crucial aspect for the test user to consider. Given
the potential for bias that many tests hold, the test user must proceed
with extreme caution in accepting diagnoses and classifications based on
test scores. In fact, it is reasonable to suggest that no diagnosis or
classification of language capabilities should be made solely on the basis
of a standardized test score. Evidence from tests must be coupled with
other types of data, including observations outside of the testing situation. Ultimately, attention must be given to the individual's use of
language in a number of different social settings before any decision
can be made regarding a child's language capabilities.

An Illustrative Case

The principles set forth above may be illustrated by turning again
to an actual test. For illustrative purposes, we have chosen the language skills subtest of the California Achievement Test (1963) which has
fairly wide distribution in various sections of the United States. We
observe that the California Achievement Test is designed "for the measurement, evaluation, and diagnosis of school achievement" (CAT Manual,
1963:2). While this is what the test claims to be measuring with reference to language, the language subtest turns out, for the most part, to
be a test in the recognition of written standard English sentences.[5]
This recognition may or may not be related to skills achieved in school.
For the speaker of a non-mainstream variety who is being taught standard
English in school, it might relate to school achievement; however, for

the speaker of a mainstream variety who comes to school speaking a main-stream variety, it has no direct relation to what is being learned in the schools. There is, then, a discrepancy between what the test claims to be testing and what it actually assesses for different groups of speakers (Principle 1).

The test makes two important assumptions about the test-taker's par-ticipation in the task (Principle 2). For one, it assumes reading ability. Although the recognition of standard English may exist independent of reading, it cannot be tapped here unless the child can read. Furthermore, the test presumes familiarity in a mutually exclusive response format such

as *He* $\left\{ \begin{matrix} are \\ is \end{matrix} \right\}$ *my cousin.* One additional point in terms of the task involves

the instructions to "make an *X* on the one you think is correct in each sentence." This direction requires that a child extract from the typical real-life situation, where the *X* is used to cross out wrong answers.

The specific items which may vary in this test for the AE speaker as opposed to that of the speaker of a mainstream variety are seen on p. 144 in Table 34 (Principle 3). In this case, the answers considered correct according to the test manual are italicized. In those cases where an alternant form would be acceptable according to the rules of AE, we have listed the section in Chapter Four where the particular rule is discussed.

Of the 25 items in the test, there are 15 in which the alternant form in the list of choices is a legitimate AE linguistic item. In these 15 cases, the AE speaker who intuitively follows the rules of his dialect will obtain answers which would be marked incorrect. The speaker of a mainstream variety, however, should obtain correct responses here simply by following intuitively the rules of his dialect.

The scoring of the test may provide a breakdown in terms of the individual items if hand-scored (Principle 4). It is unclear if the alternate procedure involving machine scoring allows for the retrieval of answers to individual items, but such information would appear neces-sary to see how much influence the speaker's intuitive rules of AE may actually have on his answers.

The interpretation of results for the speaker of a non-mainstream variety can best be done by comparison with what the results may mean for the speaker of a mainstream variety (Principle 5). For the majority of items, the mainstream dialect speakers are tested on the recognition of their mainstream dialect rules in writing. Following their intuitions in terms of the rules they have acquired from their community, they should obtain correct responses without assistance from the school. For speakers of a non-mainstream variety, however, it measures the ability to recognize written standard English, a dialect different from the one they have ac-quired in their community. Dependence on intuitions from the dialect they have acquired would lead them to responses quite different from that of mainstream dialect speakers. If standard English is being taught in the school, then the test might tap some facet of school achievement in language for the speaker of a non-mainstream variety. It is, however, inappropriate to compare results from the mainstream and non-mainstream speakers as aspects of school achievement, since the test may be measuring quite different things in each case.

In connection with the observations made above, the test user should know what legitimate assessments can be made on the basis of this test (Principle 6). As an indicator of the recognition of written standard English in a particular testing format, it may hold some validity. How-ever, as an assessment instrument of basic school achievement in language skills, it must be viewed quite cautiously, for the results may lead to

Table 34

Stimulus with "Correct" Item According to Test Manual	Section in Chapter Four Where AE Alternant Discussed
1. He {are/is} my cousin.	
2. Can you {go/went} out now?	
3. Beth {come/came} home and cried.	Irregular Verbs
4. We {were/was} told to sit down.	Subject-Verb Concord
5. Mark read the poem {too/to} the class.	
6. My sister {am/is} six years old.	
7. I have read {those/them} books before.	Object Pronoun Forms
8. She {were/was} a nice girl.	
9. He {run/ran} all the way to school.	Irregular Verbs
10. She {see/saw} the cow in the barn.	
11. I {am/are} a good pupil.	
12. A man {came/comed} to the door.	Irregular Verbs
13. I didn't hear {no/any} noise.	Multiple Negation
14. There {were/was} no ducks on the lake.	Subject-Verb Concord
15. I try not to talk {too/to} much.	
16. Is {this here/this} your pencil?	Object Pronoun Forms
17. He {can/may} read very well.	
18. She will give me {them/those} dolls.	Object Pronoun Forms
19. We have {run/runned} many blocks.	Irregular Verbs
20. When {can/may} I come again?	
21. She {doesn't/don't} read very well.	Subject-Verb Concord
22. She and {I/me} are good friends.	Object Pronoun Forms
23. I just {began/begun} my lessons.	Irregular Verbs
24. I have just {wrote/written} a poem.	Irregular Verbs
25. {Isn't/Aren't} most houses painted white?	Subject-Verb Concord

California Achievement Test with AE Alternant Forms

unfounded conclusions.

LANGUAGE ARTS AND DIALECT DIVERSITY

There are several different educational issues related to language
arts and dialect diversity. These include the teaching of spoken standard
English, written standard English, and the role of the study of dialect
diversity as a part of the general educational background of the language
arts student. Although these different aspects are inter-related in many
ways, we shall discuss them separately here.

Spoken Standard English

One of the most controversial educational issues related to the study
of non-mainstream varieties concerns the teaching of spoken standard
English. Many linguists and educators hold strong convictions about this
issue. There appear to be essentially two dimensions of this controversy,
one relating to the philosophical position on whether standard English
should be taught and the other relating to the reality of the prospects
for success in teaching spoken standard English.

There are several different goals that an educator may have in teaching standard English. One possible goal, which has fairly solid historical roots, has become known as *eradicationism*. The goal of eradicationism
is to eliminate the various phonological and grammatical forms that are
socially stigmatized replacing them with their standard English counterparts. For example, eradicating such features for AE speakers would involve an attempt to eliminate the use of multiple negatives, various AE
patterns of irregular verbs, or perfective *done*. At the same time, the
goal would be to replace each one with its standard English correspondence.
In many cases, the motivation for this position is based on the conviction
that nonstandard forms are simply corruptions of standard English that
lead to cognitive deficits and learning disabilities. The indefensibility
of this view as discussed previously weakens the position of eradicationism
from the perspective of most linguists. A different incentive for this
position comes from the premise that nonstandard English forms, although
they are linguistically and cognitively the equal of their standard
English counterparts, still confer a social stigma on their speakers.
For this reason, some educators feel that such features should be eliminated in order to allow the student the full opportunity to enter mainstream society. In this case, the position is not advocated on the
basis of a belief in the linguistic inferiority of non-mainstream varieties, but rather as a means of accommodating the "social realities"
of our society. It should be noted, however, that such accommodation
assumes the inevitability of existent language prejudices, and is
therefore open to question on this basis.

An alternative to eradicationism is *bidialectalism*. In bidialectalism, standard English is taught, but with no effort to eradicate the
student's non-mainstream variety. At the end of the teaching process,
the student ideally would be able to use either standard or nonstandard
forms as the situation required. Bidialectalism overtly rejects the
notion that nonstandard English forms are inherently inferior, but like
eradicationism, it does assume that the social stigmatization of nonstandard English is both significant and inevitable. Some object to
this position because it accepts the existent linguistic prejudices of
American society while others have questioned bidialectalism on the
basis that it often has the same end result as eradicationism rather
than achieving the espoused goal of co-existent varieties appropriate
for different situations.

The third alternative is to maintain non-mainstream dialects with no
attempt to teach standard English either as a replacement for the non-mainstream variety or as an addition to it. This position has been set forth
most strongly in two articles by Sledd (1969; 1972). Sledd maintains that
attention should be devoted to an attack on the negative language attitudes
of those who impose their linguistic prejudices on others. While some support this moral ideal, there are those who point out that attitudinal
change is often slow and incomplete. Meanwhile, those who are penalized
on the basis of their speech are asked to bide their time until society
changes its attitude toward them. The practical consequences for the
speaker of a non-mainstream variety, given current language attitudes,
may not be justified in terms of the moral ideal.

Various arguments could, of course, be extended in favor of or in
opposition to each of the positions given above. Our purpose here is not
to be exhaustive in our treatment, but simply to set forth the possible
alternatives. It should, however, be noted that there is no "safe" position among the alternatives. Advocates of eradicationism face the ire
of many who accept the legitimacy of non-mainstream varieties. To endorse bidialectalism invites the criticism of traditional educators and
language purists on the one hand, and on the other hand evokes objections
from the more outspoken critics for compromising moral ideals for the
sake of "social reality." And, the position that standard English should
not be taught brings strong opposition from those who, for one reason or
another, believe in the importance of knowing standard English in our
society.

Even if we take the position that standard English should be taught
for one reason or another, we are still faced with the question of how
successful we can expect to be in teaching it. Past history seems to
indicate that there is considerable reason for pessimism. It is quite
possible to come to the conclusion that the influence of the school
teacher with respect to the teaching standard English is minimal at best.
Speakers who start out speaking a variety of non-mainstream English but
then find it necessary to use standard English will learn it. On the
other hand, many students have been quite resilient in resisting the
attempts of the school to teach them standard English. The reason is
that learning spoken language is different from some other types of
learning and it cannot be brought about with methods and materials alone.
It appears that the desire on the part of the learner to become a member
of the group represented by the speakers of the new language variety is
a crucial motivational factor in learning success. Herman (1961:162-163)
notes:

> If, as our analysis would indicate, group references
> play an important part in the choice of a language,
> it would follow that the readiness of a person to
> learn and use a second language may depend in part
> on the measure of his willingness to identify with
> the group with which the language is associated--
> or, at any rate, on his desire to reduce the social
> distance between himself and that group.

Language learning is somewhat different from other types of learning
in that it depends very heavily on a psychological factor of group reference. If this motivation is present, non-mainstream dialect speakers
can be expected to learn standard English, with or without formal teaching. After all, the schools, in one form or another, have attempted to
teach standard English, but for some time, it is only those individuals
from non-mainstream groups who are upwardly mobile in their social status

or aspirations who consistently learn and use standard English forms.

If the group reference factor is present and the student is oriented toward learning standard English, a well-designed program may aid in guiding a student toward this goal. There are various methodologies which have proposed, including the utilization of techniques developed by linguists for teaching foreign languages to speakers of English. (For a summary of one such technique, see Feigenbaum, 1969; 1970). Rather than detail here the various types of methodologies which might be used, it is more appropriate to set forth some guidelines that may serve as a basis for the development of adequate strategies for teaching standard English.

1. *The teaching of standard English must take into account the importance of the group reference factor*. As mentioned above, the group reference factor may be the most essential variable in the success of teaching spoken standard English. This is, unfortunately, the most difficult aspect to incorporate into materials since it is so dependent upon social relation networks and aspirations often not under the control of the formal educational system. Efforts to motivate students in terms of future employment opportunities are often illusionary and pretentious. In many cases, the motivational factor must be assumed before the formal teaching of standard English begins. Because of this assumption, there are some educators who feel that formal instruction in standard English should be an optional rather than an obligatory part of a school curriculum. In this way, systematic instruction is provided for students who want to learn standard English while those who feel no need for it are not subjected to a curriculum that would probably be ineffectual for them anyway.

2. *The goals for teaching spoken standard English should be clearly recognized in the teaching program*. It is essential to keep the goals clearly in the forefront in establishing an effective program for teaching standard English. The curriculum should be reflective of the goal both philosophically and methodologically. If, for example, the goal is bidialectalism rather than eradicationism, then such an approach must be formally integrated into the materials. It is questionable whether a program can be effective in terms of bidialectalism if all the materials are structured unidirectionally; that is with all of the exercises involving some type of translation from the nonstandard to the standard form. In such a case, the materials may end up looking like they endorse eradicationism even if the overtly stated goal is bidialectalism. One of the innovations of Feigenbaum's materials (Feigenbaum, 1970) is the active use of strategies which require both the teacher and student to use nonstandard forms in the course of the exercises, so that the translation exercises flow in both directions.

The goals of the curriculum must also consider the appropriateness of language usage in terms of the nonstandard and standard English forms. Just as there are contexts in which standard English is appropriate, there are contexts in which a non-mainstream variety is appropriate. The teaching of standard English must be fully cognizant of this contextual sensitivity and include it as a part of the teaching strategy. Although there may be a number of different methods by which learning activities toward this goal can be structured (e.g. role playing, setting up different contexts of real life situations), the integration of this sensitivity into the curriculum is crucial.

3. *The teaching of standard English should be coupled with information on the nature of dialect diversity*. Students should know that the reason they are learning standard English is not related to any linguistic inadequacy of their own system or their failure to learn the English language. They should be taught about the systematic structure of their own

language system and the patterned nature of language differences. Speakers of a non-mainstream variety should be given the social basis for learning an alternative system instead of a fallacious linguistic reason.

4. *The teaching of standard English should be based on an under-standing of the sytematic differences between the standard and nonstandard forms.* Materials will be most effective if they are based on a knowledge of the relationship between the features of the mainstream variety and its non-mainstream counterpart. For example, any attempt to teach a main-stream alternative to AE should start with a knowledge of the systematic differences between the varieties, such as those described in Chapters Three and Four. An understanding of the similarities and differences in the rules of the varieties provides important input into the construction of materials.

Consideration of linguistic differences in rules may also be an im-portant factor in ordering the materials with respect to the teaching of different features. For example, Wolfram (1970a) has suggested that stand-ard English teaching should start, other things being equal, with those rules which are more general in their effect rather than those affecting restricted sets or individual lexical items. An understanding of the sys-tematic differences between the standard and nonstandard forms can help eliminate many of the unnecessary features which are focused on in some current materials as well as assist in the consideration of priorities in terms of the teaching of various standard English forms.

5. *The variety of spoken standard English taught should be real-istic in terms of the language norms of the community.* The variety of standard English which is taught should reflect the local community norms. That is, the basis of any instruction should be the informal standard English norm of the regional variety rather than a formal standard English not actually used in the region. It must be remembered that some aspects of social diagnosticity are quite sensitive to regional differences. Teaching should focus on items that are socially stigmatized within the particular region rather than some of the regional characteristics which may carry minimal social stigma. Grammatical variables are more prone to have general social significance in terms of different regions of the United States, and therefore, should probably be given priority over those phonological and lexical differences which tend to be more regional-ly sensitive.

Although other guidelines might be added to those given above, the essential factor which emerges from these principles is the serious con-sideration that must be given to the teaching of standard English. If it is to be taught, a number of important issues must be dealt with in order to improve the prospect for success. It is not a subject which can be taught as a haphazard and tangential adjunct to other subject matter. If it is treated incidentally in connection with other education skills such as math, science, reading, and so forth, the failure of students to speak standard English may become an unnecessary obstacle to the acquisition of more central education skills.

Written Standard English

In the consideration of written standard English, it is important to look carefully at the needs of students in different types of writing situations. There are some situations, such as in a personal letter to a peer or family member, where it may be unnecessary to insist on written standard English in every detail. However, in most "official" situations such as filling out forms, composing business letters, etc., the ability to write standard English can be important, and so developing this ability is an appropriate goal for a language arts teacher to set for students. Even those most adamantly opposed to teaching spoken standard English would concede this requirement.

In the process of teaching written standard English, it is useful for the teacher to be able to distinguish between three different types of problems in writing. First of all, there are problems in organization and the logical progression of an argument or narration. This type of problem is, at some point, quite common to practically everyone who learns how to write and is not related to dialect differences as such. The writing process, although a derivative of speaking, is in some respects quite different from speaking and certain problems may be related to this difference. There are, for example, different stylistic conventions which characterize writing in contrast with speaking. There is also a different type of editing process which results from the visual representation of speech as opposed to the auditory editing process of spoken language. The progression of writing vis-a-vis speaking also involves a different rate of speed. For example, writing takes somewhat longer to produce than speaking in most instances, and this may cause certain types of problems for the beginning writer. There may be a tendency to "jump ahead" in the progression of writing since the time taken to write down one sentence may put a writer several thoughts ahead of what he is actually writing. These sorts of problems, however, are characteristic of the inherent difference between the written and spoken message and can affect anyone learning to write, regardless of the variety of language spoken.

Other difficulties may stem from the mechanical aspects of learning how to write. Certain types of errors in spelling, punctuation, and grammar may not be traceable to any difference in the spoken variety of a language, but are simply part of the arbitrary, but conventional usage of certain mechanisms in writing. For example, the system of capitalization in English writing, the use of periods, commas, and certain arbitrary spellings are aspects of the English system that any speaker of English must master, regardless of their dialect. Thus, the spelling of *to* for *too* or *laied* for *laid*, the failure to use commas in a series of items, the failure to use quotation marks, and so forth, are simply related to the mechanical aspects of learning to write in English.

There is, however, a third type of problem caused by dialect differences. In these cases, grammatical problems or spelling errors may be based on influence from the spoken language. While formal differences between written and spoken language certainly exist in all varieties of English, the extent of the influence of spoken language on writing may be greater for the speaker of a non-mainstream variety. Viewed in terms of a continuum, we may present the differences between the spoken and written language in Figure 6.

Figure 6

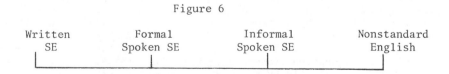

| Written | Formal | Informal | Nonstandard |
| SE | Spoken SE | Spoken SE | English |

Continuum of Difference in Written and Spoken Language

In this continuum, we see that non-mainstream varieties of English would be further removed from written standard English than either formal or

informal spoken standard English, although none of the spoken varieties
may be exactly identical to the written standard language.

In the strictest sense, those aspects of writing related to dialect
differences are not errors at all, but are simply the reflection in writing
of the differences in grammar, phonology, and verbal expression between the
non-mainstream dialect and the standard one by which the writing is being
judged. In one set of freshman compositions written by non-mainstream
speakers, over 40 percent of all items marked by teachers as errors could
be related to the influence of speech (Wolfram and Fasold, 1974:203).
While the extent of spoken language influence may not be this high in all
cases, it must be recognized that the influence of spoken language on
writing can be substantial. For example, suppose a writer spelled both
pin and *pen* or *tinder* and *tender* with an *i*. Although this might, on
initial glance, simply be considered a mechanical error, it may instead be
a reflection of dialect influence if the speaker does not contrast the *i*
and *e* before a nasal sound. Similarly, a speaker of AE who pronounces
once as *oncet* might be tempted to place the *t* on this item in the writing
(see Chapter Three). In such cases, the commonly used suggestion to
"sound out" the spelling might turn out to confuse rather than clarify
the writing problem. Similar problems may relate to grammatical rules.
Thus a speaker of AE who writes a sentence such as *Yesterday it was a man
come in the house* might be reflecting influence from his spoken language
in several instances. For one, the choice of the expletive *it* corresponding to *there* in standard English could be derived from a feature of
his spoken dialect. The use of the present form of the verb *come* in a
past tense context may also be reflective of the AE system with respect
to irregular verbs (see Chapter Four). Finally, the absence of a relative
pronoun is not necessarily due to a careless omission of a word in writing,
but may rather be a result of the relative pronoun deletion rule operating
in the dialect. There is, then, a considerable amount of spoken dialect
divergence which may be responsible for certain types of writing problems.

In the teaching of writing, the first step toward effective instruction involves an accurate diagnosis of the various types of potential
problems. To treat these different categories as one general problem may
confuse the student so that it becomes difficult for the teacher to ef-
fectively deal with the writing problem. Naturally, the differentiation
of dialect influence from other types of writing difficulties presumes
that the teacher knows what the predominant features of the spoken dialect are and how they operate. In this regard, the descriptive aspects
of AE given in Chapters Three and Four may be used as a reference to the
areas where spoken forms could potentially have an influence on the
writing of AE-speaking students.

The accurate identification of different dimensions of writing problems may be a first step in setting priorities in the development of
writing skills. Thus, for example, theme development and the logical
progression of a thought may be given first priority at one stage of development, followed by an emphasis of mechanical skills at another stage,
and dialect influence at still another stage. Although the writer may
eventually need to deal with all types of writing problems in developing
capabilities in written standard English, the eventual goal might be
reached most efficiently by structuring methods to deal with different
problems at different stages. Furthermore, the dimension of dialect influence in writing may call for the development of pedagogical materials
which are qualitatively different from currently available materials.
For example, certain types of editing processes and exercises related to
dialect influence may be different from those relating to mechanical types
of problems. Thus, contrastive drills analogous to those set forth by
Feigenbaum (1970) for spoken standard English might be used for teaching

written standard English.   Aspects of dialect influence in writing may
also be utilitzed in teaching about the nature of dialect diversity and
the difference between written and spoken language.

Integrating Dialect Diversity into Language Arts

In addition to the considerations of standard spoken and written
English discussed above, we should note the potential that the study of
AE has for the investigation of dialect diversity and general linguistic
inquiry as a part of language arts.   In a number of the more recent language arts materials developed for both primary and secondary levels,
the nature of dialect diversity has been given some attention.   Within
this context, the study of AE can provide a rich data source for the
first-hand observation of such diversity.   For the most part, individuals
within the Appalachian range are aware of language differences between
this area and other regions of the United States.   Unfortunately, in
many cases, such diversity is often seen in terms of unwarranted stereotypes rather than as a valid object of study in order to determine the
nature of these differences.   Data from the AE system can provide a base
from which an accurate understanding of the systematic nature of linguistic diversity could be developed.   Both individual introspection and
the collection of samples from other residents in the area may serve as
a data base.
The knowledge of a language is a somewhat unique kind of knowledge
in that a speaker has it simply by virtue of the fact that he speaks a
language.   While much of this knowledge is, to be sure, on a tacit rather
than a conscious level, it allows the potential for systematic tapping
that few disciplines can match.   Examining how a speaker of AE uses his
language provides a natural laboratory for making generalizations based
on an array of data.   In this context, our knowledge of the language can
be used as the basis for hypothesizing rules which govern the use of particular linguistic items.   These hypotheses, formulated on the basis of
initial observation, can then be checked against additional data that we
provide as speakers of a language.   In a sense, then, hypothesis construction and testing as an approach to the nature of scientific inquiry
can be examined through the unique laboratory of language.   While the
formalization of particular aspects of the system may call for specific
training, it is quite clear that accurate generalizations are not the
unique domain of the professional linguist; they are open to any speaker
of a language.   From this perspective, the speaker of AE should be encouraged to use his knowledge of the system as an introduction to the
systematic nature of dialect diversity.
Although the above suggestion may, at first glance, seem somewhat
abstract and removed from the actual situation in the language arts classroom, it can readily be translated into practical language arts exercises.
For example, take an item such as perfective or completive *done*.   In an
attempt to introduce students to the systematic way in which this form
operates, a teacher might ask them to construct sentences where the time
or aspect perspective makes the use of *done* permissible.   This would then
be compared with instances where it would not be permissible.   On the
basis of the acceptable and unacceptable contexts, students may then come
up with a hypothesis which in turn could be checked against the data.
The rules must, of course, ultimately account for all but only the cases
where the form is permissible.   The significance of such an exercise lies
as much in the process as in the result.   That is, the fact that the students provide the data, make the hypothesis, and then check this against
the data is an important aspect of learning.   In this way, students may
learn about the nature of scientific inquiry in language and the systematic

nature of linguistic diversity. Many of the descriptive features in
Chapters Three and Four would lend themselves conveniently to such types
of exercises. In fact, hypotheses that students arrive at may be checked
with the analyses provided here, and revisions made on this basis. While
this type of exercise may appear to be more appropriate to students on a
secondary level, such an approach has been experimented with quite successfully on a primary level as well.

In addition to the use of introspective techniques such as those described above, it is possible to use the linguistic diversity within Appalachia itself to considerable advantage in the language arts curriculum.
For example, language change can be examined through the comparison of
speakers from different age levels. As we mentioned in previous chapters
an important dimension of the diversity within AE relates to age differences. Students could interview older and middle-aged residents and then
look for ways in which their own usage differed from that observed in the
interviews. Here again, we must point out that the expertise of the professional linguist is not necessary to make valid observations.

The use of the community as a base for looking at diversity within
Appalachia may have advantages other than the examination of age differences. For one, it may serve as an impetus to look at the roots of the
English language as it has developed through the years. In this way, the
study of the history of the English language can be a meaningful and vib-
rant subject matter for classroom discussion. Another advantage of send-
ing students into the community itself relates to the preservation of the
cultural and oral traditions of the region. There is, for example, a rich
oral tradition and verbal art which has developed around story-telling in
Appalachia. An indication of the recognition of this art is found in the
fact that most people in the community can readily recall individuals who
are recognized as "good story-tellers." Using such residents as sources
for preserving the traditions of the region could be a rewarding activity
as well as provide an opportunity to look at the art of story-telling.
The qualities that make a person a good story-teller could be investigated
by comparing different individuals recognized as story-tellers as well as
by eliciting comments from the community concerning the characteristics of
a good story. While we shall not detail them here, there are many ways
in which community themes can be tapped in meaningful educational and cultural ways. The success of Eliot Wigginton's *Foxfire* (1972) collections
attests to the cultural and educational advantages of using the community
itself as a primary source in language arts. In the context of the linguistic tradition of Appalachia, there is great opportunity for the language arts specialist to use first-hand data in a meaningful way in the
education of children from the region. In many cases, however, such resources are not going to be tapped if activities are limited to the conventional approaches to the curriculum in language arts. The creative
language arts specialist will have to go beyond such sources in utilizing
the potential of the community itself. Although this admittedly requires
a different type of preparation and some creativity, language arts specialists who invest their energy in such an effort should reap rich re-
wards for their work.

DIALECT DIVERSITY AND READING

As we saw in the last section in Figure 6, the distance from written
standard English to non-mainstream varieties of English is greater than
that to varieties of spoken standard English. This fact naturally has implications for children acquiring the skill of reading, since they bring
with them the variety of English from the community around them and are

faced with a form of written standard English as reading material. The
question that has been raised by sociolinguists and educators is how great
an effect this mismatch has on the acquisition of reading skills.
     The role language plays in the acquisition and process of reading is
an important one. In speech, language rules mediate between sound and
meaning. While the purposes for which written language is used may differ
from those of speech, the reading process must also involve these rules,
mediating instead between visual symbols and meaning. This inter-relation-
ship between language and reading is thus a crucial one and may have even
further implications for the learning processes involved. Frank Smith
(1971:45) observes:

> Whatever the relation of speech to writing, the fact
> that almost all children have acquired a good deal of
> verbal fluency before they face the task of learning
> to read has a dual significance for understanding the
> reading process. In the first place children have a
> basis of language that is obviously relevant to the
> process of learning to read - the written language is
> basically the same language as that of speech, even if
> it has special lexical, syntactic, and communicational
> aspects. But equally important, study of the manner in
> which children learn to speak and understand spoken
> language can provide considerable insight into the
> manner in which they might approach the task of learning
> to read.

     Given the influence of language in reading, we must ask how great a
problem the mismatch between spoken language and the language of reading
materials poses for the child in developing reading skills. This mismatch is present to some extent for all children, due to the characteristic differences between speech and writing. Our focus here, however,
is on those cases where dialect diversity makes the distance even greater.
While it is not yet known what degree of difference leads to difficulty
in learning to read, there is evidence that children who speak non-mainstream varieties of English show a higher rate of failure in reading than
others. While this higher rate is undoubtedly a product of other social
factors as well, it seems likely that language patterns are involved.
(See Baratz, 1973; Venezky and Chapman, 1973.)
     There are obviously a large number of areas of potential conflict
due to differing language patterns when someone is developing reading
skills. For instance, when reading aloud, a very common activity in the
earlier grades, an AE speaker might say *acrosst* when the printed word is
across. If this and other comparable features are counted as reading
errors rather than being recognized as features of spoken language, the
student's reading ability may be underestimated. Frequent correction in
these cases might also lead to confusion on the student's part, since
the task of acquiring reading skills may become enmeshed with learning
standard forms of English.
     Sociolinguists and educators who have considered the problem of
differing language patterns and reading have suggested various ways of
dealing with it. The options basically involve changing the methods or
the materials for teaching reading in order to accommodate dialect diversity. These four alternatives are discussed in detail by Wolfram
(1970b). It is not our intention to advocate any one of the options but
rather to state briefly the advantages and disadvantages each has. An
important consideration in all cases is the need for an understanding of
the features of the dialect before any special measures can be undertaken.

With an inventory of features such as that found in Chapters Three and Four, modifications in programs can be suited to the specific groups involved. That is, materials or methods designed with Vernacular Black English speakers in mind, for example, would not be appropriate for use with AE speakers due to the significant differences between the two varieties. In most cases, it would be preferable to retain programs geared to mainstream varieties of English rather than assuming that non-mainstream varieties were enough alike to allow the same approach for all of them.

Two of the alternative ways of handling dialect diversity with respect to reading have the advantage that no change in materials would be required. The first of these involves changing the child instead. In this approach, standard English would be taught before any reading instruction began, in order to reduce the gap between the spoken language and the reading materials. Then the teaching of reading could proceed, ideally with no problems caused by dialect interference. The rationale for this method takes two very different forms. Those who believe that non-mainstream varieties are deficient in some way advocate it, not only as a way to facilitate the acquisition of reading skills but also to remedy the cognitive handicap such children are assumed to have because of their language system. This interpretation cannot be justified and so any program dependent on it could not be seen as desirable. Other advocates of this position, however, recognize non-mainstream dialects as legitimate linguistic systems. They feel that standard English must be taught prior to reading to ease some of the difficulties there. In this way, the student would control both varieties and could call on the standard one during the development of reading skills.

The proposal stemming from the second type of rationale seems very attractive until the practical implementation is considered, when certain disadvantages become apparent. First of all, teaching standard English first would mean that all reading instruction would have to be postponed for some period of time. This delay might have some effect on learning to read itself and would certainly cause the students involved to lag behind the other members of their grade for a while at least. Secondly, and probably most important, it is not at all clear that widespread success can be expected in teaching standard English. If success in teaching the language forms is uncertain, delaying reading instruction until it is accomplished would not appear to be a desirable course of action.

The second alternative provides for allowing non-mainstream speakers to read in their own dialect (noticeable mainly during reading "aloud"). This has the advantage that it can be implemented immediately with no change in the student or the materials. In this case, the teacher would accept alternant forms from the standard materials as accurate renditions if they represent features of the student's spoken language variety. This approach particularly demands a familiarity with the variety on the part of the teachers so that a clear distinction can be maintained between true reading errors and dialect features. The teachers in this case must also be observers of the students' spoken language to be confident that the features are in fact part of their systems. According to this approach, an AE speaker who reads *There were four yellow flowers* as *They was four yeller flowers* would not be corrected if the teacher has noticed this type of concord, final unstressed *-ow*, and expletive *they* as features of the student's speech. It would, in fact, seem likely that such students are exhibiting good comprehension by interpreting the sentence according to their own language patterns.

There are potential disadvantages to this approach as well although they appear less severe than those for teaching standard English first. Although most of the differences between mainstream and non-mainstream varieties are apparently surface level phenomena, there is a possibility that some meaning will be missed or misinterpreted by non-mainstream speakers when reading standard English materials. Little evidence is available on this point and hence it is impossible to determine how greatly comprehension would be affected if this method is adopted. Also, those who advocate teaching standard English would object to this approach on the grounds that it would not necessarily contribute to the learning of standard forms. However, it is important to remember that learning spoken standard English and learning to read are different activities and, as goals of teaching, should be clearly distinguished.

The remaining two alternatives involve changing the materials to lessen the gap between a student's language patterns and those of the reading materials. Where modification of materials is required, there is naturally the practical disadvantage of cost. Again, it is extremely important to have available an accurate description of the variety in question, as well as some idea as to the generality and importance of the features to justify designing materials around them. The restructuring of materials would also mean that different sets would need to be developed for the various non-mainstream varieties where dialect diversity was found to cause difficulty for students in learning to read since the nature and extent of features different from standard English varies.

The development of "dialect-fair" or "dialect-free" materials, the third option on our list, is probably the less controversial of the remaining two. This proposal basically aims at reducing the problems caused by dialect differences by eliminating, as far as possible, those features in the standard English texts which have alternant forms in the non-mainstream variety. In this approach, a text intended for AE speakers would, for example, have no instances of expletive *there* due to the nonstandard concord patterns it can follow and would avoid using past tense irregular verbs for the same reason. The rationale for this approach is based on the belief that learning to read is facilitated by eliminating those features which would be unfamiliar to the non-mainstream speaker. None of the alternant nonstandard forms are used; only standard forms that are also part of the variety are included.

The major disadvantage to this approach lies in its assumption that it is feasible to construct reading materials in this way, that mainstream and non-mainstream varieties have enough in common to provide for such neutral texts. As we have seen in Chapters Three and Four, the number of features which have alternant forms in a non-mainstream variety can be quite large. To avoid them in composing a text might cause the language of the materials to be very unnatural. For instance, in materials designed with AE in mind, no relative clauses like *I know the people who lived up there* could be used due to potential relative pronoun deletion, adverbs that had standard forms ending in *-ly* such as *originally* and *certainly* would have to be avoided due to the possibility of *-ly* absence and so on. Some evaluation measure might be used, however, to determine a ranking for the features so that only the more important ones would need to be involved. In this way, the gap might be reduced without making the materials too unnatural. Constructing entirely new texts, although time-consuming, might allow for the use of this method. Attempts to alter existing materials might prove more difficult, as Wolfram and Fasold (1974:197) point out:

> Even if the overall differences between the standard
> and nonstandard dialect are significantly less than
> the similarities, the clustering of differences may
> make this strategy virtually unusable for particular
> types of passages.

Neutralization of reading materials with respect to non-mainstream varieties could have certain advantages, however. Eliminating the features that might be unfamiliar to non-mainstream speakers could simplify the task of learning to read for them. Neutralization of texts without incorporation of nonstandard forms also avoids the controversy over whether or not it is desirable to include socially stigmatized language patterns. It would be possible for teachers to use this strategy to some extent without costly revisions of materials by designing certain texts on their own, provided, of course, they are aware of which features should be neutralized.

The fourth alternative that has been suggested by certain sociolinguists and educators is the use of dialect readers for beginning materials. This proposal involves developing texts written in the non-mainstream variety spoken by the students, with a gradual conversion to standard English materials once reading skills have been established. Those who advocate this strategy (see Baratz, 1973 and the discussion of these readers in Leaverton, 1973) argue that learning to read is facilitated if the language patterns of the student's speech are more closely matched by those appearing in beginning readers. An additional advantage comes from the confidence this may give the student with respect to his speech; that is, feelings that it is somehow "inferior," which are fairly common, may be lessened if the variety is represented in printed materials and not stigmatized in the classroom.

This alternative would require not only development of early reading materials written using the non-mainstream variety but also a set of transitional readers which would gradually introduce the various alternant standard forms. An example sentence in a test intended for AE speakers might be developed in the following way, using the description of features in Chapters Three and Four. A first representation might be *They come here about three year ago*. Then, a later stage might add the plural ending, giving *They come here about three years ago* and finally, the standard form of the irregular past tense would be introduced, giving *They came here about three years ago*. Naturally, because of the development of reading skills that would be going on, as well as the fact that sets of materials would be different, the sentences would not be replicated exactly as in this example. A schema for introducing standard features would need to be devised, though, based on an accurate descriptive account of the variety and some decision procedure for establishing an order for the entry of particular forms or patterns at various levels.

We mentioned above that this strategy is the most controversial of the alternatives. Looking at it in a purely practical light, the difficulties of implementation, in terms of developing the materials alone, present quite an obstacle. The strongest criticisms, however, have come from those who believe that standard English should be taught and feel that the use of dialect readers will only reinforce the non-mainstream language patterns, and thus delay the acquisition of standard English. This objection often is voiced by members of the community from which the students come who are sensitive to the social stigmatization of the various dialect features. There is also a feeling that the use of different materials for a particular group signifies some inferiority on the part of that group, in that it is assumed they are unable to learn to read in the same way as everyone else. This types of criticism is made as well by others who feel it is the job of the schools to teach standard English and this approach can only impede progress toward that goal. Leaverton (1973) discusses the difficulty of convincing school personnel to allow dialect readers to be used even on an experimental basis to determine their effectiveness. Thus, the controversy that surrounds this approach is a disadvantage that may be impossible to overcome at this time.

Another problem with dialect readers is the identification of the population for whom they are appropriate. Care must be taken to ensure that these materials are truly reflective of the language patterns of the students, since a reverse mismatch would occur if they are not. In some cases, the texts have inappropriately been used as general remedial materials, for students having difficulty with the acquisition of reading skills when not all the students were speakers of the non-mainstream variety in question. This would undoubtedly only lead to greater confusion on the part of such students. Dialect readers are not remedial materials and precautions should be taken to prevent this type of misuse.

It should be apparent from the above discussion that none of the alternatives provides a foolproof way of dealing with dialect diversity and the teaching of reading. There is as yet no clear way to resolve the sociopolitical issues and at the same time treat the problems that occur in learning to read due to linguistic differences. Much more evidence of the effectiveness of the various approaches needs to be gathered.

There are, however, certain suggestions that can be made for those who cannot wait for this evidence because they must face the situation immediately. An important distinction that needs to be kept clear is that between the goals of teaching standard English and teaching reading. Although a policy decision on the spoken language question may limit the alternatives in terms of reading, the two activities should be separated so that the acquisition of reading skills is a well-defined goal in itself. A first step that can be taken follows the second option discussed above, that of allowing students to read in their own dialect. This can be immediately implemented, provided that the teacher has the information needed to discriminate between reading errors and valid patterns of the students' spoken language. In this way, the task of learning to read will not be confused with language instruction and the mismatch we have spoken of will be somewhat less intense.

Other activities can also be planned to supplement the school reading curriculum. In our discussion of language arts, the community was viewed as a valuable source of a number of possible activities. There are also a variety of applications of these suggestions for teaching reading, following an approach similar to the "language experience" type of program. In addition to having the students recount stories which can then be read back (the most common form "language experience" activities take), tapping the oral traditions of the community can also provide a source of reading materials. The stories that could be gathered by the students would be told in the language of the community and so would be linguistically appropriate as texts for reading in terms of the match between spoken and written language. There would, of course, be additional benefits in terms of preserving the traditions of the area, providing meaningful experiences for the students and generally adding some excitement to the task of developing reading skills. The type of interview used in the present study could be adapted, for example, for use in collecting such materials. A model for this type of activity can be found in the *Foxfire* collections, compiled by Eliot Wigginton, which have met with great success, both in terms of the learning experiences for the students involved and in its value for the community as a whole. It would appear that the model could be adapted to any grade level and would be extremely useful if implemented in beginning reading. The materials would, in a sense, be designed by the students and the community and so would be linguistically and culturally appropriate. This could be very effective in facilitating the development of reading skills, both for the beginning student and the older student needing some remedial work. It would also, of course, be a useful and interesting activity for more advanced readers.

There are certain other considerations that relate to dialect diversity and reading beyond the specific approaches to teaching reading. One aspect involves the evaluation of reading skills in the form of standardized and individual classroom testing. We saw in the previous general discussion of testing that dialect diversity has potentially a great effect on performance on standardized tests, and the implications of this are far-reaching. These comments hold as well for tests of reading since often the knowledge of standard forms of English is implicitly or overtly part of the evaluation. As Principle 3 stated, the test user must consider carefully what problems the non-mainstream speaker of English might face in an attempt to identify what parts of the test truly evaluate reading ability and what parts do not.

Another dimension of dialect diversity that should be mentioned here is the cultural and social diversity that generally accompanies it. These factors enter into the consideration of comprehension (and tests of comprehension) as well as in the concern which is often voiced for making materials "relevant." For instance, an urban student might have difficulty with a story that dealt with life on a small farm, even though the reading of the story could be successfully accomplished. In the same way, a student who had always been in a rural environment might find the reading task unduly complicated by subject matter involving street life in a big city. These types of gaps show up often as poor comprehension skills in testing situations. For example, a common type of question in comprehension tests is something like "Why do you think the author wrote this story?" This might well be answered in a way considered incorrect if the values in the cultures of the test designer and the student do not match. These sorts of problems are ones teachers and other test users should be aware of when they choose to use a test, or use its results for some evaluation of a student. Reading tests are particularly susceptible to this difficulty, due to the comprehension component.

There are, of course, many other considerations and suggestions that could be made with respect to dialect diversity and the teaching/learning of reading. This outline of some of the advantages and disadvantages of alternatives to dealing with the situations is intended to be suggestive of ways in which different strategies may be used and what sorts of problems might occur. Since none of the options emerges as the clear solution, no recommendations can be made at this time. However, programs designed with an awareness of the relationship of dialect diversity to reading are needed to minimize the effect of linguistic differences on the task of learning to read for the speaker of a non-mainstream variety.

Notes
1. For a description of an actual project related to teacher attitudes, see Shuy's (1972) "Sociolinguistics and Teacher Attitudes in a Southern School System."
2. The framework discussed here is essentially that presented in Wolfram (1975), with special adaptation for AE.
3. The prediction of linguistic interference in tests should, of course, be followed up with studies of test responses to observe the actual patterning of interference.
4. A *test user* is defined here to mean anyone who is involved in choosing a test to be used or who makes decisions based on test scores.
5. In addition to the majority of sentences in this subsection which are related to the recognition of written standard English sentences, there are several sentences related to the spelling of one item *(to/too)* and

several sentences which relate to the recognition of sentences which would violate the grammatical rules of both mainstream and non-mainstream varieties.

Chapter Six: Conclusion

The dialect today is a watered-down thing compared with what it was a generation ago, but our people are still the best talkers in the world, and I think we should listen to them with more appreciation.

—**Wylene P. Dial,** *"Folk Speech is English, Too"*

In the previous chapters, we have attempted to give a representative account of the linguistic characteristics of AE and discuss some of the educational implications of this linguistic diversity. We have seen that some of the features discussed are governed by rather detailed linguistic rules. It would be nice if some of the complexities of various points in our analysis could have been avoided, but this, for better or worse, is the nature of language. A more comprehensive treatment of AE would invariably involve even greater detail than we have chosen to include in this study.

In the course of our descriptive account, we have sometimes referred to various forms as retentions from an earlier period of English. The existence of certain *archaisms* is fairly easy to establish in AE if one has ready access to reference works on the history and development of the English language. These archaisms have sometimes led observers to claim that AE is simply a version of Elizabethan English. While such a claim may have a certain romantic charm, it is, unfortunately, too simplistic and categorical to be meaningful. Our description shows that, while certain features represent retentions from earlier periods, at the same time, there are others which are candidates for new developments in the grammar and phonology of English. No doubt, some of the features found in AE today will some day be considered integral parts of the phonology and grammar of standard American English. So the truth is, that when AE is compared with standard English, it is more advanced in some areas and slower to change in others. This is not an unusual phenomenon since differing rates of change for various features is one way in which varieties of a language differentiate themselves from each other.

As we have attempted to point out in our description, the complete set of features that we have discussed may not be revealed in an individual

AE speaker. Some of the differences between speakers may be attributable
to certain social variables. Thus, many of these features, particularly
those which are socially stigmatized, may not be found among middle class
individuals. There are also a number of features which are clearly differentiated on the basis of age. The age variable appears to be considerably more significant in Appalachia than it is in some other varieties of
English. Quite clearly, there are generational differences which indicate
that some of the characteristic forms of AE will not be found in future
generations. While the number of characteristics which distinguish AE
from mainstream varieties may have been greater 50 years ago, we should
not assume that AE will lose its distinctiveness as a variety of English
in the near future. There are still a number of features which combine
to set this variety apart from other varieties, so that the dialect is
alive and well. Naturally, many of the features we have described are
shared by other varieties of English, particularly by those spoken in
different regions of the South, but the particular combination of features appears to characterize AE as a distinct variety of American
English. Under the rubric of AE there are, of course, subsystems which
vary slightly from one another. Ultimately, then, we must refer to AE
as a somewhat idealized notion, just as we are forced to do with a construct such as standard English.

The vast majority of the socially stigmatized features of AE discussed fluctuate with what might be considered to be their standard
English variants. This type of fluctuation follows the general patterning found in other studies of non-mainstream varieties of English, in
which many of the characteristic features are variable in nature. As
noted previously, the extent of fluctuation is sensitive to social constraints such as age, status, and region and linguistic constraints per-
taining to the linguistic environment. This structured variability is
a central concern in studies of language varieties.

The discussion of the educational implications of dialect diversity
in Appalachia could have been extended considerably beyond what we have
done in this study, but our emphasis on the central importance of language attitudes would not change. The educator who views AE as a legitimate, systematic variety of American English rather than a distorted,
haphazard version of English will be more effective with or without new
materials. Such a person will be slower to make judgments of intelligence
based on the use of a non-mainstream variety; he will refrain from concluding that a child has a language disorder simply because his language
is not standard English; he will spend more time on essential education
skills rather than focusing on the "correction" of manifestations of the
child's dialect. Indeed, such an educator will use the dialect of the
area as a ready laboratory for students to learn about the nature of
dialect diversity and how languages change through time.

Studies of language do not end with a conclusion. Language is a
dynamic phenomenon which deserves continuous study for as long as it is
spoken. We wish that we could have studied AE 50 years ago, but are
glad that we received the opportunity to study it when we did. And we
look forward to looking at the development of AE in the years to come as
it preserves some features while changing others. We recognize that the
current handle we have on AE is both incomplete and transitory, but,
again, it is the nature of language to resist a complete and definitive
account.

LANGUAGES

There are no handles upon a language
Whereby men take hold of it
And mark it with signs for its remembrance.
It is a river, this language,
Once in a thousand years
Breaking a new course
Changing its way to the ocean.
It is mountain effluvia
Moving to valleys
And from nation to nation
Crossing borders and mixing,
Languages die like rivers.
Words wrapped round your tongue today
And broken to shape of thought
Between your teeth and lips speaking
Now and today
Shall be faded hieroglyphics
Ten thousand years from now.
Sing--and singing--remember
Your song dies and changes
And is not here tomorrow
Any more than the wind
Blowing ten thousand years ago.

                                    --Carl Sandburg

APPENDICES

Appendix A

Interview Questionnaires

INTRODUCTION

We're looking at what people from different parts of the country are interested in. People from different areas have different ways of doing things and they also talk differently. We're interested in these different things and the way people talk about them. We're going to tape record because we can't remember all the things you might say.

We'll just ask some questions that you might like to talk about, like what games you played as a child, what TV programs you might watch, and so on, but feel free to talk about anything you might be interested in.

Adult Questionnaire

I. Current Activities

1. What sorts of games do the kids play around here? Do you remember how to play them? How about some of the games that you played when you were a youngster? Can you remember them? Tell me about them. (See if they built forts or tree houses.) Other favorite activities.

2. How do you spend a typical day? What are some of the things you have to do?

3. Do you like to watch TV? What are some of your favorite TV programs? Can you tell me about one of the recent ones that you saw? What happened?

4. Have you ever seen *The Waltons* on TV? What do you think about the way it makes out life? Is it a good picture of the way things used to be? Why or why not?

5. Do you like music? What kind of music do you like? Why? Do you have a favorite singer? What are they like?

6. Do you have a lot of family that lives around here? Do you ever get together for family reunions or special occasions, like Christmas, or Thanksgiving? Can you remember one of those get-togethers that was the most fun? Why? What happened?

II. Everyday Living

1. What are some of the things that people grow here in their gardens? Do you have one? When's the best time to start planting these things? When do you pick them?

2. Do you ever hear of people planting their crops according to the signs? How does this work? Do you think it's a good way to plant crops? Why or why not?

3. What season of the year do you like best? How come? Can you remember a real bad winter? Were you stuck in the snow? What was it like?

4. How about floods? Can you remember a bad flood? What was it like?

5. Did your parents have any special things they did for you when you were sick? What did they do for a cold? How about mumps? How about measles?

6. How about when babies are born? Do you think it makes a difference if they're born at home or in a hospital? Why?

7. Do you have some friends who have moved away from the area -- to a big city or somewhere else? Do they ever come back? Why do you think they leave and why do some of them come back?

8. Do you think the area has changed much in the last few years? [Women]

9. Does your family preserve foods? What kinds of foods can you preserve? How do you do it? Do you remember how to churn butter, make homemade soap? (If so, how do you do it?) [Men]

10. Do you do a lot of hunting? What types of animals do you go hunting for? Have you ever heard of any dangerous hunting stories (like about bears or dogs fighting with a wild animal)? What happened?

III. Remembering

1. Do you remember your first days at school? What were they like?

2. Do you remember your first girlfriend or boyfriend? How did you meet them? Can you remember your first feelings?

3. What are some important things to remember when you're raising kids? Are there some things you should remember not to do? Like what?

4. When you wake up in the morning, do you usually remember dreams you had the night before? Is there a dream you remember real good? What was it about?

5. Do you ever remember getting lost as a child? What happened? How about brothers and sisters who got lost?

IV. Tradition

1. Lots of people talk about ghosts. Do you believe they could be real? Why or why not?

2. Do you remember any ghost stories that people tell to each other? (If so) tell it to me. Do you know of any place that they say is haunted? What do you think about that?

3. Are there stories about snakes? (If so) tell them to me. Have you ever had any scary things happen with a snake?

4. Have you ever heard of people handling snakes in a church service? Do you believe these stories? Why or why not?

5. How about healing? Do you believe people can be healed through another person? Why or why not? Have you ever heard of someone who was healed? What happened?

6. Is there somebody you know who's a good story teller? What kinds of stories do they tell? What do you think makes a good story teller?

Adolescent Questionnaire

I. Current Activities

1. What sorts of games do the kids play around here? How do you play? How do you decide who's *it*? Are there any rhymes you say? Do you build forts or tree houses much? How? Other favorite activities.

2. Do you like to watch TV? What are some of your favorite programs? Can you tell me about one of the recent ones you saw? What happened? Have you ever seen *The Waltons*? What do you think of it?

3. Do you have a lot of family that lives around here? Do you get together for special occasions like Christmas, or Thanksgiving? Can you remember a special present you got for Christmas? Are there any other holidays that you really like (Easter, Halloween, birthday)? What do you do?

4. Do you have special chores that you're supposed to do around home? What are they? What happens if you don't do them?

5. Do you have a pet? (What's it like?) Did you ever take care of a stray animal? What happened to it?

For teenagers only

6. Do you like music? What kind do you like? Why? Do you have a favorite singer? What are they like?

II. Everyday Living
      1. What are some of the things people grow here in their gardens? Have
you ever had a garden yourself or worked on one? When's the best time to start
planting?
      2. Do you have some friends who have moved away from this area -- to a
city? Do they ever come back? Why do you think they leave? Why do they come
back?
      3. What season of the year do you like best? How come? Can you remember
a real bad snow? Or a bad flood? What was it like?
      4. Do your parents have any special things they do for you when you're
sick? What do they do for a cold? Measles? Mumps?
      5. So you ever have fights with your brothers and sisters? What sorts of
things do kids fight about? How do fights usually start? Are there any rules
for fair fights? Did you ever get into a fight with somebody bigger than you?
What happened?
      6. Did you ever get blamed for something you didn't do? What happened?
      7. If you could do anything you wanted for a whole day, what would you
do? Why do you think you'd like that?
      8. Do you talk differently to your parents than you do to your friends or
brothers and sisters? How about to a teacher? What do you think the difference is? Do you think the people on TV talk the same way you do? Do you know
anybody that tried to change the way he talked?
For boys only
      9. Do you do a lot of hunting? What types of animals do you go hunting
for? Have you ever heard of any dangerous hunting stories -- like about bears
or a dog fighting with a wild animal? Tell me about it.

III. Remembering
      1. Do you remember your first days at school? What were they like?
      2. Did anybody ever play a trick on the teacher? What happened? What
happens when you have a substitute teacher?
      3. Are there any special things that happen in school that you really
like?
      4. Do you ever remember getting lost? Or a brother and sister or friend
getting lost? Tell me about it.
      5. When you wake up in the morning, do you usually remember dreams that
you had the night before? Is there a dream you remember real good? What was
it about?
      6. Do you have a favorite aunt or uncle? What are they like?
      7. Have you ever been in or seen an accident? Was it bad? What happened?
For teenagers only
      8. Do you know of anybody who got drunk and did something crazy? What
happened?

IV. Tradition
      1. Lots of people talk about ghosts. Do you believe they could be real?
Why or why not?
      2. Do you know any ghost stories that people tell each other? (If so)
tell it to me. Do you know about any place that they say is haunted? What do
you think about that?
      3. Are there stories about snakes? (If so) tell them to me. Did you
ever have a scary thing happen with a snake?
      4. Is there anybody you know who's a good storyteller? What kinds of
stories do they tell? (What makes a good storyteller?)

Sample Informant Interview

INTERVIEW NUMBER 31
(67 year old retired miner)

FW: Okay, what sort of games did you play when you were a youngster?
INF: Oh, we played hop scotch, baseball, ring around the roses, little kid games.
FW: They still play alot of that now, don't they?
INF: Uh huh.
FW: Well, Mr. Hartwick, how do you spend a typical day? What are some of the things you have to do?
INF: Do I have to do?
FW: Yeah.
INF: Oh, I don't have to do much of... I just run around trade their knives, and watches and guns a little once in a while, maybe, and set around the rest of the day and chew tobaccer.
FW: Okay, do you watch TV?
INF: A whole lot.
FW: Do you like it?
INF: Fine.
FW: What are some of your favorite TV programs?
INF: Well, news, sports and *The Waltons*, I like that. And old *Sanford and Son*. Any kind of comedy.
FW: Okay, did you see *Sanford and Son* this week?
INF: No, I haven't this week, I missed that. The grandchildren's home and they wanted to watch something else and I just give in to 'em.
FW: Okay, can you tell me about one of the recent programs you just saw, something that happened on it you thought might be interesting?
INF: Which... of the TV programs?
FW: Uh huh.
INF: Oh, I watch *Animal Kingdom*. And that's pretty interesting, you see old-what's-his-name, that's catching all those animals? He's the, he's the head of that St. Louis Zoo. What's his name? I can't think. But anyway I watch that every weekend.
FW: Have you ever seen *The Waltons* on TV?
INF: Oh yeah. I love that.
FW: What do you think about the way it makes out life?
INF: It's a typical way of life back when I grew up.
FW: Okay, you think that it's a good picture of the way things used to be?
INF: It is.
FW: You think it's true.
INF: I think it's the nearest to the real thing of anything I've saw.
FW: Well, they seem down to earth, don't you think, just good honest people.
INF: Yes, they do. Hard back Hoover times you know, nobody had any money.
FW: Hard working.
INF: Raised what they eat.
FW: Okay, do you like music?
INF: Oh, yeah, play a fiddle a little myself.
FW: Well, good, what kind of music do you like?

INF: Well, just plain old Country and Western and Bluegrass. And I watch
      Lawrence Welk a lot, I like his program too.
FW: Well, he's on every night isn't he?
INF: I don't think so now, is he? He was on just one night a week, that is
      on Channel Six.
FW: Oh, yeah, that's right, he's on Channel Six and Channel Seven.
INF: Well, we see him about twice a week. I have for the last week or ten
      or two.
FW: You know they were going to take him off of the air so he just turned
      around and bought his own network.
INF: He bought it out. And did you see that little girl that, he and his wife
      followed him around and made him listen to a recording and he hired her.
FW: He did?
INF: Uh huh, that last one he hired. They used to be down here in Tennessee
      somewhere.
FW: No, I haven't seen it real lately.
INF: I forget her name.
FW: Well, do you have a favorite singer? Who's your favorite singer?
INF: Singer? Tennessee Ernie Ford.
FW: Yeah, well, he sure is good. Ike, do you have a lot of family that live
      around here?
INF: Oh, yeah.
FW: Do you all get together for reunions or...
INF: Well, not in the last year or two, but we did. There's only twelve of
      us kids a-living, one dead and my mother's living. She's eighty-five
      and she taught us about all, any of us ever knew, that is, until we got
      up to get out on our own.
FW: Do your children come in for Christmas or Thanksgiving?
INF: Well, not all of 'em at the same times. They sometimes happen in at the
      same time for Christmas and Thanksgiving but hardly ever. Usually one or
      two of 'em in.
FW: Well, do you remember one that was outstanding or one that you have...
      you can remember real well that was a lot of fun or something?
INF: With my children?
FW: Uh huh, a family get together?
INF: Oh, yeah, my oldest one, he's dead now, yeah, he was an awful lot of fun.
      Enjoyed life awful well. He died the first of February, sixty-eight.
FW: How did he die?
INF: Liver failure.
FW: Good gracious, did he have children?
INF: Five.
FW: Five children.
INF: Four or five, I believe, is right.
FW: Did he live around here?
INF: Right in Springfield, Virginia, when he died.
FW: Ike, what are some things people grow here in their gardens?
INF: Oh, potatoes, tomatoes, or did you want me to say 'maters and 'taters?
      Tomatoes and potatoes, peppers, corn, and uh, cabbage, carrots, radishes.
FW: Did you have a garden this year?
INF: A small one.
FW: Small one? Do you know anything about when the best time is to start
      planting things?
INF: Well...
FW: How do you plant?
INF: We always planted our corn around the tenth of June or tenth of May, and
      beans in June, tender beans, tough beans a little later on, and, I don't
      remember the dates we plant the cucumbers, but it's always, my mother in
      the Twins, when the sign was in the Twins, she would plant her cucumbers.
      She claims she'd get two for one by planting them in the Twins.
FW: Okay, when do you pick?

INF: You mean gather the garden and stuff? As it ripens and matures.
FW: What's usually last coming in?
INF: Tough hull beans. I'd say would be the last thing that you'd gather.
FW: And it takes awhile for the corn, and the corn...?
INF: Yeah, it usually cut corn in September and October. Or pick it, what-ever they do. We always just cut and shucked ours.
FW: Yeah.
INF: Didn't have any pickers.
FW: Well, did you hear of people planting according to the signs?
INF: Oh yes, plenty of people yet.
FW: You think they still do?
INF: A lot of 'em do yet, yes.
FW: Do you think it works?
INF: Well I never could tell it did, but, they bet on that. Now, I saw a fellow Parks down at Jolo, he wouldn't kill a hog only on the dark of the moon.
FW: Why?
INF: He said if you killed it in light moon that the meat, when you fried it, would turn up around the edges. You've fried it when it would do that? And when you, if you fried it in dark, killed it in dark moon it'd lay down flat when you fried it. And it had more grease in it, in the dark moon if you killed it. And always feed 'em corn the last two or three months before you kill 'em, it makes their meat solid and firm.
FW: What, is that grain feeding them?
INF: Uh huh, feed them corn.
FW: You have to take them in, don't you? Oh, do you think these things work? Planting by the signs, and killing, and...
INF: I wouldn't say that they do or don't, but I don't pay it any mind, I just plant when I get the ground ready and the ground gets warm enough to, so the seed won't rot.
FW: Well we have so much cold weather and stuff you just have to plant when you can. What seasons of the year do you like best?
INF: Well, it's hard to say. There's parts of all of it. I used to like winter the best. But now that I'm older I don't.
FW: How come you liked winter?
INF: Well, you get out and hunt and do a lot of things in winter you couldn't in the summer, 'possum hunt and, such as that, rabbits and squirrels, pheasant.
FW: Well, can you remember when we had a real bad winter?
INF: Yes ma'am, nineteen seventeen.
FW: Good gracious.
INF: That's the worst one I can remember. Oh, I'll tell you that, my uncle lived about a mile from where we did and I sold papers, and I'd have to walk out there and half the time during seventeen you couldn't go the road, you'd have to go through the fields where the wind had blowed the snow off and there was drifts you couldn't see the fence out through there in places.
FW: Good gracious. Were you stuck out in the snow? Did you ever...?
INF: Oh yeah, we'd get out and I never was stuck up in it but we would get out in the snow and romp through it. My dad and me used to go down to a fellow by the name of Burke, barefooted every night nearly. Him and Roy would come up to our place.
FW: He'd walk up barefooted?
INF: Barefoot. They would, to our house, it was about, oh, five hundred feet I guess, maybe a little better. Then maybe the next night we'd go down barefooted. My dad and my ma would play "set back" in the winter. There's a lot of fun in the winter time, sleigh-riding, playing games, and, when you can't get out and do a lot of other things.
FW: Uh huh, do you enjoy fishing?
INF: Oh yeah. Yeah, I used to fish a lot when I was a little boy. Now I got so short winded that I can't. Can't do the walking 'ere is in it.

FW: Uh huh, do you still hunt very much?
INF: Oh yeah, I hunt a little bit.
FW: What do you like to hunt?
INF: Oh, squirrels, and turkey, and rabbits, pheasant, quail.
FW: Well, Ike, is there a special way to cook wild game? You don't...
INF: Well, now I never cooked anything other than coon.
FW: How do you cook that?
INF: Well, I don't know. Some says one way and some another. Now my wife
     just put it on in a pot and pressure cooked it, but I didn't like it,
     didn't like coon but, now all the other I mentioned, the pheasant and
     the squirrel and the rabbit, now I like 'em fried. And the squirrel
     boiled and gravy in it. I'm a sloppy sopper when it comes to eating
     gravy. Love gravy.
FW: What about turkeys, wild turkeys?
INF: Well, you just cook 'em like you would a tame turkey, but roast 'em.
FW: You know that I heard that if you'd cook an apple, put an apple and
     grapes in 'em that it does something to that wild flavor and makes it
     even better. I saw that on *Dinah's Place* last week.
INF: Well, I tell you, we cooked a coon they said put a couple of big onions
     in it and cook it, you couldn't taste the wild, but that's all a bunch of
     crap you can't taste the onion and the meat tastes like it did without the
     onion 'cause we tried it both ways. They's no difference that I can tell.
FW: Is that greasy?
INF: Yeah, it makes it a little bit greasy. Now, I'll tell you what I do
     like. You take a squirrel and boil 'im with a piece of pork or throw
     'im in when you cooking spare ribs or back bones. Put 'im right in
     there and cook 'im with that and it makes 'im awful good.
FW: Well, do you remember any bad floods here? Can you remember when we had
     any real bad floods?
INF: Well, in nineteen and I believe it was fifty-six is about the worst one
     I can remember around here. I believe that was in April of fifty-six.
     I's working in the mines at Arista and you couldn't get to the shop with
     the car, you had to go up as far as the store and walk the rest of the
     way.
FW: Uh huh. Did anyone get killed?
INF: Not that I know of.
FW: Okay, did your parents have any special things they did for you when you
     were sick, when you were small, do you remember any of these?
INF: Oh, nothing more 'n they tried to take care of us the best they could.
     When I was a boy, you know, that's been a long time and, such as measles,
     they had a different way of treating 'em, they wouldn't give you a drop
     of cold water then, but now they want to give you ice water, plenty of
     it, to break you out. And, pneumonia they had mustard poultice and stuff
     of that sort of break it out.
FW: How do you make a mustard poultice?
INF: Well, now, my mother had a coffee mill she'd tighten up you can adjust
     it you know and she'd grind the mustard seed in 'at thing and she mixed
     it with a little flour and, vinegar. I don't know whether she used any-
     thing else in or not. Boy, it'll burn you plumb up.
FW: Do you put onion in it?
INF: No.
FW: Just mustard and vinegar?
INF: And a little flour to kinda hold it together.
FW: Did they just rub that right on your...
INF: No, they put it in a cloth and fold it over, it'd be right soupy wet, you
     know, and just lay it on you, and boy it will bring you up out of there,
     it will blister you in five minutes.
FW: Oh, it breaks up your cold then.
INF: It'll break it up, the congestion.
FW: What about the mumps? Do you remember any different...

INF: I don't remember too much about the mumps. I know one thing, I couldn't eat a pickle. I was small when, let's see, I wasn't but about nine or ten years old when I had them things. Chicken pox, small pox, I had a vaccinate for small pox and they didn't take a good hold of me, I had 'em but didn't hurt me much.

FW: Uh huh. Did you go to the doctor very much then, or...

INF: No, the doctor came to you. You'd just send for him or go after 'im. Dad would always go after 'im for us kids if we needed him, but he didn't believe in going to a doctor ever time you had a pain in your belly. They would treat us theirselves.

FW: Uh huh, and, do you remember anything else they did, like for any special ailment?

INF: Well, nothing more 'n pulling teeth, he had the blacksmith to make him a pair of forceps over at the (inaudible) and if one of us kids 'd get a toothache he'd pull it. And we held back on that all we could.

FW: Well, did he use anything on it after he pulled it?

INF: No, no, washed it out with warm salt water.

FW: And that was it?

INF: That was it.

FW: Did you tell him when you had the toothache?

INF: I wouldn't tell him if I could help it, and see they weren't anything like aspirin or pain killers back them days that you could get. They had it but you couldn't get it and take it oral like a aspirin.

FW: Did they use whiskey alot?

INF: Do which?

FW: Well, do they use whiskey alot back then?

INF: Well, now my folks never was bad to use whiskey for anything like that. Now, Dad would make a ginger stew with whiskey, give it to us kids if we got the flu or something like that.

FW: What's a ginger stew?

INF: Take the ginger, grind it up right fine, you know, and boil it in some water and put the whiskey in a little bit of water and drink it. That's the awfulest tasting stuff in the world but it'll sweat you plumb to death.

FW: And it will get rid of the cold?

INF: It will sweat the fire out of you.

FW: Okay, now, like I'm thinking if they were going to pull some teeth, did they use whiskey on it to numb it or...?

INF: Oh, sometimes if you could get a hold of it, but if you's old enough they'd let you drink it, drink you a little bit, and kinda get on, you didn't care what they done to you. They could saw your head off.

FW: Oh, that's why they used whiskey. Okay, what about when babies were born?

INF: Now, that's something that we never knew much about, they always sent us somewhere else. Out to my aunt's or one of the neighbor's houses. When it was all over then they come and got us.

FW: Uh huh, well did, like when your wife had her first children did she go to the hospital or did the doctor...

INF: No, she only went to the hospital with the last 'ns, the twins. The others were born home, Doctor Harley delivered all of them except the one, and Doctor Pack delivered the other one.

FW: Well, and he came to the house?

INF: Oh yeah.

FW: Did he have any women there helping? Like midwife?

INF: Yeah, uh huh, there'd be usually a couple of women. My Aunt Polly Hartwick, she was there when two or three of my children were born, and she was...she helped deliver me when I was born.

FW: Uh huh.

INF: Them old midwives, you can't beat 'em.

FW: Well, don't you think the women got along just as well.

INF: As far as I can see, they got along as good. Now, they'll get you up the next day after the baby's born and then they made you stay in bed ten days before you got up.

FW: You think that was good for 'em, better than getting up right off the bat?

INF: Well, I don't believe they should get up the first day or two, I believe they should rest a couple of days, you know that's a terrible experience.

FW: It sure is.

INF: Now of course I've never been there, but I's a sightseer a few times and I think that's the nearest death a women'll ever be in her life.

FW: Well, what about the babies, do you think they're all right. They just left them at home, right? Did the doctor examine the babies?

INF: Yeah, they cut the navel string and fixed that all up and back when I was a boy. Now, you see so many children with navels sticking out, you know, way out here as long as your finger and the awfulest looking things. They made 'em wear a band around 'em for so many days, you know, Ma'd grease 'em with mutton's tallow and put over the place, you know, and pin it tight on 'em. I don't know how long they would leave it, but, for a right smart while. And it wasn't a dang one of them that ever had it that kind of a-looking deformed navel.

FW: Yeah, and now they don't do anything to them.

INF: I don't think so, I know one of mine had a kind of a ruptured navel, and I kept a silver dollar in a thing right over it in a band to let heal up, that kept it down the weight and so forth.

FW: Yeah, well, do you have some friends who have moved away from the area to a big city or somewhere else? When they leave here, do you think they come back, the young people, have you noticed any? A lot of times they all think they oughta leave here, but sooner or later don't you think they usually come back? Why do you think they come back or why do you think they even leave to begin with?

INF: Well, you always heard it says, a bird comes home to roost. Now they'll take off, a lot of 'em and they come back and you can't hardly understand 'em, they can't talk, they try to pick up the lingo that they learned at the other place.

FW: Right off in a week or so?

INF: In two weeks they'll pick it up, or they'll try to pick it up. They'll come back home in a month or two and you can't understand what they're saying, and, but in the end they all filter back.

FW: Why do you think they leave?

INF: Well, they think this grass is greener on down the road. 'Course now jobs around this neck of the woods has... about mining is about all 'ere is. And there's alot of them don't like the mines and they'll go somewhere and work at different jobs, construction working and, factories and this, and when they get their barrel full or get tired of the job they come back home.

FW: Yeah, do you think they like to raise their children in big cities?

INF: Do I think they do? No. All of my children says they don't like it. And I know I wouldn't, they's too many things to get into. Out on a farm's the best place to raise children.

FW: They learn how to work, honest work, work for what...

INF: Well, you can't get these doggone old boys to work anymore. They won't work for you.

FW: No, you can't get anyone to do anything for you.

INF: And if they do, their darn hair's so long that they can't see what they're doing. Spend half their time a-raking it back out of their eyes.

FW: And they don't know how to do anything?

INF: They don't know, they've never been taught, they never will know anything. And, I's talking to a foreman the other day in a coal mine. He said, Ike, he said "You wouldn't work as a foreman anymore," I says "Why?" "Well," he said, "you show them boys something to do and they don't know how to dig even down, much less do anything else." And he says, "It's just a terrible job to try to train 'ose boys. They're good boys, but they've never been taught anything and you just got a problem."

FW: What do you think of all these young people on welfare?

INF: Well, if they're sick or their parents or the boys are sick and disabled to work why, I'm in favor of 'em having it. But they's a lot of 'em on there that is stout, able-bodied men and boys and they could make it on their own. Now, I'll tell you, people say, "Oh, I can't find a job, I can't find a job." They's a job for you if you want it. If you'll hunt for it. It may not come to you, but it's there.

FW: What, you see all these people in the grocery store, a lot of times, pull out from the grocery store in a new Buick or a new Cadillac, go inside and they pay for their groceries with food stamps.

INF: Plenty of that. Dressed a lot better than I can dress.

FW: What do you think about that? What do you think they oughta do?

INF: Well, they oughta stop it. It's just a-draining the taxpayers plumb to death and now they're wanting, Ford, they want Ford to give Nixon or Ford's a-wanting to, 450,000 dollars, just hand it out to 'im. He's no better than I am. Why don't they give me some of that 450,000 dollars? I'm retired, I could use it. He's got plenty.

FW: Uh huh. Well, do you think things have changed much in the last few years?

INF: Yes. Well, in two or three different ways. Now, you can go out any-where and buy a beer, and you see girls and boys a-running around filthy, raggedy dirty, old long hair, don't look like they've washed in six months. And the inflation, you pay now, you take your money to the store in a shopping bag and bring your groceries back in your pocket. And, used to, you took your money in your pocket and brought your groceries back in a shopping bag. It's just reversed. And, now that could be cut down, that's just some of this Republican junk and my way of looking at it, Nixon's responsible for the whole thing. Now, they's a-gonna be a end to it. It may get worse, but it'll get better some of these days, I may not be here to see it, but somebody'll enjoy it.

FW: Do you think children have changed much, young people?

INF: Well, nothing more than they think the country owes 'em a living, and they're not a-gonna work for it if they can get out of it. If things would suddenly change back like it was in nineteen and twenties and the early thirties, ninety-nine percent of 'em would starve to death, they too lazy to work. And, that's the only way you had of getting it, grow-ing it yourself mostly on a farm. I worked for a dollar and eighty cents a day and my Dad was disabled and I gave him part of that.

FW: How many children were in your family?

INF: Oh, they was twelve of us kids, not at that time, after I got old enough to work, two of the girls was married, the rest of us was home we farmed and grew about everything we eat, other than coffee and sugar, you know, the things that you can't grow around here. We raised our hogs and had cows, we had our milk and butter and cornmeal and now we didn't raise no wheat, we bought our flour but outside of that we grew the rest of it, our cornbread, butter and buttermilk, sweet milk and molasses, we made them and I used to love them things... The old cane molasses.

FW: Well, what do you think about the difference in morality? Don't you think back then people were, seemed to have more pride than they do now?

INF: Lord have mercy, you know, Betsy, when I was a boy, if you seen a woman's knee you had done seen something, and now you can just see anything they-'ve got. The girls, young girls they wear their pants down just as far as they can get 'em and then a little short shirt of a thing that shows their belly wide open to the public. I don't think that's decent.

FW: No. Braless, all these halter tops showing everything.

INF: It's all right to look at, but, I declare, it won't do to die by. Don't you think I'm right?

FW: I agree with you. Don't you think the young people just don't care?

INF: I believe they've got a I-don't-give-a-damn attitude. Like the colored man's mule, it was blind, he'd run into everything and the man asked him, said, "That mule's blind?" "No, he ain't blind, he just don't give a damn." But, now I think that's the attitude that most of 'em take.

FW: And do their own thing. Think they can do anything they want to.

INF: And not be reprimanded for it. I think they oughta be turned across your knee and lay the lash on 'em. The parents' fault. Why, they won't make them mind you. Why, if I'd a done the things when I was a boy that the do now my Daddy'd kill me. Now, he didn't believe in this here horsing around. And, if he told you to do something, you done it, and not only my Dad, all of the parents around through the country where I was raised, when they asked their children to do something, they went and done it. If it was clean out the barn, or hoe out the corn, or the potatoes or whatever they had, build fence, cut brush, anything that come handy, we done it. And there was no belly-aching about it. And when they come to the bed of morning and said, "All right, get up boys, time to get out of here and go to work," you better come out, if he come back a second time he brought his razor strap with him. Now, that's facts, and I think it's the way you're brought up more or less that... the way you're gonna end up.

FW: What do you think about all this dope, and

INF: Oh, that's outrageous and not only that, whiskey. Whiskey should be outlawed, all kind of dope. It's just like putting a dang hog in a corn crib full of corn and say "Don't eat that corn!" Well now, that pig's gonna eat some of that corn. Same way with this other junk a-running around over the country. That dope, you know people has to try and be seen. Like, the man from Missouri, he don't believe it, he got to show him. So, all these, not all, but a lot of these teenagers, "Let me try that!" And, if they get a kick out of it, it's like taking a drink of whiskey, you take a drink or two of whiskey and it makes you feel pretty good, you want another 'n, you want to feel better. And the more you drink the better you feel 'til I reckon you feel, the first thing you know, you don't know anything. You're dead to the world. And then, a lot of 'em go on and drink every day, after they get into it and that puts 'em on the green hillside. Oh, I'll tell you, I read a little article in a paper, in a magazine, where some dude said, yesterday would make, I mean, the girls of today woulda made mothers of yesterday ashamed of theirself cooking. That the girls this day and time cook so much better. If they couldn't get it out of a tin can they couldn't cook you a can of soup. It comes out of the can and bread offa' the shelf. Well, that's ruined more good women than anything in the world this old light bread. My old woman in there has made as good a biscuits than you ever stuck in your mouth, but she's got away from it, she don't make 'em often enough. I don't care what you do, you got to keep it up in order to do it good and properly.

FW: And keep doing it better.

INF: That's right, practice makes perfect.

FW: Young women just cook those TV dinners. Whatever is the quickest.

INF: I hate them things.

FW: I do too, I think they're not fit to eat.

INF: I wouldn't give a nickel a piece for them.

FW: Does your wife do any canning? How does she preserve food? Does she do any canning?

INF: Oh yeah, she's canned, I helped her some, her hand was crippled up, arthritis, and I'd tighten the tops for 'er, help her that way, get 'em out and carry them to the basement. We canned green beans and apple sauce, and berries, hot peppers, and she made a batch of jelly, some blackberry jelly, jam, and some peach marmalade the other day, she made a bunch of that. And, we've canned, it's around a hundred and twenty-five quarts, I'd say.

FW: Well, do you freeze food too, do you have a freezer?

INF: I don't have a freezer, nothing more 'an what's in my the frigerator, it's got a small one on the top, but, we don't freeze too much stuff. She's got some corn in 'ere now, just a little bit, a fellow gave me some the other day, we didn't raise any corn and, she put some of that in there and she canned part of it.

FW: Uh huh, do you like frozen corn on the cob? Do you like that?

INF: I never tried any. I like corn on the cob very well, but I'd rather have it cut off and a thickening put with it and cook it that way. That's the way my mother cooked it, mostly all of us liked it that way.

FW: Uh huh. Do you cook it and then cut it off or do you cut it off before?

INF: Cut it off before.

FW: And then you just cook it?

INF: Yeah, put a thickening in it, kinda like making gravy or something, and cook it.

FW: Do you remember anything about churning? Did your mother churn butter?

INF: Well, I've churned a lot, I'd rather've took a beating. You have to sit there and churn that dang thing. Oh yeah, boy did we churn butter for years. Ma, let's see, oh, she hadn't been away from that, til about ten years ago. And, I used to buy butter from 'er all the time, buttermilk.

FW: How do you churn butter? What do you do?

INF: Well, she would take her cream from the cow's milk and put it over in a separate container and let it stay in there. Well, if you kept it cold, it wouldn't turn. What I mean by that it wouldn't sour enough for us to make butter. Now, a lot of people makes it from sweet cream, but I don't think it's as good. And let it 'til she'd get three or four gallon of that, and pour it in a churn, and it had a lid with a hole in it and an old homemade dasher and, a handle up through there, you'd just slosh that up and down 'til the butter come to the top. Sometimes it'd be three or four or five pound. About a pound to the gallon. And then she'd take it out of 'ere and work it, work the water out of it and salt it to taste, you know, the way we liked it and put it in a print, every pound, and lay it out kept it where we had a spring house where the water come running down, we had a little trough in there where water'd stay about a inch or two inches deep in it, and she'd set it in 'ere to keep it cold.

FW: Could you keep it a long time?

INF: Well, in the summer you couldn't keep it too awful long, of course, now you take twelve kids and it didn't last long anyhow, and hot biscuits and butter, that's good eating.

FW: Well, did she ever make soap? How do you make homemade soap?

INF: Well, she never did make her own lye, now back when she was a girl she showed me, I've seen 'ose things, it was a hopper, built you know, a little at the bottom, and bigger at the top. And they'd take the wood ashes and dump in there and as it rained in it and water, you want to pour water in it, all right, and it would drip, that's what they call drip lye. It was kind a the color of iodine, and that stuff was strong as the devil. And then they'd put meat scraps, fat, in 'ere, and, that would eat that up and they'd a boil it and make soap. I've washed a many and a many a time with it.

FW: Do you think that's hard on your complexion?

INF: I don't know whether it hurt mine or not. It'd be hard to say, not knowing.

FW: Well, Ike, do you remember your first days at school, what were they like?

INF: I remember the first day I went to school, but I, as to what went on I don't, but I remember, I never will forget it. Mother packed me a lunch in a little old half gallon syrup bucket. Put me some tomatoes I can yet, once in a while I'll get a tomato that reminds me of that and that's, that's been sixty years ago. And, she'd always fix me a good lunch and

I looked forward to that. Sit down, and all of us would sit down in the
school, if we wanted to, you could go outside and eat in the summer.
But, we'd always sit down in 'ere and eat our lunch. I'll never forget
that first days of school, only had to walk about a mile.

FW: They didn't have buses?

INF: Oh, we didn't even know what a bus was, didn't even have a taxi automobile, nothing like that. First car I ever saw was along about well, I
started to school about twelve, nineteen twelve, I guess, and the first
automobile I ever saw was along about fourteen or fifteen.

FW: And you walked how far?

INF: About a mile.

FW: About a mile, did you go all day?

INF: Yes, we uh, from nine o' clock until four. And, we'd take, we'd have,
fifteen or thirty minutes at ten-thirty, then at noon we'd have one hour,
and then about two or two-thirty, I forget which, we'd have another fifteen or thirty minutes, then when school turned out at four o'clock,
you'd go home.

FW: How many rooms?

INF: Two. Two rooms, they had, from the first grade, they didn't have a
primer them days, first grade through the third, in what we call the
little room. The little children went in 'at one. Then, in the other
room, we had four through the eighth in 'at.

FW: And one woman taught all these different grades?

INF: There's two teachers there. One taught the small children in what we
called the little room from the first through the third, in the big room
we'd call that one, they taught the fourth through the eighth.

FW: Was she strict?

INF: Some of 'em were, some weren't.

FW: Uh huh. Did you enjoy going to school?

INF: Yes, I loved it. But, I, I've went through the eighth grade twice. I
wouldn't go to high school, I got a job and went to work and, back them
days, you know, education didn't amount to much. When you got able to
work, and they'd hire you, you'd go to work, try to make a living.

FW: Uh huh. Were there many in your class, do you remember?

INF: Oh, they was, I'd say, fifteen, maybe and each, in the, let's see, fourth
grade, fifth, sixth, seventh, and eighth that's five grades, I'd say
they'd be about forty, maybe fifty in the whole, all the classes.

FW: What did she discipline you with, do you remember that?

INF: Dern board and stick, she's usually send one of the scholars out and cut
a width for her to thrash you.

FW: Do you remember getting any?

INF: No, I got one, Ray Davis, you might know Ray, from Matoaka, used to be a
federal man over Bluefield, not at the same post office, Ray, that's over
there though, he held me and Curtis Green pourt snow down my neck and
there was a set of twins there, Al Farmer's girls, they brought their
lunch in a two pound lard bucket. Well, they turned me loose and I
grabbed up one of those buckets, and cut down on them and I hit Brook in
the back of the head with it and cut a place about two inches long in
the scalp and the teacher thrashed me, that's the only one I ever got, I
would a got another one but I left, I didn't stay for it.

FW: Okay, do you remember your first girlfriend?

INF: No.

FW: You don't remember her?

INF: No. No. That is really, I'd just go with first one the other, I remember
the first one I dated regular. We had a pretty good time.

FW: Where did you meet her?

INF: Church.

FW: Church? Do you remember when you first fell in love?

INF: Oh yeah. Yeah, that's the hardest fall, isn't it?

FW: Were you sick very long, Ike?

INF: Well, not exactly, until we married I's a-hurting pretty bad.

FW: Okay, what are some of the important things to remember when you're raising kids, what do you think people oughta do now? When you're rais- ing your kids?

INF: Well, I didn't do it myself, but I think the most important thing when you're raising your children is to go to church with them every Sunday and between Sunday if it's, if you can, 'course a lot of times you can't, and grow up a-hunting with them instead a-hunting for them. 'Course now, I shoulda went with mine but I didn't. They went, the girls went, but the boys never did care nothing about going to Sunday School, but the girls went every Sunday, down Mount Olvie, and I always encouraged them to go, I didn't try to get them not to, and I encouraged the boys to go but I wouldn't go and so they said, like father like son, I reckon, and so they didn't go either. We like to hunt and we done fished, we done 'at together. Me and the boys and the dog.

FW: How many boys do you have?

INF: I did have two, I've got one now.

FW: Uh huh, and the rest girls?

INF: Uh huh, four girls and two boys.

FW: Well, do you think people ought to be strict on them, you know, try to keep them in, have rules and make them go?

INF: They should have rules to go by they can set up and watch television 'til a certain hour. If they got homework to do, do that and then watch tele- vision 'til the allotted time. A child can't lay up all night, watch television or out here at these old places a-running around, and do any good in school. Now, you've got to draw a line somewhere.

FW: And stick to the rules.

INF: That's right, have strict rules. I believe in letting 'em go but I don't believe in just giving 'em the reins and let's say, here, you go ahead, lay out all you want, I don't believe in 'at.

FW: What do you think about spanking them?

INF: If they need it, lay it on 'em. If you tell a child, now I'll give you a spanking if you do that, and if he goes and does it, then he asks for that. You done told him what you was going to do if he done that, now if you don't, you lie to him. And, if he catch you in one lie, he'll say well, Daddy lied about that or Mother did so I'll do it again.

FW: What do you think about the TV programs? Do you think TV's good for young people?

INF: Some of it is, and some of it I wouldn't care about mine watching it, although we watched anything that come along, I bought one of them things in nineteen fifty, and Huntington was all we could get, and couldn't get it very well. We'd set up on Saturday nights and watch the wrassling that come on and then other programs, but we all would stay up and watch the wrassling.

FW: Well, did the children like to watch it then?

INF: Oh, yeah, they loved it.

FW: What do you think are some of the good programs for children?

INF: Well, *The Waltons* is a good program, *Lawrence Welk's* a good program, the news sometimes it's pretty rotten, it puts things in children's head, but maybe I can do that and get by with it. You know, children has, they al- ways want to challenge the worst and what God don't want you to do that's what you wanna do. You always want to do that you're commanded not to do. Why, you tell me. But, now, they's a lot of good programs that I could mention, we see them just every little bit, I know I do, I see a lot of 'em on there that's good, clean programs. Some of these Country and Western, some of these singers come out with some pretty dirty things. It depends on, I reckon, the way you look at it, but it's not, I don't think, too awful good. Now, everybody don't have the same opinions.

FW: Yeah, have you ever seen that *Sesame Street* or...

INF: Yeah, I have, they's nothing wrong with that. That's a good program for children.

FW: Uh huh, don't you think that's real good?
INF: It is.
FW: They can learn a lot from it.
INF: I know that grandson of mine has learned a lot from it.
FW: Well they teach you, you know, how to count and the colors and things
     like that. A lot of women don't have time to spend. Do you think women
     spend enough time with their children? What do you think about women
     working?
INF: Well, now you liable to get me in a tight spot but I think that women
     that has small children should stay home with them until they start to
     school. Then, if she wants to work the hours that the child goes to
     school, that's okay. But now, you take...you take...two or three child-
     ren and Tom, Dick, and Harry looks after 'em. That child, you does one
     thing, he does another, and the third party does another, and maybe
     eight or ten will babysit with those children. Well, it's kinda like
     going to church, you get confused, you don't know which is right. Just
     like going to church, you go up here to one church and they tell you you
     go to Hell if you smoke a cigarette and the other one tell you you don't,
     you just go part of the way, and first thing you know you don't know
     what to believe. Read your Bible's the best thing, when it comes to
     that. But now, getting back to the, I think a mother should wait 'til
     her children is ready for school, then, if she wants to work, that's
     okay. What do you think about it?
FW: Well, I think that I agree with you. I think if you have other people
     raise your children, then you shouldn't be disappointed later on with
     what they do because you weren't there to train them.
INF: And it's hard to tell, You know a lot of these fellows has men folks to
     babysit with children, boys and girls, girls up to ten or twelve years
     old. Some of 'em's afraid to leave them, afraid they'll set the house
     a fire or of they's any whiskey in the house they'll drink that, and
     they will. Some of 'em will try out something new and they's been a
     lot of crimes committed right there by babysitters.
FW: Did you read in the paper, a Huntington paper, where this couple had a
     young girl come in and babysit with their six-weeks-old daughter and
     while they were away, the parents were away, this girl had some friends
     in and they started taking pills, and she apparently went crazy or some-
     thing and she put the baby in the oven, she thought that she was cooking
     a turkey.
INF: No, I didn't read that.
FW: That was in the news.
INF: But my aunt one time, she left the oven door down to put out a little
     more heat in the kitchen, it was in the wintertime, the old cat got up
     in 'ere to cool down to where he liked it and got in 'ere and set down
     and somebody come along, closed the oven door, so the next morning she
     gets up and builds a fire in the old coal range and baked the cat. She
     opened the door to put her bread in to bake it and there set the cat.
     Hide done busted off his skull and fell down and his meat just come
     off'n his bones.
FW: Oh, you're kidding!
INF: It's a fact.
FW: Oh, isn't that awful?
INF: Oh, I want to tell you one, maybe I shouldn't on this thing, but I'm
     a-gonna tell it anyway. My aunt was sick, and my uncle cooked breakfast.
     So, he washed his dishes up and everything and went out and harnessed
     up his horses to go plowing and run his hands in his pockets. Well,
     he hunted for the dishrag first, he couldn't find it. So he got him a
     new one, went out and harnessed his horses after while and went on to
     work and him, he chewed tobacco, you know, and reached his hand in his
     pocket to get him a chew of tobacco and found his dishrag. He'd stuck
     it in his pocket!
INF: Do you remember any more interesting stories, Ike? Like, cooking the

cat?

INF: No, not right off hand, now, if it come to a bunch of jokes I could tell you enough to run that thing crazy.

FW: Well, have you heard any good jokes lately?

INF: Well, they wouldn't be fit for that. Uh, I laughted at John Parker. Do you know John Parker over at Ashmeade?

FW: No.

INF: Him and me and Jack Stern, we went to Bath County, Virginia, coon hunting. Went up to Leroy Buzzie's. And before I forgets I wanna tell you there's a Leroy Buzzie lived up there, and Al Crawley and Chuck McCoy, all of 'em lived in the same hollow 'ere.

FW: Buzzie. Where did you go, up in Bath County?

INF: Bath County, Virginia. Up on Little Bath Creek.

FW: I think that's where Charley goes every year.

INF: Yeah, I expect it is. Well, now they've got a cabin back down this side of that. Way down this side.

FW: They're mountain people, aren't they, Ike?

INF: No, not really. No... They...he used to be an Army man, the old man Leroy Buzzie, see, he's dead now. He was a retired Army man, and, we went up 'ere and John supposedly had a sack to put the coon in if we caught one. We's gonna try to bring it back alive, so we tromped through the woods 'til along about six o'clock in the morning. The dogs treed up a big hollow chestnut oak, and we proceeded to cut the thing down. It's about three or four inches all the way around. About four foot through the stump. We tied the dogs and cut the thing down. Well, we cut it down and turned one dog loose, and he went down in that thing, way down in the old hollow of the tree and it forked, and we couldn't get up in there so he backed out and he tied 'im. And we's a-gonna chop the coon out if it was in there, I's a kinda halfway thought maybe it just treed a possum or something. Well, I chopped in and lo and behold, right on top of the dang coon. Eighteen pounder, Jack Stern says, kitten coon. I run in with the axe handle down in behind him to keep him from getting out or backing down in the tree. He reached, fooled around and got him by the hind legs and pulled that thing out it looked big as a sheep to me. Turned 'im loose, he said "kitten, Hell." We had an old carbide light and he turned that over and the lights were... that's all the light we had. And, we had to hunt it then and the dogs took right after the coon right down the holler and the dogs caught it and Jack beat us all down there. Went down there and he's a-holding three dogs in one hand and the coon in the other hand. And they's all a-trying to bite the coon and the coon a-trying to bite Jack and the dogs, and Jack pulled out a sack and it wasn't a dang thing but an old pillow case that Maggie had used, his wife, it was about wore out. So we fumbled around 'ere and finally got that coon in that sack and he aimed to close the top of it and the coon just tore the thing in half, in two, and down the holler he went again. With that sack on him, half of it and we caught that thing, and you know, E. F. Wurst finally pulled off his coveralls and we put that thing down in one of the legs of his coveralls and tied that coon up. He's tearing up everything we could get, we couldn't hold him he's so stout. And I brought that thing home and kept 'im about a month, fed 'im apples and stuff to eat so we could eat 'em. Well, I did I killed him and tried eat that thing, I'd just soon eat a tomcat or a polecat, I wouldn't make much difference. And, that's about the best coon hunt I believe I was on.

FW: Did you ever deer hunt any, or turkey?

INF: No, I never would deer, I object to getting killed.

FW: Deer hunting?

INF: Uh huh. There's too many crazy people in the woods shoots at anything that moves.

FW: Yeah, what about turkey hunting?

INF: Oh, I love turkey hunt.

FW: Where do you hunt?

INF: Pocahontas County, West Virginia, I've killed two, that's all I've ever killed. And, they're a smart bird, I'll tell you. They can see every direction and straight up to boot at the same time.

FW: Well, what about hearing, do they hear real well?

INF: You're dang tooting, they can hear. Why, you just break a stick and they'll...now if the wind's a-blowing real hard, they don't pay too much attention to you. That is, walking in the leaves. But, now, if everything's still, you better not move if he's one in sight, cause he'll see you move.

FW: Do you go out real early in the morning or...

INF: Oh, all hours of the day, anytime from early morning 'til dark.

FW: Do you just sit... How... What do you do turkey hunting?

INF: Well, if you're pretty good with a call, a lot of times you can call maybe you can call one out to you, if you get out and don't have any luck seeing any, get you a good spot, but that's dangerous, somebody's liable to slip around and shoot you, think you're a turkey. That's how most people know about hunting and you just call kinda like a turkey would make, you know about three counts on a caller, if they's one in hearing distance, and if you've got him fool...and are good enough to fool him, he'll answer you. And, you just keep calling and they'll keep coming to you. Now, a young one, you just make most any kind of a racket and bring 'im up to you, but an old residenter, you better not make a sour note on 'at call, if you do he's gone.

FW: Uh huh, and they're real smart, aren't they?

INF: Uh huh, they're easy killed.

FW: They are?

INF: Oh yeah.

FW: Oh, I thought they could get away.

INF: Now, if you hit one in the head, neck, you've got him. But, now hit him in the body or in the legs, 'em scoundrels, you can't hardly knock 'em down.

FW: You have to hit them in the head or neck?

INF: If you can hit 'em in the head or neck, or if you can hit 'em enough in the body you've got him.

FW: Uh huh. What other kind of hunting do you do? Other than coon and turkey?

INF: Squirrel, and rabbit, and pheasant, grouse, I think is the real name for 'em, we all just called 'em native pheasants, you know, boy they're good eating, too.

FW: I know, I've eaten them. I love them.

INF: I, too.

FW: Are they smart? Like turkeys?

INF: No, they're now, around here they won't fly up until you get pretty close to them. But up in Pocahontas County they're pretty wild. I reckon it's because so many hunters in there and shooting around. Well, I've walked by them and then they fly up and be in three foot of them.

FW: Where do you grouse hunt? Oh, in Pocahontas County?

INF: Well, no, if I was going to do any of that, of grouse hunting, I'd do it around here, around over my mother's.

FW: Do you take dogs?

INF: No, I never did use any dogs. I always just tromp around through the woods. In the wintertime you can find their tracks and track 'em up. I know one time I told my mother, I's just an old boy, and over next to Bud Hyman's, in a valley there, a lot of grapes, briar berries, I told her I was going a-pheasant hunting. After school, I got my wood and stuff ready and I lit out and I run into, oh, they's must have been six or eight of 'em flew up about the same time and scared me, I didn't know I had a gun. Never even fired a shot.

FW: They are real good. I think they're delicious.
INF: Oh, and you take the broth off a those things after you boil them you
      know, get you a cup of broth and salt it and pepper it to taste, now
      that's as good a drink as anybody would want.
FW: You boil them and then you bake 'em, brown 'em a little, don't you?
INF: Well, now, some people do. My mother always just boiled 'em and made
      gravy out of them, like chicken and dumpling. And we always was foolish
      about gravy there at home, you know, and she always tried to fix it so
      we would like it, the way we all liked it. Now rabbit, she used to boil
      'em, parboil 'em, and fry 'em, but, I like to take 'em and just wring
      your hands in the back, just about a half inch apart, plumb to the bone
      with a knife, and just put 'em in the skillet like you would a chicken,
      and fry 'em. Make gravy they's the best stuff and you ever eat.
FW: Have you ever eaten tame rabbit?
INF: One.
FW: Do you like it?
INF: I can't eat 'em with as good a stomach as I can the wild one, for some
      reason. They're good, but, no I've eat it, I've eaten it twice. Preach-
      er Kinley, one time he had some, fried some tame rabbit cooked up, and
      a fellow gave me one, weigh about, oh, a pound and a half, two pound.
      It was good, but I still lean toward the wild one.
FW: Yeah, I think they're better. Do you hunt anything else other than...
INF: No, no that's about all the hunting I ever done was for just the small
      game. I went a-deer hunting twice last year, over here above Hinton and
      saw a buck each time and didn't get a shot at either one. One of 'em
      I almost ran over the thing that morning, it was foggy, just the other
      side of the bridge there at the dam. Standing right square in the middle
      of the dang road. Well, in our lane, and I said, Allen, Allen Bentley
      was driving, don't you hit that thing, it come right back in the truck
      on us. It would come right through the windshield and I could a killed
      it with a pistol, if I'd a had a pistol with me.
FW: Were there other people there with you?
INF: Just two of us in the truck, Rob Montley and Allen Benson, we was going
      up to Rob's brothers, above Hinton, and he just jumped down over the
      field, toward the lake, the dam there.
FW: And, none of you got any that day?
INF: No. No.
FW: And, you don't like to deer hunt?
INF: I told Rob, him and me went the next day. Allen didn't go with us and
      I told Rob, I said Rob, you know, he's just got one leg, I said "You
      and me's out here deer hunting." I says "if we killed one we couldn't
      get it home. I ain't got enough of breath to pull the thing and you
      ain't got but one leg, what would we do?" He said, "My brother's got a
      truck and a long rope would get 'im at-a-way." Oh, 'ey's a lot of fun,
      we used to go up in Pocahontas County. Mary went with me, my wife, and
      the boys, and the twins, we'd camp up there about three days and nights.
      Oh, we had the best time, there's several families would go, you know,
      and we'd cook up a lot of things to eat, and I'll tell you the best thing
      you can cook to eat out on a trip like that. Potatoes and corn beef,
      just cook your potatoes and put the corn beef in there, about three cans
      of that, and about a gallon of potatoes and I'll guarantee there won't
      be any left.
FW: What, do you boil potatoes before you go?
INF: No, I boil 'em there, just build us a fire. I made me a thing in the
      shop, it was about three foot square and I welded some angle iron on it
      so it wouldn't warp, build up a little furnace and put that, cook on
      that. Now, that's some real eating. And boil your coffee in an old
      bucket of some kind, I finally did buy me a big coffee pot, a gallon one,
      white one, and just boil your coffee, wasn't no such a thing as a perco-
      lator, it's better boiled anyway, better flavor. You don't have the
      grounds in the perked coffee you have in that, but, you spit them out.

Complete List of Informants in Sample

[Note: For purposes of this study, all informants were White.]

Tape No.	Age	Sex	Occupation of Head of Household
1	15	M	housewife
2	13	M	truck driver
3	23	F	salesman
4	13	M	coal miner
5	13	M	coal miner
6	14	M	unemployed
7	17	M	salesman
8	14	M	salesman
9	12	M	coal miner
10	14	M	construction worker
11	71	F	retired
12	13	M	housewife
13	12	M	coal miner
14	11	M	coal miner
15	11	M	coal miner
16	12	M	cook
17	16	M	coal miner
18	14	M	coal miner
19	12	F	coal miner
20	11	M	coal miner
21	42	F	laborer
22	60	M	retired
23	58	F	babysitting
24	72	F	babysitting
25	29	F	unknown
26	19	F	student
27	27	F	unknown
28	42	F	cook/waitress
29	33	F	waitress
30	50	M	coal miner
31	67	M	retired
32	54	M	retired
33	30	F	purchasing agent
34	59	F	assembly work
35	22	F	furniture mover
36	27	F	truck driver
37	45	F	sawyer
38	80	F	unknown
39	29	F	social worker
40	39	F	unknown
41	14	M	unknown
42	14	M	farmer
43	17	M	grocery business
44	14	M	unemployed
45	16	M	farmer
46	15	M	federal govt. employee (retired)

Tape No.	Age	Sex	Occupation of Head of Household
47	7	M	farmer
48	9	M	factory worker
49	9	M	construction worker
50	10	M	farm tenant
51	10	M	farmer
52	8	M	farmer
53	17	M	county govt. employee
54	10	M	farmer
55	12	M	farmer
56	12	M	laborer
57	10	M	truck driver
58	11	M	laborer
59	9	M	factory worker
60	7	M	truck driver
61	14	F	coal miner
62	14	F	unemployed
63	14	F	unemployed
64	15	F	state employee
65	15	F	contractor
66	17	F	saw mill worker
67	16	F	construction worker
68	15	F	truck driver
69	6	F	school bus driver
70	13	F	farmer
71	11	F	housewife
72	7	F	laborer
73	8	F	painter
74	11	F	unemployed
75	10	F	construction worker
76	9	F	teacher aide
77	11	F	carpenter
78	7	F	factory worker
79	6	F	factory worker
80	9	F	constable
83	93	F	retired
84	group	M and F	unknown
85	78	F	unknown
86	10	F	factory worker
87	24	M	maintenance engineer
88	15	F	unemployed
96	77	M	farmer/miner (retired)
97	81	F	teacher (retired)
98	87	F	farmer (retired)
121	11	M	coal miner
122	13	M	coal miner
123	13	M	coal miner
124	11	M	coal miner
125	8	M	lawyer
126	8	F	laborer
127	8	F	unknown
128	17	F	retired
129	8	F	lumber company worker
130	10	F	laborer
131	10	F	laborer
132	11	F	unemployed
133	11	F	unemployed
134	11	F	unemployed
135	55	F	coal miner

Tape No.	Age	Sex	Occupation of Head of Household
136	11	F	truck driver
137	9	M	unknown
138	9	M	unknown
139	9	F	janitor
140	16	F	secretary
146	52	M	coil winder
147	13	F	coil winder
148	13	F	unknown
149	18	F	waitress
150	13	F	coal miner
151	18	F	machinist
152	64	F	retired
153	83	F	unknown
154	13	F	machinist
155	17	F	coal miner
156	20	F	welder
157	52	F	unknown
158	25	M	medical technician
159	20	M	grocery store employee
160	56	F	railroad worker
161	32	F	laborer
162	44	M	educational administration
163	60	M	unknown
164	33	M	custodian
165	57	M	educational administration

Bibliography

Allen, Harold B. 1971. "The Primary Dialect Areas in the Upper Midwest" in Harold B. Allen and Gary N. Underwood, eds., *Readings in American Dialectology*. New York: Appleton-Century-Crofts.

Anshen, Frank. 1969. *Speech Variation Among Negroes in a Small Southern Community*. Unpublished PhD Dissertation, New York University.

Atwood, E. Bagby. 1953. *A Survey of Verb Forms in the Eastern United States*. Ann Arbor: University of Michigan Press.

Bailey, Charles-James N. 1973. *Variation and Linguistic Theory*. Arlington, VA: Center for Applied Linguistics.

Baratz, Joan C. 1973. "The Relationship of Black English to Reading: A Review of Research" in James L. Laffey and Roger W. Shuy, eds., *Language Differences: Do They Interfere?* Newark, DE: International Reading Association.

Belcher, John C. 1962. "Population Growth and Characteristics" in Thomas R. Ford, ed., *The Southern Appalachian Region: A Survey*. Lexington, KY: University of Kentucky Press.

Bickerton, Derek. 1971. "Inherent Variability and Variable Rules," *Foundations of Language*, 7:457-492.

Bolinger, Dwight. 1972. *Degree Words*. The Hague: Mouton and Company.

Brown, James S. 1972. "A Look at the 1970 Census" in David S. Walls and John B. Stephenson, eds., *Appalachia in the Sixties: Decade of Reawakening*. Lexington, KY: University of Kentucky Press.

Butters, Ronald. 1975. *Variability in Indirect Questions*. Unpublished manuscript.

Christian, Donna. 1973. "Deletion of Inital *d* in Fast Speech." Unpublished Manuscript.

Cicourel, Aaron V. et al. 1974. *Language Use and School Performance*. New York: Academic Press.

Cofer, Thomas M. 1972. *Linguistic Variability in a Speech Community*. Unpublished PhD Dissertation, University of Pennsylvania.

Coles, Robert. 1972. *Migrants, Sharecroppers, Mountaineers*. Boston: Little, Brown and Company.

Fasold, Ralph W. 1970. "Two Models of Socially Significant Linguistic Variation," *Language*, 46:551-563.

_____. 1972. *Tense Marking in Black English: A Linguistic and Social Analysis*. Arlington, VA: Center for Applied Linguistics.

Feagin, Crawford. Forthcoming. *The Verb in White Alabama English*. PhD Dissertation, Georgetown University.

Feigenbaum, Irwin. 1969. "Using Foreign Language Methodology to Teach Standard English: Evaluation and Adaptation" in Alfred C. Aarons et al eds., *Linguistic-Cultural Differences and American Education*. Special Anthology Issue, *The Florida FL Reporter*. North Miami Beach, FL: Florida FL Reporter, Inc.

_____. 1970. "The Use of Nonstandard English in Teaching Standard: Contrast and Comparison" in Ralph W. Fasold and Roger W. Shuy,

eds., *Teaching Standard English in the Inner City*. Washington,
DC: Center for Applied Linguistics.
Glenn, Max. 1970. *Appalachia in Transition*. St. Louis: Bethany Press.
Gordon, David and George Lakoff. 1971. "Conversational Postulates,"
Chicago Linguistic Society, 7:63-84.
Green, Georgia M. 1974. *Semantics and Syntactic Regularity*. Bloomington:
Indiana University Press.
Guy, Gregory R. 1974. "Variation in the Group and the Individual: The
Case of Final Stop Deletion," *Pennsylvania Working Papers on
Linguistic Change and Variation*, 2:4
Hackenberg, Robert. 1972. *A Sociolinguistic Description of Appalachian
English*. Unpublished PhD Dissertation. Georgetown University.
Herman, Simon R. 1961. "Explorations in the Social Psychology of Lan-
guage Choice," *Human Relations*, 14:149-164.
Jespersen, Otto. 1933. *Essentials of English Grammar*. University, AL:
University of Alabama Press.
Illinois Test of Psycholinguistic Abilities. 1968. Urbana, IL: Univer-
sity of Illinois Press.
King, Pamela. 1972. *An Analysis of the Northwestern Syntax Screening
Test for Lower Class Black Children in Prince George's County*.
Unpublished MA thesis, Howard University.
Krapp, George Philip. 1925. *The English Language in America*.
New York: Frederick Ungar Publishing Company.
Kurath, Hans. 1949. *A Word Geography of the Eastern United States*.
Ann Arbor, MI: University of Michigan Press.
Labov, William. 1964. "Stages in the Acquisition of Standard English"
in Roger W. Shuy, ed., *Social Dialects and Language Learning*.
Champaign, IL: National Council of Teachers of English.
_____. 1966. *The Social Stratification of English in New York City*.
Washington, DC: Center for Applied Linguistics.
_____ et al. 1968. *A Study of the Non-Standard English of Negro and
Puerto Rican Speakers in New York City*. USOE Final Report, Research Project Number 3288.
_____. 1969. "Contraction, Deletion, and Inherent Variability of the
English Copula," *Language*, 45:715-762.
_____. 1972a. "Some Principles of Linguistic Methodology," *Language
in Society*, 1:97-120.
_____. 1972b. *Sociolinguistic Patterns*. Philadelphia: University of
Pennsylvania Press.
_____. 1972c. *Language in the Inner City: Studies in the Black Eng-
lish Vernacular*. Philadelphia: University of Pennsylvania
Press.
_____. 1973. "Where Do Grammars Stop?" in Roger W. Shuy, ed., *Mono-
graph on Languages and Linguistics*, No. 25. Washington, DC:
Georgetown University Press.
Laffey, James L. and Roger W. Shuy, eds. 1973. *Language Differences:
Do They Interfere?* Newark, DE: International Reading Associa-
tion.
Leaverton, Lloyd. 1973. "Dialectal Readers: Rationale, Use and Value"
in James L. Laffey and Roger W. Shuy, eds., *Language Differences:
Do They Interfere?* Newark, DE: International Reading Associa-
tion.
Meier, Deborah. 1973. *Reading Failure and the Tests*. New York: Work-
shop Center for Open Education.
Morgan, J. L. 1972. "Verb Agreement as a Rule of English," *Chicago
Linguistic Society,* 8:278-286.
Motley, Charles B. 1973. *Gleanings of Monroe County, West Virginia,
History*. Radford, VA: Commonwealth Press, Inc.

Photiadis, John D. 1969. *West Virginians in their Own State and in Cleveland, Ohio*. Morgantown, WV: Center for Appalachian Studies and Development.

Pyles, Thomas. 1964. *The Origins and Development of the English Language*. New York: Harcourt, Brace and World, Inc.

Roberts, Elsa. 1970. "An Evaluation of Standardized Tests as Tools for the Measurement of Language Development" in *Language Research Reports*, No. 1. Cambridge: Language Research Foundation.

Robertson, Stuart and Frederic G. Cassidy. 1954. *The Development of Modern English*. Englewood Cliffs, NJ: Prentice-Hall.

Shuy, Roger W. 1972. "Sociolinguistics and Teacher Attitudes in a Southern School System" in David M. Smith and Roger W. Shuy, eds., *Sociolinguistics in Cross-Cultural Analysis*. Washington, DC: Georgetown University Press.

_____ et al. 1967. *Linguistic Correlates of Social Stratification in Detroit Speech*. Final Report, Cooperative Research Project Number 6-1347, U.S. Office of Education.

Sizer, Leonard M. 1967. *Measures of Social Change in West Virginia, 1940-1965*. Morgantown, WV: Center for Appalachian Studies and Development.

Sledd, James. 1969. "Bi-dialectalism: The Linguistics of White Supremacy," *English Journal*, 58:1307-1329.

_____. 1972. "Doublespeak: Dialectology in the Service of Big Brother," *College English*, 33:439-456.

Smith, Frank. 1971. *Understanding Reading: A Psycholinguistic Analysis of Reading and Learning to Read*. Toronto: Holt, Rinehart, and Winston.

Stewart, William A. 1967. *Language and Communication Problems in Southern Appalachia*. Washington, DC: Center for Applied Linguistics.

Stoffel, C. 1901. *Intensives and Down-towners: A Study in English Adverbs*. Heidelberg: Carl Winter's Universitats buchhandlung.

Summerlin, NanJo Corbitt. 1972. *A Dialect Study: Affective Parameters in the Deletion and Substitution of Consonants in the Deep South*. Unpublished PhD Dissertation, Florida State University.

Ter Horst, Gerald. 1972. "No More Pork Barrel: The Appalachia Approach" in David S. Walls and John B. Stephenson, eds., *Appalachia in the Sixties: Decade of Reawakening*. Lexington, KY: University of Kentucky Press.

Traugott, Elizabeth Closs. 1972. *A History of English Syntax: A Transformational Approach to the History of English Sentence Structure*. New York: Holt, Rinehart, and Winston.

U.S. Department of Commerce. 1973. *Characteristics of the Population, West Virginia*. Washington, DC: U.S. Government Printing Office.

U.S. Department of Labor. 1968. "Doing Your Best on Aptitude Tests." Washington, DC: U.S. Government Printing Office.

Vance, Rupert B. 1962. "The Region: A New Survey" in Thomas R. Ford, ed., *The Southern Appalachian Region: A Survey*. Lexington, KY: University of Kentucky Press.

Venezky, Richard L. and Robin S. Chapman. 1973. "Is Learning to Read Dialect Bound?" in James P. Laffey and Roger W. Shuy, eds., *Language Differences: Do They Interfere?* Newark, DE: International Reading Association.

Walls, David S. and John B. Stephenson. 1972. *Appalachia in the Sixties: Decade of Reawakening*. Lexington, KY: University of Kentucky Press.

Weatherford, W.D. and Earl D.C. Brewer. 1962. *Life and Religion in Southern Appalachia*. New York: Friendship Press.

Wigginton, Eliot. 1972. *The Foxfire Book*. Garden City, NJ: Doubleday and Co., Inc.

Williams, Joseph M. 1975. *Origins of the English Language*. New York:
     The Free Press.
Wolfram, Walt. 1969. *A Sociolinguistic Description of Detroit Negro
     Speech*. Washington, DC: Center for Applied Linguistics.
_____ . 1970a. "Sociolinguistic Implications for Educational Sequenc-
     ing" in Ralph W. Fasold and Roger W. Shuy, eds., *Teaching
     Standard English in the Inner City*. Washington, DC: Center
     for Applied Linguistics.
_____ . 1970b. "Sociolinguistic Alternatives in Teaching Reading to
     Nonstandard Speakers," *Reading Research Quarterly*, 6:9-33.
_____ . 1973. "On What Basis Variable Rules?" in Charles-James N.
     Bailey and Roger W. Shuy, eds., *Studies in New Ways of Analyz-
     ing Variation in English*. Washington, DC: Georgetown Univer-
     sity.
_____ . 1974a. *Sociolinguistic Aspects of Assimilation: Puerto Rican
     English in New York City*. Arlington, VA: Center for Applied
     Linguistics.
_____ . 1974b. "The Relationship of White Southern Speech to Vernacu-
     lar Black English," *Language*, 50:498-527.
_____ . 1975. "Levels of Sociolinguistic Bias in Testing" in Deborah
     Harrison and Thomas Trabasso, eds., *Seminars in Black English*.
     Silver Spring, MD: Lawrence Erlbaum Associates.
_____   and Ralph W. Fasold. 1974. *The Study of Social Dialects in
     American English*. Englewood Cliffs, NJ: Prentice-Hall.
Wyld, Henry Cecil. 1936. *A History of Modern Colloquial English*.
     Oxford: Bail Blackwell.
Zwicky, Arnold. 1970. "Auxiliary Reduction in English," *Linguistic
     Inquiry*, 1:323-336.